Soul-Led Living

Soul-Led Living

Discover your soul's true path
and become brave enough
to follow it

NIKKI NOVO

NIKKI NOVO

Soul-Led Living: Discover your soul's true path and become brave enough to follow it

First edition

ISBN: 978-0-9908042-2-2

COVER ARTWORK Natalia Aristizabal
BOOK DESIGN Laura Wrubleski
EDITORS Danielle Goodman, Kat Morzewska and Marisa Leon
PUBLISHING SUPPORT The Self Publishing Agency

Soul-Led Living LLC
www.nikkinovo.com

For my daughter, Aly.

May this book be a reminder of the power that lives within you.

And may it find you when you need it the most.

Thank you for supporting me the whole way through.

Thank you for being you.

I love you, eternally.

Contents

INTRODUCTION 9

CHAPTER ONE Remembering Your Soul 17

CHAPTER TWO Discovering Your Soul's Path 39

CHAPTER THREE The Road to Your Soul's Path 55

CHAPTER FOUR Breaking Free from Identity Webs 79

CHAPTER FIVE Becoming Your Soul Self 111

CHAPTER SIX Your Soul's Work 139

CHAPTER SEVEN Losing Trust 179

CHAPTER EIGHT Manifesting Your Dream Life 205

CHAPTER NINE Learning to Lead 251

CHAPTER TEN Healing Foundations 297

CHAPTER ELEVEN The Creation Process 323

ACKNOWLEDGMENTS 331

Introduction

There was a scared, young boy stuck behind his 43-year-old eyes. Curious to understand what I was seeing, I softly brushed his thick brown hair back in hopes of locking eyes together. I needed him to see me, seeing him.

"I'm only doing this once," I said gently, but sternly. He nodded in agreement.

"You're going to be okay. We're going to be okay. Our family will be okay," I promised, reluctantly.

After one, joint deep breath, he turned away from me and walked toward the building we both desperately hoped would heal him.

The truth is, I didn't know if we would be okay. I didn't even know how we had gotten here. Seven years earlier, when we were married, we had been full of hope for our future. I had dreamt of building successful careers together, making tons of money, raising happy children, having a perfectly decorated home, and taking fancy vacations so we could later brag about it on social media.

But none of that was happening. Instead, I was checking my strong, loving, and beloved husband into a rehabilitation center, for an addiction I didn't even know he had until three months prior. Somehow, I had to go back home to care for our three young children, run the company I built with my husband (one that made me feel suffocated), and manage to pay all our bills... all without falling apart.

This was not the dream life I had imagined for myself when I was younger. In fact, I had not intended to create this life at all. I found myself wondering, *How did I get here?* and *Where did I go wrong?* Perhaps the scariest question I asked myself was *Am I even meant to have my dream life, or is this it?*

Raised by two Catholic Cuban parents, I was brought up to follow the rules: go to college, build a respectable career, get married, buy a house in a nice neighborhood, have kids, and get a dog. I did all of that. And yet, I felt restless...more restless than most of my friends.

They seemed more content than me. Their nine-to-five jobs were just fine. The standard life of working during the week, ushering kids to sports in minivans, and drinking while brunching on the weekends was enough for them. Why couldn't this be enough for me?

Instead, I found myself constantly wrestling with my purpose and wondering whether I even had one or not. Deep within me, I wondered whether my soul had a true path or a destiny. And if that were true, how could I find it? How could I live it?

Despite my husband's health, I had a beautiful life. The only problem was that I was starting to realize it was *someone else's* beautiful life. To me, it often felt boring and anticlimactic. At the same time, it felt messy—like it might all crack at any moment.

Obviously, my intuition wasn't too far off. When I discovered that my husband was sick, my life did actually crack. Surprisingly though, the crack felt like the most authentic moment I had experienced in years. The crack turned out to be an opening. And as my foundation began to crumble, it was as if the door of the cage I was stuck in finally busted open, and I was invited to walk out.

At first, I thought about literally walking out. You know—leaving my husband, trading in my suburban home for a tiny bungalow in the hippie part of town, downsizing my work, and just saying F-it to the life I had unintentionally created.

But if I was being honest with myself, blowing it all up is not what I really wanted. Instead, what I deeply, truly wanted was to just rearrange and reimagine my life so that it could be aligned with my most authentic self. And I believed that there had to be a better way to live, outside the constant grind we were living in.

A few months after my husband began his recovery, we began to have honest conversations about the fact that our system was not working. My husband was working himself to death and I was drowning with three kids, while trying to fight for my own little business. And despite showing up, every day, at 100 percent, we were barely making ends meet. We didn't love where or how we lived. What we were doing was not working.

My intuition was telling me it was time to be brave and start intentionally creating the life that I felt in my heart I was meant to live. Not only was I ready to create what I felt called to, but also what I knew would be the best thing for my family. It was time to lead.

I knew this meant leading a whole new lifestyle—one that was intentional, fulfilling, and reflected more of who we truly were as individuals and as a family. We decided to sell our house in the city and trade it all for 30 acres of land in the country. My husband sold his business, and we pivoted our focus to my digital company, so we could have the freedom of time and flexibility of location we were dreaming of.

To make this work, my husband and I had to rethink our roles. Turns out, we each wanted the other's job! He wanted more time with the kids, and I wanted more time to grow my business. We figured out digital and passive ways to make money, so that neither of us would be burdened with the pressure to join the rat race to survive.

You might be thinking, "But what about the kids?" After all, we did move them from everything they know. Well, it turns out that what is best for you is often what is best for your family. All three of my children's teachers have used the word "thriving" when describing our kids.

I do believe you know what is best for you and your family. It may not be super clear, and you may not know how to get there or how to become the bravest version of yourself, but I do believe the vision you hold for your dream life is accurate. I believe the calling comes from your soul.

And not only is it accurate, but it is possible. Beyond it being possible, it is your soul's true path, and therefore, you are destined to live it.

Sure, you may not know how to get there. You may even find yourself in a messy situation like I was. Well, guess what? That doesn't mean you're doomed or stuck. It just means that there's an opportunity to reconnect with your soul's voice, so you can live the life that was truly intended for you. The good news? This book is designed to do exactly that.

Why should you trust me? Well, this story about turning my life around to live my soul's true path is actually not the first time I've done this. Since my early 20's, I have constantly been seeking my authentic path. I've landed on it several times, and then accidentally fell off, only to find it again. My search led me to change careers from film publicity to fashion and beauty writing to becoming a sought-after intuitive with a waitlist of more than 1,000 people. My Catholic parents never saw that one coming!

My work has given me the honor to perform more than 800 intuitive readings on people, where my main intention is to find the soul's true path and purpose. Hours of case studies have taught me that we are, in fact, not crazy when we search to connect with the deepest part of ourselves: our soul. It is trying to guide us into a life of fulfillment and full expression. We just need to remember how to hear its guidance.

It's true, we are mind, body, and soul. And that little, persistent voice or feeling is your intuition telling you that there is a better way to live. What's most amazing about this "better way," is that it's custom-fit to your soul. Which means, most people around you are just not going to get it. Because most of us are led by the blueprints created by others.

While you, my friend, are soul-led.

This means that you are not satisfied with the mediocre. You don't believe in the grind. Your heart tells you there is something, better and greater. All you need is to become brave enough to follow the calling of your soul.

After performing hundreds of intuitive Soul Readings, I have observed how the soul works; I have come to understand how it communicates, and how it doesn't. I have learned how to distinguish our ego and fear from the soul and intuition (a.k.a. the soul's voice). I've discovered how to decipher the difference between the true soul's path and a default path (the life we create by accident).

But most importantly, I have learned how to *live* the soul's path — without throwing away everything I love about being human. As we commit to a soul-led life, we don't have to fear losing the material things and people we love — or the lifestyle we like to live. Our soul is not asking us to suffer, or to leave everything behind and go meditate at the top of a mountain. Even a billionaire can live a soul-led life. It can be accomplished even if you're living in the busiest city, and whether or not you're eating a non-vegan diet!

In this book, I will share with you these findings in the hopes that you remember your soul, its callings, and how to feel brave enough to follow it. As a result, you will begin living your soul-led life. And when you live soul-led, the life of your dreams begins taking form. Because your soul placed all those dreams you long for, in your heart. This book is designed to help you bring them to life.

While most books are best read in sequential order, this book was not written linearly. This is because soul-led living is not accomplished in one, straight line. Rather, we achieve a soul-led life after going through a somewhat creative process of examining different aspects of our life and tweaking it until it feels just right. And what feels just right now, might change as you evolve and grow.

With that said, please feel free to use this book intuitively. Read it in order or flip it open to a chapter that speaks to you. You will notice many of my own stories creating a thread throughout the book, but know that those stories were not written in sequential order. May these stories help you find inspiration and give you space to reflect on your own life and the stories that have created you.

In addition to being inspired, I have included several tools that have helped me and my clients to discover, create, and live our soul-led lives. Keeping a notebook and pen next to you will be helpful when exploring the prompts and exercises included in this book. And as extra support, I created several meditations to aid you in this process. These meditations can be found at nikkinovo.com/soul-led-book.

My intention for you is that by the time you finish reading this book, you feel brave. Brave enough to acknowledge your soul's desires. Brave enough to admit what is currently not working in your life. And brave enough to trust yourself toward the creation of a soul-led life.

No matter how complicated your current situation may appear, remember you have called this book into your life. It may not feel like it just yet, but your soul does know the way. And I am honored that you have decided to start your journey toward your soul-led life, here with me.

CHAPTER ONE

Remembering Your Soul

I came home to a nearly empty house, small reminders of our family's memories scattered throughout. The glider from Ethan's baby nursery—the chair where I had nursed both our boys and created lullabies with my voice—stood by the front door, lifeless. The Swarovski crystal Champagne flutes my mother had gifted us for our wedding day, forgotten on the kitchen counter, sat next to a crumpled bag of fast food left behind from the mover's lunch.

"Nikki, we have to leave today," my husband Benny said, as he kissed my cheek and rolled my luggage into our very bare house.

"Tonight?" I asked, still shocked by everything that he and the movers were able to pack while I was gone.

"Our beds are in the truck, the kids are ready, and the animals are packed. We're leaving tonight," he said sternly.

Five months earlier, Benny and I had taken a weekend trip to Western North Carolina, curious to see if it was finally time to move our family to the country. My parents stayed with our three kids in Miami, FL, while we searched for land amongst the Blue Ridge Mountains.

For five years, we had been dreaming of owning farmland—a place for our family to roam, grow our own food, and experience nature. We always imagined it as a vacation home, but in 2020 Benny's health was taking a turn for the worse, and our entire family structure needed to change. By 2021, we knew it was time to make the move.

Despite discussing our plans with friends and family, no one really believed us. Even our realtor in North Carolina (a childhood friend of Benny's who was originally from Miami) didn't believe us. She thought she was stuck driving a city couple around for the weekend, a couple who was simply *dreaming* of moving but would never really pull the trigger.

In their defense, Miami kids rarely leave Miami. Especially, when you're born to Cuban exiles. When our families left Cuba, they rooted in Miami, claiming it as their new land. As a community, there was a desire to rebuild what was lost. The exiles hoped that keeping their descendants in one place would erase the past, placing a tremendous burden on children like Benny and me.

The more I travel and meet people from around the world, the more I realize that this pressure is not unique to me, or children of Cuban exiles. We are all connected to our land, especially after many generations of settling. There is an expectation to stay and make it work at all costs, even if staying is to the detriment of your mind, body, and soul.

But what happens when new land calls us, and our families? Will we be brave enough to follow?

Benny and I drove the surrounding areas of Asheville for three days, searching for land the way one might search for a lover on dating apps, a lover they don't yet know, but one they know exists in their heart. We drove eight hours each day and discovered all sorts of land. We found high-up land, steep land, no-cell-service land, breathtaking-and-expensive land, and everything in between. But still not *our land.*

We did not know exactly what we were looking for. Raised in Miami, FL, all we knew were one-acre-or-less plots of land, placed on a straight grid. In Western North Carolina, the neighborhoods looked disorganized to me. My eye was conditioned to look for manicured lawns, houses on a straight grid, elaborate landscaping, and gates and hedges to protect your property. Where I came from, everything was tamed, polished, and groomed. Everything appeared perfect. Here, everything was wild.

The day before we were scheduled to fly back to Miami, our realtor led us to one last property. It was February; the trees were bare, the ground brown, and the air cold, but the sky was incredibly blue. We drove down a windy road into a neighborhood filled with homes where not one single aesthetic fit the other. They were all cousins that seemed completely unrelated. There was no rhyme or reason, and I was starting to get dizzy.

"I have a good feeling about this one," Benny said as he continued to drive.

My heart sank. I was scared because I recognized this feeling in my body. It was the same feeling I'd felt the first day I walked into Benny's home, on one of our early dates. "I'm going to live here. I'm going to marry this man," I had said to myself.

Just because you are brave, doesn't mean you are unafraid when you know that life is about to change.

We parked our car at the foot of the property and took a good look. It had everything we were dreaming of: flat land with a creek, a barn, and even hiking trails. Although covered in vines and overgrown foliage, Benny and I began hiking the land.

A few weeks earlier, while in meditation, I had asked for guidance. I wanted to know how we would know when we had found the right land. What I heard was, "Follow the white wolf." As we continued on our hike, a large white wolf-looking dog appeared. A dog we now affectionately know as Emily, our neighbor's dog, guided us up the mountain and to the first look-out point on the property. It was absolutely breathtaking.

Benny's mind was already racing, imagining where the house would go, and where he would build a fort for the boys, where the animals could live, and where I would hike in the mornings. I asked him to slow down and reminded him that we needed the permission from the land first.

I crouched down to the dirt, while Benny placed his hand on a tree. "We would like to be stewards of this land. Is that okay with you?" we asked.

A gust of wind came rushing through the forest, using the trees as rattles, to signal their approval. It felt like a celebration led by giants, and we were their guests. I looked up to find the bluest sky I had ever seen, and was taken aback by the sight of the big, bright moon in midday. "Benny, her name is Luna," I said.

We made our way down the 30 acres of land and back to our realtor. We told her we really liked the land, but we needed the evening to think and meditate on it.

The next morning, it was still dark out, yet Benny was already awake. "Nikki, I think we need to see the land one more time before we go," he said to me. We'd knew we'd be cutting it a little close to get to the airport on time, but we both really wanted to go back.

Without enough time to get permission from the realtors, we decided to head out on our own and risk trespassing. We had been walking around for about 10 minutes before an old farm truck pulled up to the property, and out of the truck came the closest thing I've ever seen to a rancher.

"Can I help you?" the older gentleman yelled out to us in a thick Southern drawl. "Benny, this man is going to shoot us," I whispered in a panic.

It turned out that the rancher was the owner of the land and we were, in fact, trespassing on his property. As Benny walked toward him to chat, the owner signaled to his wife in the truck to come speak to me. Benny introduced himself and shared his intentions for the land as if he were asking my father's permission to take my hand in marriage all over again. I spoke to his wife about our kids and how we were so excited to give them a life here, grow gardens, and fill the barn with animals.

Our conversations were coming to an end and all four of us were standing together when the man looked at Benny and said,

"We received an offer for the land earlier today, but we want you and your family to have it instead. Put in an offer today for the full amount. Don't insult me."

"Yes, sir," Benny replied.

"And son, you have the money, right? We don't play games around here," the man said.

"Yes, sir. I'll give it to you in cash," Benny responded.

The owner told us he was looking forward to our offer and followed it up with a good old-fashioned Southern handshake. We called our realtor, put in the offer, and drove off to the airport. Just before the flight attendants told us to turn off our phones as we boarded the plane, she called us back to tell us that our offer had been accepted. We could hardly believe it.

I plopped down into the airport seat, looked at Benny and said, "You know we don't have the money, right? And you offered the guy cash."

He laughed as he stored our luggage in the overhead compartment and said, "Nikki, when have we ever let money get in our way?"

We found the land in February of 2021, but didn't close on it until May. Those three months were a rollercoaster. During that time, we refinanced our Miami home and took out the cash we needed to buy the land. "So this is what rich people do to buy vacation homes?" I thought.

This was a great hack; it got us what we needed to buy the land, but it still wasn't enough. Our land did not come with a house, so we knew we needed to sell our current house at a particular price to cover both the land and construction cost of the new house. We were completely functioning off of faith. We hustled, followed our intuition, and worked our schemes, but ultimately we knew that we were not in control.

Despite not having sold our Miami house yet or having a home to rent in North Carolina, we decided we would move in August in time for our three kids to start school. Miraculously, two weeks before our scheduled move date, a house became available for us to rent *and* we received an offer on our Miami home at the just price we needed. We took this as a sign that moving was our true calling.

Despite knowing that we were doing the right thing, this time was not without stress. School start dates and availability of the rental home made for a very tight schedule for us. Our teenage daughter Aly, who had joined the cheer squad at her new high school, needed to be in Asheville earlier than our move date to attend cheerleading camp. So I flew with her to Asheville, dropped her off at camp, and flew back down to Miami to drive with the rest of our family for the full move up.

Expecting to have a few days to pack my final things, I arrived at our Miami home to find that there was nothing else to pack. Benny had taken it upon himself to hire help in order to give us the final push we needed to make the move. Knowing me too well, he knew that I was too nostalgic when I packed, and that if he left it to me I would be packing boxes for another three months.

Our two boys ran to meet me at the door. "Mom, we're ready for our adventure!" they squealed. Over the last six months, we had been visiting the land and had positioned our move to the kids as an adventure that our family was about to embark on together. After all, we were moving them away from everything they knew, their friends, and extended family. But Benny and I were so ready to leave Miami, and we were very excited for our new life. Our energy must have been contagious, because our children seemed equally as enthusiastic.

Benny was set to drive the largest moving truck we could rent, with a small trailer attached to it, which housed his tools. I was assigned the task of driving our family SUV, with our two boys and our dog. Attached to my SUV was a small animal trailer (with "Luna Farms" and a happy face spray-painted on it by Benny) loaded with our farm animals. We lived on a rare, agriculturally-zoned street in Miami that allowed us to have small farm animals, so we were traveling with three goats, a pig, a bunch of rabbits, and several chickens. Looking back, I realize that somehow I got the short end of the stick driving all our humans and animals, while Benny just drove our stuff.

I grabbed a few final items scattered throughout the house that hadn't made their way into boxes and began throwing them into the car. Although I had spent the last two weeks saying goodbye to friends and family, I still somehow felt like I was escaping, running away, and lying.. My best friend showed up to give me one last hug as friends who lived in the same city. My eyes filled with tears as she left, knowing how much love I was leaving behind.

"Why can't I just be happy here like everyone else?" I secretly thought.

As she left in her minivan, my father arrived at our house. Saying goodbye to our loved ones was hard, but saying goodbye to my father felt like a mix of betrayal and survival. My soul was going to die if I stayed, but my heart broke as I left.

He looked at me and said, "This is going to be very hard, but

I know it's going to be a good thing for your family."

I was the last of my siblings living near our aging parents, and us leaving meant they would eventually want to move closer to one of their children. I was not only rocking our foundation, but I was rocking theirs too.

He asked me not to drive at night. I lied and told him we would leave in the morning, already knowing that Benny wanted to hit the road right away. My father gave his grandsons a kiss on their foreheads, and left.

Just as the sun began to set, Benny and I started the cars, and we slowly drove our loaded vehicles out of the white iron gate of our Miami home. My car's bluetooth synced to my phone and Tom Petty's "Free Fallin'" began to play.

Our oldest son (eight at the time) rolled the window down in the back seat, stuck his head out and yelled, "Freedom!" Our three-year-old quickly followed suit. They recognized the song, but didn't know the lyrics, so instead they sang "Freedom! We're free!" Attempting to keep up with Tom Petty, they continued their song of freedom as we caravanned out from all that we knew and into the unknown.

THE TRAILBLAZER

The boys were right. We were all seeking to be free. The same way my grandparents and parents fled communist Cuba for the freedom of the United States, here we were again, seeking the same thing. But a country alone cannot give you freedom.

The true freedom we seek is from the molds, the blueprints, and the templates we are told to follow. Whether someone told us to follow them or we subconsciously understood this to be the only way, we have been stuck on paths that are not really ours. They may be good for some people, but that does not mean they are meant for all of us.

Sometimes that is the hardest part. When you look around and realize that your friends and family seem just fine living what you consider to be a mediocre and, quite frankly, boring life. You know there is more for you, but you don't exactly know what that means, and you don't know how to get there.

All these feelings can mean only one thing: You are a trailblazer. You are not meant to follow the paths paved before you. To follow these paths would mean your truth would have to be hidden, your heart in hibernation mode, and your intuition ignored.

I, too, am a trailblazer and know that although we seek freedom from the molds, we also long to feel confident in our decisions. The hope is to make choices that are true for us, but to also feel good when making them. Which is why the trailblazer must identify her own compass.

As trailblazers, we must first understand that the reason we feel so different from the pack is because we somehow have managed to remember our soul's tone. While many of those around us seem to follow the beat of a drum played outside them, we faintly hear a calling that comes from within.

Most likely, you call this tone your heart, your inner voice, or maybe your gut. But what it most wants to be known as is your soul. As humans, we are souls that exist in a vehicle known as the body, which is driven by the mind. This is the trinity: the mind, body, and soul.

The mind and body are new, while the soul is old. And with old age comes wisdom. The soul is the wisest part of us. It knows more than our human minds can comprehend.

However, despite all this hidden wisdom, we are here to experience human life. This means, our memory of the soul—and what it's been up to for many lifetimes—is limited. But although it's limited, it does not mean we do not have access to it. Our soul is always making regular contact with our human self.

Contact is made through a moment of presence, where we are unbound from our judgements, our biases, and our close-minded logic. There are several ways the soul can get through to us, but I have found the most effective syncing happens when we are connected to our intuition, activating our bravery, following curiosity, leaning into self-trust, and betting on ourselves. Let's look at each of these so we can better understand the moments when our soul comes online.

INTUITION

Your intuition is the voice of your soul. Depending on how you receive your intuition, you may describe this random experience in various ways.

"My gut tells me to go this way."

"I can't help but listen to my heart."

"I just know there is something not right about this."

"This feels off."

"I heard a voice within me telling me which way to go."

I wish there was more scientific research dedicated to intuition so we can better understand it (and therefore describe it), but what's most important for now is that you learn to understand your own. We may not be able to study intuition as a whole right now, but we can study our own.

When we are feeling lost, unsure of our next move, or in the middle of a transition, we tend to look outside ourselves for the answers. Despite years of intuition training, I have often found myself doing the same. In fact, this habit is actually one of the reasons I started performing intuitive readings on others.

Before my business became focused on intuition and the soul, I was a writer with a blog, desperately trying to figure out how to monetize my spiritual hobby. I wasn't a fashion blogger. I wasn't a life coach. And I wasn't an expert on anything. I felt like I didn't know who I was, or what I had to offer the world, but at the same time, I knew I was meant to do this work.

This confusing calling was driving me crazy, so over the course of two years I visited dozens of psychics and hired several business consultants to tell me who I was and what I should do. My all-time favorite memory of this was when I had two brand consultants present an entire Powerpoint slideshow to me on who I was.

All of this outside information just made me more confused, so I went to visit yet another psychic. As we sat in her tiny, purple room, as she began sharing her intuitive information. Every single thing she told me, it seems like I already knew. That's not to say she wasn't accurate, there just wasn't any new information to give me. I had all the answers within me.

On that day, I told myself I wouldn't visit another psychic for at least two years. Still to this day the only readings I have received are from my students and that's because I love to experience their talent and, well, because they are the best in the industry. Even when I'm lost, I do my best to go within because there is no better place to look for answers. Any outside guidance I bring into my life, I see as collaboration, rather than a replacement for my own intuition.

Throughout this book, I will teach you several ways to access your intuition. We'll even go into how to read energy! But for now, I want you to try catching yourself when you seek answers outside of you. Notice the habit. When you see yourself about to reach out beyond you, schedule some alone time with yourself. Go for a walk or write in a journal. And remind yourself that the answers are within you.

Without detoxing from the constant need to receive outside opinions and guidance, we'll never get to understand how our intuition works. It's like the soul is calling us on a phone. The phone is ringing, but we don't answer it, because we don't recognize the sound. Give yourself space so you can learn to decipher the ring.

In chapter two and chapter nine, I give more details on how you can develop your intuition, but the first step is to respect your own. You have your own compass, and it will always be more accurate than anyone else's. Not because they are faulty, but because they do not have your compass.

BRAVERY

The next sign that our soul is trying to come online is bravery.

This is probably my favorite way to connect with my soul, mainly because it is active. Intuition is about receiving information, and bravery is about acting upon that information.

When you use this tool, you are always rewarded. You may not be rewarded in the way you hope for, but nonetheless, your life changes when you act with bravery. One act will give you a change in the norm, but several acts, back to back, can create the kind of life people dream of.

This is why I believe that bravery is a personality trait you must commit to. Any time you find yourself afraid to make a move, you'll remember that you are a brave person. And brave people take action even when they are afraid.

The reason bravery is a portal into the soul is because it creates focused energy. When you are acting bravely, you decide to block out any distracting factors. You're "in the zone," which means that you have managed to connect to the energy source of love. This is what we refer to as God, and what I will refer to in this book as the Divine.

Bravery offers us a focus, because we understand that what we're about to do is a must. Think about the energy of something you must do, versus the energy of something you maybe will do. *Must* is tight and lean—there is no other option. *Maybe* is like the guy who is dating someone great, but insists on continuing to play the field. He can't commit, because he is entertaining distractions. Therefore, his future is in limbo.

The soul is synonymous with truth. It is our true essence. When we use bravery, we know our truth. We respect it, so we follow it.

The reason we often can't act with bravery is because we have become distracted from our truth. If bravery is focus, fear is distraction.

When we are in fear or doubt, we are distracted by all the maybes and the opinions of others. We can't actively move toward our intuitive hits, because we are stopping to hear the outside noise.

If we are not using our own intuition to receive guidance, but instead are trying to use someone else's, we will not be able to activate the magic of bravery. Bravery will only follow our truth, our essence, and our soul. It knows not to trust anything or anyone else.

CURIOSITY

Often, between your intuitive hit and brave action is curiosity. When my husband and I decided to visit North Carolina in search for land, we were curious. We had a faint feeling that we were meant to move, but we needed to investigate that feeling first. Instead of curiosity, we could have right away given into fear, worrying about what others would have thought and scared that our children wouldn't thrive. If that were the case, we would have never visited, and the more we refused to listen, the faint feeling would have become muffled.

Curiosity does not know the answer, but it's willing to find out. The reason curiosity works so well, especially in times when we don't have a concrete answer, is because it does not believe either side just yet. While it may not believe its intuition yet, it also does not believe the fear. All curiosity wants is space to explore.

When teaching students how to connect with their intuition, I always ask them to use curiosity to receive intuitive information. What blocks us from our intuition, and therefore our soul, is our logical, judgmental mind. When information tries to come through us, the messages are filtered by our mind. In order to keep us safe, our mind tries to place the downloads into categories. While it tries to keep us safe, the result is that we remain close-minded and therefore, our life remains small. We start to receive guidance from our biased mind rather than our intuition.

If we can bypass the logical mind by being curious, we're much more likely to discover something new. We can start to break free from the patterns that hold us back from living soul-led. Curiosity is how we can get access to truth instead of old patterns. Once we get that truth and believe in it, it's easier to be brave. But bravery may need one more piece of evidence before fully committing. This evidence is self-trust.

SELF-TRUST

Self-trust is the safety of knowing that when we leap or make a big move, that we will be there to catch ourselves. It's safety at its core. When I moved our family to North Carolina, I could not be sure that it was the right choice. My intuition guided me, but it would never give me guarantees.

If the move had proven to be a horrible mistake, my ability to trust myself would have stepped in saying, "Ok, so this is different than we thought. We are not going to blame ourselves. We're proud of ourselves for taking the risk. And now, let's explore why this feels wrong, and what we need to do to feel okay."

The small part of us, the part that is often unsure and scared, wants to know that if it does make a brave move, that the big part of us won't abandon it. Another way to look at this is that our inner child does not want to be scolded by our inner mother, if the brave move turned out differently than expected. To make brave moves, we need to know that we have our own back, no matter the outcome.

When my daughter, Aly, entered middle school, she struggled with girlfriend relationships. Being that she was my first child, I did not understand that this struggle was quite normal. Instead, I assumed something was wrong with her. When the other mothers would call me to discuss the situation between their child and mine, my initital instince was to trust the mom and believe in what she was saying. After all, she was an adult. She must know better! Right?

Well, it took me about three tries to realize that maybe instead of trusting them, I should trust my own daughter and what she had to say about the situation. Those first few times that she struggled with friends, I abandoned her by blaming her for a less than perfect outcome. I did not have her back. I trusted others before I trusted her.

Eventually though, I caught this pattern. I corrected it, and I asked her forgiveness. To feel brave enough to make moves, she needed to know that I would have her back no matter what. If not, she would have learned to play it safe.

This is a story of trust outside myself, but this is the best way to show you how we often abandon ourselves. If our inner child cannot trust that we will be there after a leap of faith (especially the ones that work out differently than we hoped), it will not allow us to jump. Bravery cannot exist in this environment.

Self-trust is a stable reaction to the unknown, the unplanned, and the uncharted. Stable means that something is there to catch us when we leap. We are there — there for ourselves.

Like me, you have probably abandoned yourself many times. Even as I write this book, I am afraid—afraid that if I receive criticism for who I am, I will believe the person criticizing me over myself. This has happened before. I grew up in a very critical environment as a child, and I always believed in others before myself.

Eventually, I learned to block out the noise. In fact, in the next chapter, I'm going to tell you about the time I called off a wedding just two months before I was schedule to walk down the aisle. This was the first time I actually trusted myself over others. The pain of trusting others became so intense that the only way out was to trust myself.

I was in my 20s then, and I wish I could tell you that I never abandoned myself again, but that wouldn't be true. Every once in a while, my unconscious patterns kick in, and I don't realize that I have left my inner child on her own. I tend to do this when I believe the people who criticize me, or when I believe that someone outside of me has the answer to my life's challenges.

If self-trust is the opposite of self-abandonment then, simply put, self-trust is about being there for ourselves — no matter what. Being there for ourselves sends the message that we are worth trusting. This makes us willing to follow ourselves into the unknown because we know the leader, and we know she would never leave us behind. We can now be brave because we have a leader we can count on. She may not know the way, but she always figures it out.

When developing self-trust, it's important to look back with compassion and forgiveness,at the times we let ourselves down. I let my daughter down often during those early teenage years, but she gracefully extended me forgiveness. She gave me a second chance at being a better leader for her.

Just as my daughter forgave me, a soul-led life cannot be achieved without self-forgiveness. If we refuse to forgive, we will continue to use the ego to fix ourselves, rather than using the soul. Forgiveness is love, and love is the energy of our soul. We deserve love no matter how many times we have abandoned ourselves. The reason we abandoned ourselves in the first place is because we become disconnected from our truth, and instead allow ourselves to be guided by our programming. We will learn more about programming in chapter four.

BETTING ON YOURSELF

After we have learned to access our intuition, activate bravery, utilize curiosity, and develop self-trust, we are then ready to bet on ourselves. Betting on ourselves creates soul alignment. If we think of bravery as sprinting through fear, betting on ourselves would be having the stamina to run a full marathon.

When we bet on ourselves, we enter into a long-term commitment with our intuitive guidance. We've learned to hold focus for a longer period of time than just receiving one intuitive hit and taking action on that. Betting on yourself requires a constant cycling of intuition, bravery, curiosity, and self-trust. As you cycle these qualities, fear and self-doubt are less likely to take hold. When fear takes over, we fall off our soul's true path and end up on a default path. (We'll talk more about this in Chapter Three.)

Betting on yourself also requires a bit of history. When you're faced with a leap of faith, you'll want to look back at all the times you jumped and succeeded. This is a great time to make a list of all your past, unrealistic accomplishments. We all have them. Maybe you survived a traumatic childhood, landed a job when there were hundreds of applicants, ran an actual marathon, left a toxic relationship, finished a challenging degree or certification, raised tiny humans, and so on.

Whatever it is that you accomplished, write it down in a notebook for you to see. Who needs fancy diplomas on a wall when you have your fancy list of unrealistic accomplishments?

A soul's true path is filled with leaps of faith. Moving my family from everything we knew was a leap of faith that landed all of us in deeper soul alignment. I didn't walk here. I leaped here. And we can only leap when we believe we are a solid bet.

Betting on ourselves also involves our worthiness. To feel fully worthy can be a difficult and long-term concept. To bet on ourselves we may not fully, truly believe that we are worthy. We just need to see that we deserve a chance to try — a chance to throw our hat in the ring. Why not us?

You have a gift, a talent, a calling, a desire within you. It is not there by accident. You deserve to follow it. You deserve to bet on yourself.

CHAPTER TWO

Discovering Your Soul's Path

By the time I was 20 years old, I was engaged to my high school sweetheart.

Dressed in an adorable pink lace dress, I remember holding up a glass of champagne in my parents' backyard during our engagement party and thinking to myself, "I'm old enough to get married, but I'm not old enough to legally drink."

Almost everyone at that party knew I wasn't meant to get married to this boy. Yet, we all played along. My friends bought me gifts. Guests smiled for pictures. My father reluctantly paid the vendors.

When I wasn't around, those closest to me were deciding whether or not to stage an intervention. They whispered about who would break the news to me. They gossiped about my latest inappropriate behavior. And they shared their collective sadness and concern for me.

It took them months, but my best friends eventually did it. We were traveling through Europe after our college graduation, and my girlfriends thought it would be fun to come home to our sketchy hostel (after a night of bar hopping in Salamanca) and tell me that I was making a mistake by getting married. What a buzz kill.

Of course, I disagreed with them. I countered their arguments by repeating a line that, looking back, I'm sure I picked up from a Freddie Prinze Jr. movie. "He's my everything," I said repeatedly.

The next day, I protested their attempted intervention by ignoring them. If we were on a bus, I made sure to sit as far from them as possible. When we went to lunch, I would eat my tortilla in silence while they told hilarious stories of the night before. While they shopped, I sat alone on a bench.

The streets of Salamanca were vibrant—full of joy, adventure, and possibility. A complete contrast to what I was feeling inside. As we walked those streets, I thought to myself *What awful friends I have.* I did that ugly female thing that so many of us do when we refuse to connect to our inner voice. Over and over, I soothed myself by saying, "They're just jealous."

In my heart, though, I knew that the opposite was true. I knew they loved me. And I knew that they knew, that I was really freakin' lost. Despite all this, we never spoke of that drunken conversation again. They had said their piece. And if I was about to blow up my life, then at least they could rest knowing that they tried.

THE SIGNS OF BEING OFF PATH

Before this trip, the signs of my unhappiness, fear, and despair were obvious. Unlike my other friends who were in relationships, I was alone the majority of the time. My fiancé was a professional baseball player, which meant that he was away from home often. Even when he was a college player, he was constantly traveling. He would spend summers away at elite baseball camps, while I would enjoy Hot Girl Summer with my friends. Looking back, it was probably the perfect arrangement when you're in a relationship that doesn't make you happy!

All this time alone made me feel like I was a single, 20-year-old woman living it up in Miami, not an engaged-soon-to-be-married 20-year-old. Growing up Latina in Miami means that your social life *is* life. There was always a party to go to, a club to be seen at, or a bar to dance around. There was so much fun to be had. Yet here I was in the midst of all this, expected to behave.

Well, behave I did not. I never went so far as to cheat, but suffice it to say that I was definitely a free spirit. I was constantly on the scene, and I flirted like it was my job. From the outside, it might have looked like I was looking for attention. And in a way, maybe it was. But to be more accurate, my behavior was a cry for help. I was secretly hoping someone would save me from my princess tower. I needed help breaking free from the prison that was my life.

Since I could remember, all I really wanted in life was freedom. It's not lost on me that my parents are Cuban exiles who came to the United States to seek freedom, but as their child, I did not feel free at all. I felt bound to an imaginary contract that read, "Good Cuban-American daughters shall only leave their parents' home in a wedding dress or a casket." Leaving in a wedding dress sounded more reasonable.

My quest for freedom felt a bit like taking a prescription drug that would cure one ailment only to then cause another. You're just trying to reduce inflammation from that cyst on your face, and before you know it, you're constipated. I had sought out a husband to get me out of my house, but then I needed someone else to get me out of this marriage! Or so I thought.

HEARING THE VOICE

Two months before our scheduled wedding date, I flew to New York City with my girlfriends to visit another friend who had just moved for graduate school.

Typically, if you're having a wedding in two months, you're probably spending every last minute finalizing planning. But not this bride! I was in complete denial and looking for every last possible adventure as a single lady. Little did I know that this trip wouldn't be the end but, in fact, the beginning.

After sleeping a few hours in a musty NYU dorm room, we made our way to Rockefeller Center for some hot chocolate at Dean & DeLuca. While my friends waited in line, I hung back. I stood resting my arms over the railings, staring at ice skaters as they attempted to check the box "Go ice skating at Rockefeller Center" off their holiday bucket list.

If you've ever been to Rockefeller Center, you know it's really loud and buzzing with people. Yet, somehow, it was there that I could hear the most subtle voice. It was the voice that my friends were begging me to connect to while in Spain, but I refused. Looking back, I know denial was my strategy because I was afraid that what I would hear would be too painful or too hard to follow. I honestly wasn't sure if I was even strong enough to hear it. During my engagement, the thoughts and feelings would bubble up just enough for me to say, "Hey Gut, you got the wrong girl. I am not brave enough for this. I'm not brave enough to do what you are trying to ask me to do." So I plugged my ears and pushed it down because I also knew that once I heard the *real* truth, it would be impossible *not* to follow.

But something happens when you leave the busyness and predictability of your regular life. Some sort of magical window opened up when I decided to tell my fiancé, my mother, and all the wedding vendors that I was unavailable for the weekend. I was no longer willing to carry all the balls in the air or follow the imaginary contract I thought I was bound to. And so, the voice found an opening. Amidst all the noise, for the first time in a really long time, I heard the voice of the Divine within me. A voice that I now know as my intuition.

"You are meant for something bigger," is what I heard. It was so clear and carried so much authority. When I wasn't paying attention, the voice snuck in, completed its sentence, and caught me by surprise. The damage was done.

At that moment, I knew I couldn't continue on this fake, forced path. That phrase changed everything. It saved me. I was always looking to be saved. I just never thought it would come from inside me.

As tears rolled down my face, I felt my fear surrender. There was something about that voice that felt so trustworthy and confident. That tiny phrase carried an energy that made me feel as if everything would be okay. In fact, it somehow made me believe that life would be better than just okay; it would be magical. And that was the kind of life I wanted to live. All I had to do was to follow the voice of my intuition.

That moment taught me that you could feel sad, scared, and excited all in one breath. Now I know that to feel a juxtaposition of emotions in one instant is to be alive. I couldn't feel anything for so long because I was numb. I was in denial. I was too afraid of what I would find inside myself.

Consumed by emotion, at that moment I decided I would go back to Miami, call off the wedding, and break up with my fiance—no matter the pain and discomfort that it would cause others and me. My effort to keep others from feeling pain and discomfort for a moment in time, was causing a very slow death within myself. A death, I thought, I could ultimately avoid.

In life, we are constantly experiencing the cycles of life and death. One chapter ends, so that another can begin. Nature's most iconic metaphor for this cycle is that of a butterfly. After a few days as an egg, it pops out and is introduced to the world as a caterpillar. For a few weeks it lives the path of a caterpillar. If you didn't know any better, you would assume that this was a caterpillar and nothing else. But from a higher vantage point, like a butterfly, you would know that life was about change for this little guy. Next thing you know, it's entering position to form a chrysalis. Again, without knowing any better, you might worry that the caterpillar was sick. This is not unlike the anxiety a parent feels when their child is entering puberty and their behavior becomes...well, crazy. *Have I failed as a parent?* we worry. Nope, it's called adolescence.

Thankfully, the caterpillar gracefully surrenders to this process. It understands that the caterpillar stage is ending, only to find a more expansive life as a butterfly. As for humans, we're not so trusting. As soon as life feels or looks different, we typically try to control it by creating some artificial environment, when what we're really meant to do is surrender to the voice within.

Choosing to date my boyfriend was not a wrong choice. In fact, it was a great choice for many years. Where I went wrong was in not recognizing the signs of decay. My misstep was in my refusal to recognize death.

Instead of pausing to see that this relationship had run its course, I encouraged my boyfriend to artificially move us to the next step by proposing. It didn't feel natural or organic, but I thought perhaps it would give us a new life. Instead of slowing down, I pushed along by packing my schedule. This way, I could continue on a straight path — checking all the societal norms off my checklist — rather than accept the fact that my life was screaming for a detour.

My path had been meticulously laid out in my imaginary contract: Go to college. Major in something secure that can score you a safe job upon graduation. Find a boyfriend. Stick together long enough to elicit a wedding proposal. Secure a job. Buy a house. Get married. Get a dog or become pregnant. The end.

The only reason I didn't want to hear the voice earlier was because I was afraid of what would happen if I jumped off my linear path. *Could I ever get back on? If I don't want this, then what* do *I want? If I stop taking these steps, then what is the next step?*

Isn't it funny that most of us want to live a free-flowing life, yet we are the ones who keep ourselves chained to a linear path? I was a self-described free spirit, yet I was judging myself off of the blueprints of others. That voice I heard in New York snapped me out of my trance—the trance of my programming.

Before that experience, I didn't really comprehend that I had my own inner voice that was trying to guide me to my true path. It was a path I didn't yet know, but deep in my heart I knew it existed. I had known several *other* voices in my life: my parents' voices, my friends' voices, society's voice, my own perfectionist, desperate-to-feel-good-enough voice. There were so many voices within me, but none of them were truly mine.

It wasn't until that moment in New York that I realized that I had a divine voice within me. This was my first conscious encounter with the voice, so I was by no means an expert. What came next was years of relationship building, experimentation, and hours spent reflecting in order to hone in on this innate power. Throughout this book, I'll share with you what I learned, but remember it's not linear, so stay curious!

CLUES OF THE VOICE

One of my earliest observations was that the voice was short, simple, and to the point. It would typically either give me a long-term vision with no specific steps to follow — like a flash of the future — or just one step to move forward without any confirmation of where I was going.

For example, in New York, the voice flashed me a feeling of the future. It felt magical, and I was told I was meant for something more. Which was awesome and very inspiring, but I received no plan. For someone had been following a strict linear path until then, I would have loved some sort of itinerary, preferably one created by a Virgo. All I received was the first step: break off the engagement.

Here's the trick: you must follow the first step blindly. Do not worry about not knowing the next step. This is not always easy, because the promise of the future is so much more fun than the responsibility of being grounded in the current moment. We like to dream about what it might mean or look like to be "made for bigger things" more than we like to follow the steps we are being instructed to take.

Also, we often do not like to take divinely inspired steps unless there is a guaranteed outcome. Take my client Sarah's story for example. Sarah was searching for her next career. She was a burnt-out accountant looking for more joy, flexibility, and purpose. Sarah would show up to our sessions telling me she had no idea what to do. Really, she just wanted me to use my intuition to tell her what to do because she was under the impression that mine was better than hers. Spoiler alert: yours will always be better than anyone else's. Which is why developing your intuition is a worthy investment.

After putting her on the spot with several questions, Sarah admitted that she liked planning parties. In fact, she was so good at it that even her friends were asking her to organize parties for them. Deep down, she knew that her next step was to try planning a few parties for others and seeing where it would take her. No one was asking her to quit her career. All that was being asked of her was to plan a party for payment. But she was refusing to take the steps. Why? Because she didn't know where this move would take her.

What she *really* wanted was for the voice (like Mufasa in "The Lion King") to tell her:

"Sarah, after you plan these small parties, the biggest party planner in L.A. is going to discover you and hire you. This way, you will have a steady paycheck. Clients are going to love you so much, they'll be paying you $100,000 per event. You will start your own company and be wildly successful. Your parents will be proud. Your husband will be supportive. Your friends will cheer. You will buy your dream house and then have a child. You will be so well known that you will stay at home with your child as everyone else makes you money. There's a Netflix deal somewhere in the future. Go forth, my child."

Sound familiar? Only after the voice spells out the plan and puts it in writing do we want to take the first step. But sadly, that is not how our intuition works. Here's why.

THE SOUL'S TRUE PATH

Intuition is the voice of the soul. Being human means that we are composed of mind, body, and soul. For a large portion of our lives, we identify heavily with our minds and bodies, and forget that we are souls. At some point, the soul begins to communicate with our human selves. This is what we refer to as a spiritual awakening. Our intuition starts to break through and catch our attention.

Before this lifetime, our souls made a little itinerary or plan for this human incarnation. This is also known as the soul's contract. Deciding to partake in the human experience means that, for some time, we forget what we really are: spiritual beings playing as human characters, hoping to evolve and better understand our essence.

A few weeks ago our 9-year-old son, Oliver, was playing with his virtual reality game system. He popped his head out of the goggles and asked me, "Mom, how do we know if this life is real life?" The metaphysical geek in me was so excited to have this conversation with him.

Off I went. "Well, there are different ways to look at this topic, but many big thinkers believe that Earth life is an experiment. Your soul planned the whole thing. You just forgot. It's like if you forgot that you were a human operating an avatar in your virtual reality video game," I said.

Oliver tilted his head slightly and said, "Mom, I don't understand that, and I don't want to understand. It's okay that I don't remember my soul."

I laughed and thought, "That is the most old-soul thing one could say."

Right now, our son is nine and he wants to keep doing the human thing without remembering. This is by design. In fact, his higher self was probably saying, "Good call, Oliver. Let's stick to the schedule."

At some point, when the time feels right, he'll probably start to ask life's big questions, like *What is my purpose, What's the point of life*, and all those other existential crisis questions we ask ourselves at some point or another. When we start to think this way, our human self starts to describe this reflection time as "being lost." But the truth is, we are on the cusp of being found. This is your soul initiating the remembering process by activating the voice of your intuition.

The whole point of remembering is to bring you back to your soul's path so you can complete your soul's purpose or mission. In my case, I was very close to using my free will to make one very big choice (getting married) that would significantly derail me from my soul's path. After trying to get through to me in small ways, I imagine that my higher self found an opening in New York City and was screaming, "Mayday, Mayday! It's time! Activate remembering mode." And just like that, in Rockefeller Center, I had my first conscious spiritual awakening, which guided me back to my true path.

Now, if that voice would have told me to call off the wedding, followed by all the steps that led me to becoming a professional intuitive and the author of this book, I would have been extremely overwhelmed. Like Sarah, I *thought* I wanted all the steps, but in that moment, knowing all that was to come would have paralyzed me from moving forward.

Our higher self is speaking to us through intuition. The higher self is a wise parent that knows what we can handle and when we can handle it. If we can't follow the first little step our intuition gives us, what makes us think having ten steps would make us feel more safe? The most important thing is that we take a step toward getting back on our soul's path.

Speaking of staying on path, I mentioned earlier that I was using my free will to go off course. What I'm referring to is that although our soul has a plan before we come into this lifetime, we are each given the power of free will. This means that despite the soul's contract, your human self can still do what it wants by utilizing free will.

If you grew up Christian like me, you may be familiar with the phrase, "Your will versus God's will." This is referring to the thought that perhaps I'm trying to bend life toward my own human will (or ego, if you prefer), instead of considering the direction God's will is taking me. The idea is if we can live in alignment with God's will (A.K.A. the soul's true path), we can then begin to live our destiny.

Living our destiny is that flowy, life-is-working-for-me type of life we all dream of. It's the embodiment of soul-led living. The tricky part is that mastering soul-led living is not taught in a written manual. And you can't track your soul's progress on an app (although that would be so amazing). Instead, we must go through the process of awakening and aligning, which ultimately moves us into soul-led living.

Awakening was my moment in NYC. Aligning was going back to Miami and calling off the wedding. Soul-led living is living life guided by no other voice but your own.

This is why I'm starting this book discussing the voice. The voice is just another word for your intuition. Your intuition is your own custom Siri who dictates your soul's path for you while you navigate the map of this lifetime. Getting to know and understand our intuition is the best chance we have at remembering our soul's path and therefore living it.

CHAPTER THREE

The Road to Your Soul's Path

After calling off the wedding, I was sad for about two weeks. Yes, it was all sorts of messy, but you know when you mourn something before it's over? So when it's actually over, you kind of already did all the processing? Well, that's what happened to me. The relationship had ended a long time before it actually did. I was just waiting for someone to tell me that I could get off the train and start thinking about my next adventure.

What a relief! The decision that I thought would kill me, actually gave me life. I finally realized that I had always been free. No one was really holding me back, except for myself.

When you first start listening to your intuition, it might be hard to decipher whether you're on the right path or not. And while, yes, there are a lot of moving pieces to living a soul-led life, one very simple clue is found in how you're feeling.

After choosing to follow the directions of my inner spirit, I was initially scared, and then sad. But once I broke the news to my friends and family, I found I no longer felt scared or sad. What I did feel was lost — but in the best way.

Up until that point, I had lived life on a *very* predictable path. When I made the decision to get off that train, I immediately realized that there were no more plans. I had no absolutely no idea what was ahead, but I had a strong feeling that good things were in store. Walking a path that was no longer predictable meant opportunities, excitement, and freedom. This new road is what I like to call the detour.

After we make important decisions that take us off the default path and towards our soul's path (also known as the soul's true path), there is oftentimes a detour we must take. It's not the real road just yet. It's just the road that carries us over to the soul's true path.

THE SOUL'S PATH VERSUS THE DEFAULT PATH

Before we discuss the detour road, let's first examine the soul's path versus a default path. In my practice of intuitive readings, I typically start by looking at the soul's path, which is a zoomed-in snapshot of the soul's contract. The soul's contract is a soul's itinerary for this lifetime. It's filled with possible pit stops, people you may encounter, and different levels of paths (think: regular classes, honors classes, and AP classes). As souls, we do our best to prepare a soul's contract that will give us a chance of evolving this lifetime.

The reason I focus less on the soul's contract in my readings is because it is always evolving depending the decisions we make and the collective consciousness on Earth. If you're about to head out on a five-hour road trip you might enter the address of your final destination on your map app, but the paths will constantly update based on traffic and unforeseen disruptions. The soul's contract works in a similar way; it makes adjustments while we're on Earth, making it harder to track and predict.

Instead, I like to focus on the soul's path, which I actually refer to as the soul's true path because it is aligned with who you truly are. I like to examine the true path; it's like focusing on a journey rather than trying to think about every stop and turn on the map to your destination. Paying attention to your true path is like focusing one bite-size task at a time, all part of a larger goal. With practice, you can learn to attune to the energy of your true path, which will let you know what it feels like to be on the true path versus the default path.

In my readings, the vision I receive in my mind's eye is typically two parallel vertical lines. The line to the left is the default path and the line to the right is the true path. Unfortunately we are usually on the default path. The good news is, though, that most people who come to me are already making their way towards their true path via the detour. But to head to our true path, we must first understand the default path.

Like a good, fake luxury handbag, the default path can be hard to spot. It's not unbearable, it's oftentimes comfortable, and it's usually endorsed by the people in our lives. Rarely does the default path appear awful from the outside. It's on the inside where it feels a bit 'off'.

What keeps us from acknowledging that we might be off-path is the fear that our lives will change too much. We're afraid that the true path will ask us to leave our partners, quit our jobs, or move to another country.

Some paths will, absolutely, ask us for drastic changes. My particular path indeed asked me to leave a fancy editorial career to become a professional intuitive, to prepare for divorce, and to leave a comfortable city life for unchartered country living. But more often than not, the true path is just asking for more honesty from us. Self-honesty can be achieved in small steps or big dramatic moves. I do believe that each soul decides on its own particular level of drama.

Believe it or not, there are those of us who fear the small steps. For some of us, small changes toward our truth can feel excruciating, like slowly pulling off a bandaid rather than ripping it off all at once. If you're a "Go big or go home," kind of person like me, I trust that your soul will give you a grand, dramatic collapse of your default path, complete with a side of fireworks!

For the souls who have no interest in theatrics, you can set the intention that the road to your true path be discovered softly and with grace. Take a moment now to breathe into your heart and ask for the support you need as you move toward your true path. Here's a prayer you can repeat, or feel free to make it your own.

Dear spirit of the creator within me,

I am ready to walk my truest and highest path.

Please guide me with ease, joy, and safety along this road.

May my journey be filled with support, protection, and love.

And may it be done in my highest and greatest good and the highest and greatest good of all those involved.

And so it is.

After setting your intention, you can feel safe to examine your current path. There is no need to fear a default path because your true path is divinely supported. This shift is only taking you to the life of your deepest desires.

While everyone's paths look different, there are some characteristics that all default paths have in common. On a default path, all choices are being made from the desire to manage and soothe our own anxieties. We live afraid of the future and the unknown, and thus we are constantly searching for a guaranteed, safe route that comes with a plan and a blueprint. When on this path, we look outside ourselves for approval and make choices based on how we will appear to others. We choose things that we think will make us seem "better," "smarter," and "more successful" than the rest.

A default path gives us the illusion that we are in control and making our own soul-led choices, but in truth, we are being dictated by our fear.

The true path requires much more courage and a strong connection to your intuition. There isn't an absence of fear on this path, but rather an emphasis on duty—on what must be done—to live in alignment with one's truth.

When walking the true path, we are no longer afraid to walk alone, experiment, or go down a winding road. There is no longer an attachment to linear movement. We are comfortable with receiving the first step, following it, and then simply waiting for the next. On the true path, there are often premonitions about where we are headed. We may see the future, but we don't yet see each of the steps that will take us there.

The feelings behind both paths:

True Path	Default Path
Curious	Controlling
Trusting	Need to Know
Heart-Guided Action	Extreme Logical Action
Jog	Sprint
Winding or Web	Linear
Trailblazer	Blueprint Seeker
Internally-led	Following the External
Experimental	Guaranteed
Free	Rigid
Possibilities	The Known
Allowing	Forcing
Knowing	Doubting

If you suspect that you might be on a default path, you have nothing to fear. This book is designed to guide you to your true path chapter by chapter. You're not doing too badly; after all, you've already taken the first step!

You'll learn more as you go, but for now, I want you to feel the energy of each word listed in the chart above. What does it feel like to be curious? Maybe your jaw gets lighter and your breath deeper.

Or maybe, curiosity makes you feel intimidated or uncomfortable. That's also great information. Most of us think that the true path is paved with only good feelings. But good feelings can also just mean comfortable feelings. And when we're comfortable, that usually means we are following a "safe" blueprint. If you're not feeling uncomfortable pretty often, then you're probably not being curious enough. As you reap the benefits of being uncomfortable and getting to the other side, your brain will begin to register this discomfort as excitement and nervousness that ultimately leads to new opportunities.

How about feeling into the default path? What does it feel like to be controlling? Maybe it feels like life is in order and predictable. That may feel safe, but it's also not creating new possibilities for you. The life of your dreams cannot be created in this environment because dreams are created from living outside the norm of your regular default settings.

Become familiar with the energy of each word, and as you go throughout your day, notice if you're predominantly in true path energy or default path energy. And if you're feeling really ambitious, when you find yourself in a default path energy, see if you can switch your state into true path energy.

DETOUR ROAD

As I mentioned earlier, as we make our way from the default

path to the true path, we'll find ourselves getting there by taking a detour road. In my Soul Readings, I see this as the space between the default path and the true path. By nature, the detour road is uncertain because it's not a long-term path. It's the in-between. And while we would love to believe that everything on the true path is set in stone, the detour road actually influences the true path. If I were performing a Soul Reading on you right now and looking at your true path, I would see several outcomes or options based on how you navigate the detour road.

The detour road is the space of creation. The state in which we live it, affects the final creation. Think of a pregnant mother. Yes, there is a baby forming inside of her, but how she cares for herself and how she feels during pregnancy can have tremendous influence on the soon-to-be child.

At first, we're excited to live more truly, but then we quickly recoil due to the lack of familiarity. We realize that we are in the unknown.

This is usually the moment when we seek a psychic and maybe the most regimented life coach we can find. As highly sensitive beings we're constantly looking to control life because, let's be honest, it feels pretty damn scary and unsafe over here. But, being controlling and wanting to know every single step is what got us into trouble in the first place. It is what created the predictable, default path that we are trying to move away from.

The detour road may seem blurry, but it can also feel so fun. Repeat after me: "Surprises are exciting." The unknown creates new possibilities. If we look at our lives and the predictable future feels depressing, then we must jump into the unknown. And we should feel gratitude for it because we know it is cooking up something new and exciting for us — which is always better than that lame road we walked previously.

Perhaps living in the unknown sounds way too risky for you? You may identify as someone who is risk-averse. Here's the truth: The reason you don't like to be in the unknown is because you don't like how your body feels when you're there. There is a part of you that believes that your body may break under all the pressure and that you'll ultimately turn into dust. Why do I know this? Because it takes one to know one!

I am a Cancer sun and rising. Astrologically speaking, I should be living in a cave, while snuggled up in a fleece blanket and crying out my feelings. Which don't get me wrong, I do often. My natal chart is dripping in this crab energy. Because of that, I constantly have to monitor my self-sabotaging behavior. But at some point, our dreams must outweigh our desire to protect ourselves.

Take writing this book for example: At the beginning of this process, it pained me to sit here and write. There's a part of me that loves writing (and double loves the idea of a finished book with all the praise and benefits that come with having a published book), and there's a part of me that just wants to run into my husband's arms so he can protect me from the world. It really does feel that dramatic for me.

During this process, I ended up in the hospital for non-stop vomiting. My diagnosis? Nerves. Emotionally, I was worried about the future and anything that could possibly go wrong as I allowed myself to be more exposed through the pages of this book. When you step out of your comfort zone and begin introducing something new (like writing this book), you're inevitably changing the trajectory of your life. It becomes unpredictable. I don't know what's going to happen after I write this book. I don't know if my body will explode from the pressure and turn into dust.

It probably will. Or maybe it won't? Regardless, I'm going to push myself to the edge and here's why: I've gone outside my comfort zone before, and I have always been rewarded. When you're thinking about leaping or letting go of control, call to mind a time where you allowed yourself to feel uncomfortable. When was the last time you let yourself complete a task that made you feel afraid? How did it feel afterwards? Did life reward you?

Anytime I'm afraid to leap into the unknown, I remember all the times my inner courage has rewarded me. You must keep those memories in your back pocket when you're trying to live bravely. Remember, bravery is not something we are blessed with at birth. It is something we develop and grow, like a muscle. The more we exercise it the bigger it gets.

Speaking of exercise, this is my second trick for living with more courage. Some people exercise to make their butt look better. I exercise so that I can follow through on scary stuff. And my butt looking tight is just an added bonus!

All jokes aside, introducing a difficult workout into your routine will teach your mind that you will not break when you do something hard. On the contrary, what your brain is going to obtain after finishing each and every intense workout is the high of endorphins. Over time, it will learn that going outside its comfort zone leads to reward. This is how I train myself to do hard things.

You may be wondering, "But Nikki, you said soul-led living is about living in flow and not pushing." Yes, that is true, but understand this: When we align with the flow of our lives, there will be times we need to push — even when it feels uncomfortable to do so.

This internal ability to know whether to push ourselves (or not) can be seen as our inner mother's wisdom. Sometimes, when we push or try to control our external environments, it's really an attempt to bubble wrap ourselves and protect us from the harm in the world, and from all our sensitivities. What we're creating is the worried mom at the playground who micromanages her toddler's every move.

But what if your inner mother actually believed in you? What if she could watch you get rough on the playground of life and think, "I don't need to protect her. If she falls down, she'll get back up. My child is strong and resilient."

This is the inner mother you really want—the one who encourages you to be resilient, to face challenges, and to move through your sensitivities with strength and grace. The mother who, when you fall, says "That's okay, buddy. You're strong. Do you feel okay?" The kind of mother who believes in her child's ability to heal, to adapt, and to thrive. This is the kind of mother you want, and the kind of inward-focused "pushing" I'm talking about.

Our middle child has taught me a lot about sensitivities and how to mother more supportively. As a young child, Oliver could not stand brushing his teeth or cutting his hair. It was deeply uncomfortable for him. The feeling of a loose hair tickling his neck was unbearable. The sensation of the toothbrush bristles rubbing up against his gums was enough to turn him into a monster. It was challenging to be his parent at these times.

We eventually decided to bring him to a sensory specialist who worked with highly sensitive children like Oliver. I was excited to receive all her tips. In my mind, I assumed she would introduce me to a new way of brushing his teeth or maybe provide some mantras for relaxation.

Instead, she handed me a blue, spiky finger condom, like the kind you use to brush a dog's teeth and said, "You're going to massage his gums every day, twice a day." Which I then responded to by saying, "No, I don't think you understand. He will bite me, and I will bleed."

Instead of working around his sensitivity, her expert advice was to *desensitize* him. I was shocked by this concept. I thought I was supposed to protect him from pain, and instead she was asking me to subject him to more of the activity he so desperately hated. Honestly, I wasn't sure he could do it. I didn't believe in him. I didn't believe in myself.

At the time of writing this book, Oliver is nine and I am happy to report that his teeth are clean and his breath smells fine (most of the time, anyway). We followed the expert's advice of gently rubbing his gums for a few months. Eventually, the uncomfortable became comfortable — for both Oliver and mom.

When we find ourselves in front of a detour road, we need to embrace it with the voice of the balanced inner mother. She is gentle and supportive, but she also firmly believes we can do hard things. She believes we can move through our sensitivities, and face our challenges.

While it's very easy to worry, experience doubt, and feel lost during this season, we want to make sure we keep our vibe high. In other words, we want to take care of ourselves emotionally, spiritually, and physically. In this stage of your journey, you are both shedding an old life and growing a new one. In your past season, you were in a constant state of "push mode." There was likely very little genuine inner care. You might have been caring for yourself, but only in an effort to perform and achieve results.

On the other hand, this new kind of care is centered around compassion. We must be aware of how fragile we are in this stage. We are a work in progress. Our bodies are sensitive, we're developing each day, and we're a bit confused about what is going on around us.

HOW TO CARE FOR YOURSELF IN-BETWEEN PATHS

I want you to take a minute and think about the best mother you knew growing up—the one who always knew what to say when times were tough. Perhaps you are blessed, and this mother is your own. Maybe you saw a mom like this on T.V. Or maybe you have a vision of this kind of mother within your heart.

Imagine that this mother is now your inner dialogue. She is your cheerleader and best friend.

When you find yourself feeling lost or down, ask yourself "What would my inner mother say?" Allow that compassionate and wise dialogue to guide you.

Your former inner dialogue might sound more like a sergeant. I know mine was. I would constantly catch myself saying things like "Come on, Nikki, get it together," or "Nikki, you are such a mess." Maybe these comments don't seem like much, but little by little they destroy your confidence and keep you chained to the default path.

We may think that it's the outside voices that affect us, but it's actually the dialogue within that stops us from living up to our full potential. If someone outside you is saying awful things to you, it can only affect you if the *inside you* agrees with their words. If your internal dialogue is strong enough to understand that what they are saying says more about them and not you, then exterior words cannot harm you. Maintaining a solid inner dialogue is critical in protecting us from going off path.

As a sensitive person, I used to automatically assume that if someone was criticizing me, then I must be bad. It wasn't until I sat with a therapist who asked me, "Nikki, if I tell you that I don't like your shoes, are we learning more about who you are? Or are we learning more about who I am?" that I finally understood. Her comment about my shoes gives us more information about her and her preferences; we don't learn anything new about me. It's not about *me* or *my* taste in shoes. It's about *her* and *her* taste in shoes.

A balanced inner dialogue will be able to respond to others' opinions of us by saying, "Oh, that's so interesting that they see the world that way. But this is a perspective and not the final truth."

Before we learn to shift our inner dialogue, we must first observe it. This is not always easy; our inner dialogue has a tendency to hide. I've had several students tell me, "I don't really think I have a mean voice talking to me. I don't think I have any voice at all." Yet, they find themselves living a scared life, never following their dreams.

If you have a supportive inner dialogue, you will be living authentically. You will be pursuing your dreams, feeling inspired, and loving yourself along the way. If you're not living that way, then its likely that your hidden inner dialogue is judging you, over protecting you, or simply being so chatty that it doesn't let you focus on what is important.

Sometimes we catch the tone of our inner dialogue, just by chance. You may hear yourself say something out loud that reflects your inner dialogue. For example, if you're talking to a friend about wanting to find love and she suggests going on dating apps, you may hear yourself say. "People on dating apps are creeps." Is that statement absolutely true? No, it isn't. You know there are good people on dating apps, and you know many who have found their matches on dating apps.

We become so accustomed to believing our inner dialogue that we start to see it as truth and fact. We never stop to question it. We never stop to wonder "Is this dialogue keeping me small?"

This dialogue isn't trying to kill us. It's trying to protect us. That's what the ego does. Just like that helicopter parent who wants to keep us safe, they will do so at any cost, even if it means making up lies in an effort to contain us.

If we can't catch our inner dialogue spontaneously through the way we speak, we can always observe it through meditation. Have you ever tried to sit in silence for 20 minutes? Yeah, I bet you hate it. You've probably even convinced yourself that it's boring, that it doesn't work for you, or that you're just not a meditator. And that's exactly what a self-sabotaging inner dialogue would say. We have to laugh at how basic our scared inner dialogue can be!

Instead of listening to that dialogue, try meditating. Simply sit in silence for 10 minutes and try to focus on your breath. Your inner dialogue may say all sorts of things. Maybe not mean things, but it'll talk just enough to make you confused. When we're confused, we don't take action. We become paralyzed from overwhelm.

Or maybe when you sit in meditation, you may find your dialogue to be negative, skeptical or impatient. You may not see it as negative. To you it may seem discerning, realistic, or logical. We often pride ourselves in being logical as it seems like a positive attribute, but let me ask you this: Does your life feel expansive and inspiring? Or does it feel small and boring? Being realistic, logical, and discerning can simply be code for being closed-minded.

Whatever you may find when you start observing your thoughts, know that your inner dialogue will inevitably have to change in order to guide you to your true path. The detour journey is about shifting your energy to that of your true path. The way we think and talk to ourselves is part of what makes our vibration. The more expansive, open, and encouraging your mind is, the higher your vibration will be.

As you make your way to your true path, your inner dialogue will be balanced and strong (or at least, you'll be able to catch it when it's not). But for now, as we explore the detour journey, let's just focus on creating encouraging inner dialogue that is open to change. The tone of this voice is non-judgmental, curious, and it can admit that it doesn't have all the answers. It's an open box, rather than a sealed container.

Below are a few supportive affirmations that can help you create a more balanced and trusting inner dialogue as you walk this path:

"I don't know exactly where I am going, but I do know I'm on the right path."

"I am supported."

"Everything is working out in my highest and greatest good."

"I'm excited about what's to come."
"I am scared, but I know I am protected and guided."
"It's natural to be scared when stretching into new possibilities."
"I love you. I'm proud of you. And you're doing great."

ENERGETIC INFLUENCES

In addition to adopting a gentle inner dialogue, consider what people, places, and things make you feel positive and which ones bring you down. This way, when you're feeling a little off, you can take a look at the energy you are currently consuming and determine whether or not it needs adjusting.

We are consuming different kinds of energy all day long through media, the people we surround ourselves with, our activities and outings, the things we eat and drink, and our sources of entertainment. Some of this energy will be a positive influence on our vibration and others will cause a negative impact. To take good energetic care of ourselves, we need to know what works for us and what doesn't.

Ask yourself the following questions:
Who in my life leaves me feeling drained?
Who in my life leaves me feeling energized?
What media leaves me feeling anxious or less than?
What media makes me feel inspired?
Which activities make me feel bad, uninspired, or bored?
Which activities make me feel renewed and happy?

In a perfect world, we could stay away from everything that drains us, but it's not always possible. Let's explore the most obvious example: children. We may love our child, but they may also be the person who drains us the most. Rather than abandon or ignore them, we need to dig deep within ourselves to find out why this relationship drains us and how we can rearrange it so that it's something that gives us energy instead. This is a great time to introduce a therapist into your self-care kit.

There may be other things in our lives that are stealing energy from us, but we hold on to them for one reason or another. This could be as simple as a coffee habit that we can't seem to break; to as complicated as staying in a job that doesn't fulfill us.

Remember, when we're in between paths we are in a stage of transformation. You will be asked to shed anything that does not serve you. Change is inevitable. This is happening because you are ascending, your energy is rising to a higher vibration. And at that higher vibration lives the life of your dreams.

As you start to understand what gives you energy, you will want to keep those influences in your back pocket. On the days where you find yourself doubting this new road, you'll want to tap into your high-vibe survival kit. We'll build yours together, but first let me show you how it works.

After breaking off my engagement, I felt compelled to return the ring to my ex-fiancé. He was living in a townhouse we had purchased together. Driving there and giving him back what was his felt like a proper good-bye.

As I sat on the couch — a couch I had picked out — I wondered if I was making a mistake. After all, this place was so comfortable, broken-in, and familiar. Was I really about to leave all of this comfort for an adventure that offered me no guarantees?

Despite my inner fears, in that moment I handed off the ring and quickly disappeared into the darkness of the night. Scared and in tears, I sat in my car in the desolate parking lot of my now former townhouse. I hated myself for being so complicated. Why couldn't I be like other girls who were content with a good guy, a decent townhome, and a simple career?

Tortured by my inner critic, I began to hear the voices of anyone who had ever told me that I was a brat, unrealistic, and ungrateful. Worse than hearing the voices, I was just about to begin believing them.

As I was feeling the weight of my crumbling life, my phone rang. It was my best friend, calling from Los Angeles. Maybe she had felt my energy? Or maybe the divine guidance that is with me prompted her to call me in that moment? I don't know what it was, but it worked.

This was a friend who always gave me life. She had big dreams way before I knew I was allowed to have them too. By the end of our conversation, I felt completely renewed. This is why she will always be in my high-vibe survival kit. A high hit is sometimes just a phone call away.

Not all pick-me-ups are as serendipitous as that phone call I received that night. Most of the time, we'll need to do the work ourselves and reach into our high-vibe survival kit to make the phone call, listen to an uplifting audio book, or take a drive to a place that we know will shift our energy. During these energy dips, we must take good care of ourselves. Because trailblazers, like you, need vibrancy and inspiration to get to the other side — the place where dreams are fulfilled.

Let's build your kit together. Grab a piece of paper and some color pens if you have them. Write My High-Vibe Survival Kit at the top, followed by the headlines below and your responses.

Place

List a place that can shift your energy from low-vibe to high-vibe by the time you leave. I can go into my backyard hiking trails distraught, and leave inspired. List your place.

People

List the person (or people) whose energy shifts you. This does not need to be someone who emotionally cares for you (this is a high-vibe kit, which is different from a soothing kit), but rather someone who is can life you up just by being themselves. Our youngest son Ethan, our dog Molly, and a few of my favorite Peloton instructors do this for me by just being themselves. List your people.

Activity

List any activities that help you clear your mind, quiet spiraling negative thoughts, or pick your energy back up. For me, just give me some markers, stickers, and paper and I'm transported back to my teenage years where I would spend hours decorating my agenda or writing notes to friends. When I'm in this creative space, nothing else matters. It not only shifts me, but it gives me a break from the stresses of everyday life. List any activities that give you a similar effect.

Music

List songs that give you a high-vibe feeling. The more danceable the better! Music really does it for me, so I tend to categorize my songs according to the vibration I'm trying to achieve. Write your songs here, but also consider making a playlist by category wherever you listen to music for easy access. Some categories can be for songs that make you feel happy and motivated, while other categories can include songs that give the middle finger to the world (because we all know those songs definitely uplift your vibe). The categories are up to you. List your songs here.

Food (or drink)

List any food or drinks that lift your vibration. My brain likes to think that eating a cookie will give me high vibes, but in reality it gives me more of a self-pity feeling; so this one can be tricky. If I'm really looking for a high vibe hit, then I'm going to reach for a tangerine, something with ginger, or a matcha green tea latte. Foods that are yellow, orange, and green are usually the ones that are going to raise your vibration, because they are associated with the sacral, solar plexus and heart chakras, which (without going too deep into this) are happy energetic centers that help to move us away from a scared, survival state. List your foods.

Media

List media, books, podcasts, or any other content that gives you the high vibes you seek (hopefully this book is on that list!). What works best for me is typically a magazine or book on art, creativity, or inspiring places. I love to learn, but when I'm feeling down, content with an emphasis on learning can create additional unnecessary pressure. So, I tend to turn off social media and opt for beautiful words or pictures instead. Also, there are some podcaster's voices that just work for me. List your media.

Now you have your high-vibe survival kit! It's yours so feel free to add to it as you discover what creates a shift in you. In addition to reaching for this when we're feeling a lull in energy, this kit is also great to use as a preventive tool to keep our energy balanced.

During my journey, I learned to love my high-vibe survival kit and began seeing it as a partner—one that would support me throughout all the wild and exciting changes that the detour road often brings.

CHAPTER FOUR

Breaking Free from Identity Webs

After deciding to get off my default path, my detour road began revealing itself. Fully aware of my newfound freedom, I felt ready to spread my wings and fly. Literally and figuratively, I was ready to fly my way out of my hometown Miami.

At the time, the decision of where to go next was between Los Angeles and New York. These two cities made the most sense; I worked in media production and had friends in both cities—friends who could hopefully help me find work. My decision-making process was a mix of logic and intuition. Both cities were logical choices. I wasn't spinning the globe and letting my finger decide my next move. But once I had narrowed it down to two cities, I needed to feel pulled towards one. Los Angeles had palm trees and warm weather, which felt like a natural place for my Caribbean blood.

The reason I share my process for decision-making is because once we become convinced that soul-led living is for us, we can quickly become anxious over every choice, afraid that we will make the wrong ones and find ourselves off-path again. It's in these moments that we begin to ask ourselves, *What is the line between spirituality and superstition*? It's a superstition if you're making the decision out of fear.

It's really not about what choice you make, but instead how it feels when you make it. Living soul-led is not about making perfect choices. It's about making choices that our hearts feel led to in the moment.

Los Angeles was pulling me. That's not to say that New York wasn't also a great choice. It was an easier flight to Miami, and being originally from New Jersey meant New York felt familiar to me. But in the end, I could only live in one place, and the West was calling.

I could have spent weeks in my own head, micromanaging the path and wondering, "If I pick L.A., will I miss out on meeting my soulmate? What if my soulmate is in New York? What if I miss out on my dream job? What if I'm going down the wrong road?"

Intuition does not speak in an anxious voice, asking a bunch of questions. If you find yourself in that dialogue, give yourself permission to ignore it. Your intuition may ask you to look deeper at your choice. It might ask you to wait a little bit before you jump. But the tone you hear should be that of a wise mother rather, not a friend who's hyped up on too much coffee. If we were to mistakenly follow that anxious voice, we could find ourselves slowly slipping into another default path.

Following the road to our soul's true path may be guided by our intuition, but we must be prepared to feel several emotions at once. It's rarely feels like an unopposed "Hell, yes!" More often, it feels like a mix between nervousness and excitement. Think about how you feel when standing in line for an extreme drop water slide. You are jumping up and down with excitement, but also kind of feel like you might poop your pants!

That's how I felt about my move to L.A. My close friend (and future roommate) Tracy, put it best: "Nikki, nothing is permanent," she said. Of course she was right. I could change my mind later if I hated it. That advice was my intuition speaking through Tracy. While my move couldn't guarantee me anything, I was curious enough to follow.

It's important to note here that as it related to this move, I did feel a certain level of safety. Yes, I was taking a leap of faith, but I felt like I had a net beneath me. I had a friend I could stay with for a while, a good resume, a degree in the relevant field, and contacts in the industry. In other words, I felt confident in my ability to find a job and in my ability to survive. If I had not felt safe with my ability to survive, then I would have had to start by working on my survival skills.

Maybe you're currently working on your own survival skills?

That's okay! In fact, it's better than okay. You're taking care of yourself by creating a foundation you can grow upon. This skill building may not be the most glamorous stage, but it's a process you can't skip over. These skills are critical in affording us the safety we need to take leaps.

If you're wondering "What are survival skills? Do I have them?" let me give you some examples. A survival skill is something you can fall back on while you're investing in your dreams. For example, my client Olivia is toying with the idea of becoming a photographer. She is not a skilled photographer (yet), she isn't known in the industry, and has no client base. She cannot depend on this skill to survive just yet. It's still in the dream phase.

But she is the oldest of five children, which means she is an excellent babysitter. She feels confident in this skill, and she has a network of people who already come to her for these services. It's not what she wants to do long-term, but she can depend on it while she works on building her photography business.

You may already have some skills that you just haven't recognized yet. Or perhaps you have skills that aren't fully developed. Identifying and developing your survival skills will help you feel safe enough to gamble on yourself because in the back of your mind you'll know that you have something to fall back on if it doesn't work out. It gives you a net to fall on, which is why survival skills are worth investing in.

Survival skills can also include the network of people who surround you. Your parents or partner may be able to provide you with shelter, food, and other necessities while you are busy building your new life. That totally counts! In my case, my friend Tracy shared her space with me until I got my bearings, and my father bought me my new bedroom furniture.

Think of survival skills as preparation. Imagine that you were going on a journey into the forest. While you might not know what to expect. you'll probably pack some tools—a map, some food, and something to use for shelter. You wouldn't necessarily walk into the forest with only sandals and half a bottle of water.

When we take leaps within the detour road, we are being groomed to be the person who walks a true path. We're never really fully ready or prepared, but we feel safe enough to move ahead knowing that we are creating the next version of ourselves.

Two months after calling off the wedding, I packed up my car and drove across the country. My father accompanied me. Despite him having lost considerable sums of money on non-refundable wedding deposits, he was by my side the entire way. Shoutout to those soulmates in our lives who cheer us on as we make our way back on-path, no matter the inconvenience it may cause them. Despite all the drama, my father was proud of me for following my heart. (He was also probably trying to get me as far away as possible from my mother who, unlike my father, was sorely disappointed over the cancelled wedding and forfeited deposits). I had no job lined up, less than two thousand dollars in my bank account, and no permanent place to live.

Moving to L.A. was the first time I actually saw how the Universe assists you when you take your first leap toward your true path. You know what I'm talking about, right? When you take that somewhat calculated step because you know you're being called to, but you have *no idea* if there is a net to catch you if you fall.

Sometimes the Universe throws a little bit of beginner's luck your way. It's almost as if the Universe is rewarding you for making the brave move to follow your heart. During that small window of time, the world maneuvers its way to make your predictions come true — at a hasty speed. It feels like dumb luck.

I moved in with my best friend Tracy, who shared her Beverly Hills studio (and her bed) with me until we found a two-bedroom apartment that would fit us both. Shortly after, I landed a job at a film studio working as a Hollywood assistant— just like in the movies.

After a few weeks of helping me get settled, my father was finally ready to fly back to Miami. As we said our goodbyes at the airport, he left me with this bit of wisdom: "You're about to change a lot. Let the change, change you," he said. With those words he was giving me the permission to change, and so I did.

WHO AM I?

It was the first time I had ever lived on my own. When applying for college, it never occurred to me to go away for school. As we already know, good Cuban-American girls stayed in their parents' homes until, well, marriage. So living somewhere else just never seemed like an option.

I had attended the local state university, just like all my other friends, who were also children of Cuban parents. And my parents were friends with all of my friends' parents. To paint you a picture, when we were old enough to start "clubbing" (because that's what you do when you grow up in Miami), our parents would drop us off at the South Beach night club and then they'd all go to dinner at the restaurant next door while we danced the night away.

Bizarre, I know. But this is what immigrants do. They form tight-knit communities because they are so unfamiliar with this new world they live in. Existing this way meant their kids were less likely to get in trouble because there were several other pseudo-parents watching over you in case your parents weren't able to.

Looking back, it was a beautiful upbringing, but it was also very much a bubble. I felt suffocated, but I didn't truly understand why. It wasn't until I arrived to L.A., looked around at my friend's studio apartment, and asked myself, "Wait, where are all the grown ups?" that I understood that I was free.

I didn't know this but up until that day, all of my choices had not been my own. They had been fed to me. While the tight-knit communities I grew up with are special, it can be hard to find your individuality in them, particularly for sensitive souls who absorb everyone else's thoughts and emotions.

A few weeks into my new life, I realized that I had been stuck in an identity web— which was part of the reason I'd been stuck on my default path. I didn't know who I truly was.

These identity webs are so constraining, but they are also so subtle that many times we don't even know we're in one. The community around us silently lists its expectations of how we should live, and we end up walking to the rhythm outside of us, rather than taking the time to listen to the unique beat within.

The outside voices can become so loud that they drown out the inner voice. As a result, we become like a cookie from a mold and only show individuality when the risk is low. The remainder of our inner gold remains hidden until the day we are brave enough to explore outside the confines of our community.

At the core of the identity webs is the fear of survival. We are, after all, tribal creatures and we know that we need a tribe to survive. Abandonment can mean death. Thinking outside of the tribe's group mind can mean making others upset, uncomfortable, and angry. So, we vow to stay within the reins of the web.

Identity webs are also useful when we lack the bravery needed to examine our inner selves. Allowing others to make decisions for us and to tell us who we are is effortless. Handing off our power to others is easier than building the muscle to carry it on our own.

My awakening in New York gave me the permission I needed to step out of old rhythms and structures, and to remove myself from the web that was telling me who I was. Los Angeles danced at a different pace, and it required my full attention in order to learn the steps. I could no longer cruise on autopilot like I did in Miami. I needed my inner compass, I no longer had other people's maps to follow.

My first plan of action was to figure out what I liked, and what I didn't. If our heart is our inner compass, I needed to discover what felt aligned with my heart and what didn't. Naturally, I started this journey with food.

I feel like every time I move to a new place, someone is always trying to convert me to their religion. Luckily for me, my West Coast friends practiced brunch. In this part of the world no one goes to church on Sundays. They go to brunch. Sidewalk seating and eggs benedict *is* religion in California.

It was at this place of worship where I was born again. The waitress/actress/podcaster/bathing suit designer came to our table and asked us for our orders. One friend ordered the Huevos Rancheros, another the gluten-and-dairy-free pancakes (which, by the way, is not a pancake), and the friend to my left ordered a cheeseburger with an egg on it, which qualified as a breakfast burger.

Then it was my turn to order. But first, I needed to get over my shock. This is what was going through my head as the waitress/actress/podcaster/bathing suit designer patiently waited for me to decide:

Wait, you're telling me that we can all order different things?

There isn't a secret look that we give each other to signal that we must all order gluten-free?

You actually want me to choose for myself?

Should I go with the Huevos Rancheros because I am Spanish-speaking?

Or should I go with the gluten-and-dairy-free fake pancakes because it sounds like a healthy thing to do?

Or maybe I should just go with the egg burger because my mom always insists that meat is good for me?

And then unexpectedly, something took over my body, spoke through me and said, "I'll take the eggs benedict florentine with a side of home fries."

Gasp! Had I just been possessed by the devil in the holiest of places? Who told me to order that?

Right there, at the corner breakfast spot, my true heart's desire took over. And for the first time, I realized that no one cared what I was going to eat for brunch. There were no expectations of me here, and no one was judging me. I was free to be me. And as it turns out, I was a mostly-vegetarian who liked carbs. This discovery was miraculous. Brunch was indeed a sacred place, after all.

WHO ARE YOU, REALLY?

Leaving a default path for a true path means discovering our true essence and rhythms. We seek to understand what is innate versus what is learned.

This part of the journey is where we begin to unwind, shed, and rediscover. Becoming curious about our preferences is an easy entry point. My brunch might seem silly—restaurant food choices may seem inconsequential. But who we truly are is hidden in both big and small desires. Don't underestimate these "small" self-discoveries.

You may not have paid much attention to your desires in the past. But now that you are on this journey, you will begin to realize that some of your choices are soul-led and others have simply been programmed within you. As you start to move toward your true path, the programming may begin to feel wrong. You may not have been able to count on your body's signals in the past, but now that you have made the decision to live authentically, what is not in alignment will really frustrate you.

This is one of the hardest parts of healing and shedding old programming. You begin this inner work to improve your life, but oftentimes the work reveals more cracks. It gets worse before it gets better. Something that used to be tolerable can all of a sudden feel intolerable.

Don't be afraid to feel your own intolerance. These feelings tend to be more heightened, making them easier guides to your true path. You may not know what foods are good for you, but once you eat something that you have sensitivity to, it's easy to tell that something isn't sitting well with your stomach. In the same way, these unwanted feelings are powerful indicators of your truth.

Shortly after our move to North Carolina, my husband took me to a fancy furniture store. It was impeccably designed, it felt luxurious. But as soon as I flipped over one price tag, I became angry. Almost everything in the store was well beyond what I was willing to pay for new furniture. Knowing that I was just at the beginning of furnishing our new North Carolina home, this store made me feel deeply discouraged. I felt that I would never have a nice home.

The next day, he invited me to go to a flea market with him. I'm from Miami. We do bright, new, and shiny things, definitely not flea markets. In fact, the Miami aesthetic is the opposite of flea market chic. It's about showing what you have, what you have accomplished, and what you can afford.

As I tiptoed into my first-ever flea market, I quickly began to get lost in all the eccentric pieces and quirky people. I forgot that I was shopping. I forgot that I was with Benny. I forgot what shopping here might say about me. I forgot myself — or what I thought was myself.

A few hours later I plopped into the passenger seat of our car, admiring the adorable porcelain peacock I'd just bought for $4.

"You were so happy shopping there," Benny acknowledged.

"Was I?" I responded. I hadn't even noticed because I'd been so present in the moment. I was in total wonder.

Had I walked into that fancy furniture store in Miami, I would have found a way to buy something. Like an addict justifying her addiction, I would not have been angry, but rather determined to find a way. Also, had I been in Miami, I would not have walked into a flea market. Period.

My move to North Carolina was a step towards authentic living. My recent choice to move and live more authentically had placed me on a current, which was pushing me away from my former programming and pulling me closer to my true self. This explains my reaction to the over-priced furniture store, which was a stark contrast to the happiness I felt in the flea market.

Standing in that over-priced furniture store, my ego wanted to convince me that I was giving up on my money goals. It tried to convince me that I needed to find ways to make more money, and that if I couldn't afford these things then I was simply failing at my ambitions.

Thankfully though, my journey had taught me a few things, and I knew to just let those feelings pass in that moment. I didn't know why they were coming up. I didn't know what to believe. But I also knew that I didn't need to know at that precise moment. I knew that the message would be revealed to me in due time. All that I could do at that time was let go, but I knew the Divine would fill in the gaps for me eventually.

I know that the Divine speaks through people, especially the people we love the most. So when Benny pointed out to me how happy I was at the flea market, I became curious. What made me so happy about other people's junk and lost treasures?

As I questioned myself about what brought me so much joy there, I realized it was several things. First: I loved the artistic expression of furnishing your home with things that are unique. Second: It made me conscious of the impact that our desire for new things has on the environment. Third: I felt like I was honoring my money in a way that felt right.

The discomfort I felt at the furniture store led me to a gold mine of inner truths. "Oh, so *this* is who I am," I thought. Unfiltered. Uninfluenced. *This* is me.

Now, it's your turn. What bothers you? What no longer fits? What are you wrestling with?

Below are some steps to help you discover your true desires. Keeping a journal can be helpful in this exercise.

Step One

Commit to feeling the uncomfortable feelings. Remember you are doing this is in search of old programming and buried truths. To help yourself along, put your hand on your heart and say "Please give me the courage to feel it all so that I may see who I truly am."

Step Two

When you find yourself feeling uncomfortable or intolerant of things that previously did not bother you, observe your feeling but don't try to fix it. Don't worry about solving it in that moment. Allow it to show its ugly face and then let it leave when it's ready.

Step Three

Ask the question "Why?" With an open heart (one filled with gratitude and humility), ask the Divine why you are feeling this way. You are not asking yourself this question. It is not your job to answer. You are asking the Divine, a source with much higher perspective than you.

Step Four

Trust the process, and know that the answer will come when

the time is right. But continue to look out for moments when you feel the opposite of that discomfort. Pay attention to the moments when you feel the joy of truth.

Step Five

When you find yourself feeling the opposite, with curiosity, ask yourself why. Ask yourself what your truth is in this matter. Write it in your journal.

WHAT TO KEEP AND WHAT NOT TO KEEP

If my former self—impatient for results and answers—were reading this book, I would probably be thinking about moving and breaking off all my relationships. After all, if it worked for the author, then it should work for me!

Unfortunately, results are not that simple. This portion of our work together is about observation and getting to know yourself. If you were to get rid of everything uncomfortable in your life, you would learn nothing about yourself.

Ridding ourselves of all our stresses and moving to the top of a mountain to meditate all day is easy. The real spiritual heroes are those of us who are in it and still connecting to our souls despite the chaos that surrounds us. I'm talking about the mom staying home with three young children with not a minute to herself, the person trying to leave her toxic job to figure out how to support herself through her passions, and the person who goes on date after date, year after year, hoping to find their soulmate. This is the real spiritual work we came for.

You may not know why your soul has chosen to come to Earth in this lifetime to live a physical existence. But hopefully, based on what you're learning, you can be more curious about your soul's choice rather than resist it. Often, our instinct is to "check out" and bypass these very human scenarios, but that won't make life any better. Going through them is where we'll find the soul's master plan.

This is a process. We are all in the process. In the meantime, please don't put pressure on yourself to be perfectly aligned. I'm talking to you, the overachiever who thinks they can figure out life by chapter three. I know you, because I am you. Instead, let's practice breathing through the anxious feelings of wanting to know and fix it all in this one moment. Let's allow ourselves to let this book do the work it intends to do with us. Deep breath in. Exhale out. Repeat after me, "I allow."

HEALING THE STORIES ABOUT OURSELVES

The biggest threat to the true self are the old stories we tell about ourselves. Uncovering our true self means shedding false beliefs and programmed behaviors. Think of it as stripping a piece of furniture from its paint in order to expose the wood's true nature. As you do this, the furniture piece will look and feel different. The same goes for you.

Before stripping the nightstand of its blue paint, one might assume that it is, in fact, a blue night stand. But then you begin to sand it and strip it, and find that the night stand, in its natural form, is a light oak wood.

Before stripping yourself of your need to please, your negative outlook, your toxic environment, or anything else that is not true to your nature, you will appear a certain way. But as you begin to realign and release what is not yours, you will change.

Man, do we hate change. And the people around us don't like to see us change either. We're going to explore all of these dynamics, but first, let's talk about how we get so comfy with stories about ourselves that are not true. These stories can be one of the biggest hindrances in calling in our soul-led lives.

I used to think I was lazy. This is a story about myself that developed during childhood and through adolescence, and stayed with me as I became a young adult. Yet, I had no idea I was up against this lie.

I was once in my Downtown Miami apartment, cooking very complicated Chicken Parmesan for my new boyfriend and his friends. (I had just moved back home from L.A. We'll talk about this in the next chapter.) My effort in the kitchen screamed *I'm wife material, I swear!*

One hour deep into this new recipe, my boyfriend tried to distract me with conversation and asked me how my writing was going. When we had first started dating, I had proclaimed that I was writing a book. So naturally, he was just following up on that conversation.

"I can't get to it. I just think I'm lazy," I responded.

"Lazy? You? You're the opposite of lazy," he said.

I was in shock that he thought that about me. After all, I had cared very little about schoolwork growing up. In high school,

I never practiced my ballet turns enough to be a legitimately good dancer. My brothers always seemed to be studying longer and harder than me. And my mother had definitely directed the word *haragana* (the Spanish translation of lazy) towards me often enough for it to stick.

Therefore, I thought I was lazy. But my boyfriend thought otherwise. He began to list all the ways that I was not lazy. Everything he said was fact. He wasn't even trying to be nice (He was a Scorpio, and Scorpios don't know how to be nice.)

"Maybe you're a little unfocused at times, but I wouldn't call you lazy," he said. I was taking all this in and thought, "No, that's not it either. What I am is scared."

Not only was this story about being lazy causing me to work extra hard, like making an unnecessary, overly complicated home-cooked meal for 20-somethings who would eat anything you serve them, but it was hiding the root cause of *why* I wasn't writing.

As long as I kept thinking that I was lazy, I would never be able to overcome the challenge of not being able to write. "Lazy" and "unfocused" was covering up the truth. My truth. Which was that I was afraid of what could happen if I wrote what was in my heart.

You might be thinking, "Well, being afraid isn't a good thing either, Nikki. It's no better than being lazy." But it is. Because my truth is that I am a sensitive person—I feel a lot. Which means, I am scared often. Lazy just isn't my truth.

Funny enough, without these sensitivities, I couldn't be a writer, an intuitive, a caring partner, or an in-tuned parent. All the things I love about myself are possible because of my sensitivities. Sometimes my sensitivities show up as fears, which may look like being unfocused, and which may seem lazy. But, as long as I know the truth, I can help myself through whatever I'm going through.

Not only are our negative stories about ourselves not true, but they're also hiding a deeper need. You may identify as being controlling, but you may just have a need to feel safe. You may think you're not smart, but perhaps you just learn differently and you were overlooked growing up. You may say you're afraid to put your voice out there, but what you're really afraid of is losing your privacy and independence when you become heard. All of our stories have greater truth that can serve us in the most liberating ways.

Similar to hearing your inner dialogue out loud, you may find yourself stating who you believe you are. If the belief is working for you, great, keep it. But if when you say it, you feel shameful, down, or embarrassed, ask yourself if there is a deeper truth you're missing.

STORIES TOLD BY OTHERS

These stories are not only told by us, but often they are told by the people closest to us. While in a conversation with a friend, you may find them telling you something about yourself that you no longer want to be or be identified with. Maybe when you talk about dating, they state that you're picky. Rather than feel proud about that statement like you usually do, perhaps you notice it feels a little off. Stop to ask yourself, "Am I really picky? Or is there a greater truth for me?" Perhaps "picky" is a code word for, "I am afraid of getting hurt again, so I'm trying to protect myself from what has hurt me in the past."

Other stories told by loved ones can keep us stuck. Growing up, my younger brother was a big sleeper. Or at least that's what it appeared to be. He is five years younger than me, and seven years younger than our older brother. When he was in high school, we were in our twenties. His very normal teenager behavior looked abnormal to two twenty-something year olds. So we labeled him as a sleepy-head.

Fast forward years later, as adults, we were all visiting my parents in our childhood home. I walked half-awake into the kitchen looking for breakfast, surprised to see my younger brother awake before me.

"You're up early," I said.

"What are you talking about? It's 8:30 a.m." he responded.

"I just assumed you would sleep in like you always do," I said.

"Nah, I don't do that anymore," he responded.

I mean, who was I to talk about his sleep schedule? I hadn't slept in the same house as him for years. Yet here I was, holding a snapshot of a moment in time, and telling him who he was.

People will hold pictures of us and tell us who we are based on a short period of time in our lives. If it doesn't feel accurate to us, we don't need to listen or believe it. We are ever-evolving creatures. We are allowed to shift and change as often as we like.

Pay attention to what others say you are and then decide if it feels true to you. There may be a partial truth, but always remember that you get to dig deeper. The best way to do this is to be curious about it. See it as an interesting discovery that has just shown itself to you. And then inspect it, with no judgment.

My brother could have reacted defensively toward my comment. Instead, he realized that I was just thinking of a former version of him. He knew that the story I had of him was wrong. He observed it, and corrected it.

ANCESTRAL STORIES

I once had a client who wanted children, but was also deeply afraid of becoming a mother. Her understanding of children was that they end your life. All fun, all freedom, and all joy are gone after you become a parent.

Coincidentally, my three children would often interrupt my sessions with her. They would pop in to say hi, tell me a funny story, or ask for guidance. Although a part of me was embarrassed by these interruptions, I also knew that she needed to see this more than she needed to speak to me.

After yet another interruption, I turned to her to apologize. She looked at me with curiosity and said "You're friends with your kids."

I had never thought about it that way, but yes, I see my children as souls. They can each be much older souls than me. They've had way more experiences than just these few years on Earth. So I don't usually feel the pressure to be everything for them. In this game, I just happen to be playing the role of mom.

My client had been raised by a young, single mother. When she was born, her mother's life, as she knew it, did end. And because she could never overcome this resentment, she grew up feeling that this story was true. In fact, she thought it was her own story too, rather than understanding that it was her ancestral story. It wasn't until she witnessed another story was she able to start writing her own.

We are created of all the ancestors that come before us. Their triumphs and their struggles are within us. The unhealed parts of them remain inside of us until we're ready to discover them.

Rewriting your story sets them free. It makes all their hardships worth it. They couldn't figure it out, but they are grateful you can. Don't be afraid to reject some of the oldest stories told in your family. Don't be afraid to solve some of the greatest challenges in your family.

A few years into my intuitive practice, I was exhausted. I was so grateful to have gained popularity as a talented intuitive through word of mouth, but at the same time, I felt trapped. I was performing readings for about five hours a day, day after day.

I didn't feel like I could stop or even slow down. My husband, Benny, was showing signs of illness (more on that in later chapters), and I knew that I was soon going to be the main financial provider for my family. *I just have to keep grinding*, I thought.

The funny thing about ancestral patterns is that they have a tendency to show up in your body. As I was deeply in this state of overwork, my right knee became swollen. I was diagnosed with arthritis at three years old, so I am no stranger to inflammation. But when she comes, she usually comes to teach.

I did all the medical things I knew I needed to do. But I also went to my favorite mystics, also known as energy healers. In one of these sessions, as I lay on the massage table, the healer asked me to put all my attention on that right knee. And just as if I were watching a movie, I flashed back to my childhood, watching my father see patient after patient in his medical practice.

In my early teen years, my father bought a large group of pediatric practices, along with another pediatrician. But my father and his partner were doctors, not business operators. And a few years into starting the business, it started to collapse.

My parents did the best they could to keep the crisis away from us, but the tension was thick, and we were all scared. So, my dad did what he knew to do: he started to see patients again. He saw a lot of patients. And worked long hours. Within a year, life was somewhat back to normal. And he never took a risk again.

When my knee swelled up, I was working like my dad. Doing what I knew to do to provide for my family. But I was tired, and I wanted to take a risk. I wanted to teach others how to be intuitive. And I wanted to teach them in a group setting, like an academy for wizards.

But I didn't know how to do this. I didn't know how to run a school. And I was scared to scale back on my client hours to invest my time in an entrepreneurial vision that had no guarantee. It didn't work out for my dad, so why would it work out for me? This was my ancestral story holding me back.

I was scared and stuck, and my knee knew it. In that energy session, I decided to stop working like my dad... and my grandfather, and my grandmother, and who knows how many more generations back.

I decided that I would learn to be both a practitioner and an operator. I believed I was already a smart businesswoman, and anything I didn't know, I would figure out or learn along the way. I was ready to break this ancestral story.

I was still scared, but I could feel my entire lineage behind me cheering me on. After years of connecting with so many souls through my readings, I have learned that who we are on Earth is quite different from our true essence. Our overprotective, risk-averse family members are trapped in a fearful human body, using the limited parts of the brain. When they pass and are now free in the spirit form, they begin to understand the limitations of their human lives. Our ancestors who have passed often look to us to cleanse the lineage.

I could sense that my ancestors wanted me to heal this, too. And if I wouldn't brave those waters, I would be leaving the journey behind for my children. So I jumped in.

When you find yourself about to hit a milestone where your mother, father, or ancestors once walked, and you're hitting a wall, feel into their stories. You can do this by playing music that reminds you of your lineage. Close your eyes, and feel any pain stuck in your body. Their memories will lodge themselves there. Write down what you find. And then rewrite what you decide will be true for you.

For additional support with this, try my ancestral healing meditation located at **nikkinovo.com/soul-led-book.**

EXPANDING IDENTITIES

It's not just the negative stories that get us, but the positive ones do too. For example, some of us like to identify as being a positive person, but sometimes we're just afraid of feeling sadness. Or how many of us identify with being a hard worker, but can never find time to rest?

My general rule of thumb is to get curious about anything you say which follows the two holy words, "I am." These are very powerful words. Once we use them, we create a bubble of truth around us. This bubble contains us, and we will only grow as big as the bubble allows us to.

This is why you may have heard spiritual teachers talk about losing our identities. Anything that comes after "I am" is an identity. Our identities, at worst, limit us and, at best, keep us safe. We can only go as far as the identity suggests.

As a grounded spiritual guide — someone who honors our choice to incarnate as human beings — I don't believe in fully releasing identities all at once. Yes, they limit us, but they also contain us while we expand at a natural pace. The same way I wouldn't allow my four-year-old to leave the house and drive a car (assuming his little legs could reach the pedals), I do believe identities keep us safe until we're ready for the next step.

You want to see identities as little fences that expand as we are ready to expand. Too big a fence too early, can cause overwhelm. We want to expand the fence with intention.

Over the next few weeks, as you observe yourself, notice any "I am" statements. Decide if they need expansion or if they're good for now. If you decide to expand, I suggest picking an identity that might be a little bit of a stretch, but not so far out there that you can't believe it.

For example, perhaps we're trying to expand our identities when it comes to money. Maybe we decide to start telling ourselves that we are millionaires. We start writing notes all over our house that say, "I am a millionaire."

Repeating this affirmation and seeing visual reminders is great, but it's only helpful for someone who is ready to believe it. If I'm in major debt and have no career ambitions to speak of, then repeating "I am a millionaire," will only make me feel more anxious and defeated.

Instead, I'll start off with something that still feels ahead of me, but nonetheless closer. Like, "I am debt free." Changing that habit of being someone who is used to being in debt is going to be a few steps ahead of being a millionaire. So I'll start there.

Or let's say you're trying to be a more trusting parent. A parent who sees their child as a soul rather than a piece of clay that they are responsible for molding. To tell yourself, "I feel in complete flow as a parent. I'm doing a great job," might feel a little unsettling. Instead, you may want to narrate the next steps you are taking. A better story would be "I am starting to see my child for who they really are. I don't know all the answers, but I am supported and guided in this process. It is all coming together."

The trick is to start introducing a wider identity. Something you can grow into, but not feel overwhelmed or defeated by.

REWRITING STORIES

The detour road is all about rewriting stories so that they align with who you truly are and who you are becoming. The stories we tell ourselves are meant to be supportive, not punishing. You are innately good. You don't deserve any of those negative or limiting stories. You have so many bigger things to do this lifetime!

Unearthing limiting stories is a lifestyle, not a hack. If you are dedicated to living your true path, you will always be stretching. Which means, you'll always be unlearning the lies you have picked up and re-learning the truths that have been forgotten.

Here are some moments where you might want to check in with your stories:

When you're feeling stuck.

Ask yourself:

"What do I believe I can't change about myself?"

"Who do I believe I will hurt?"

"What do I believe I can't do?"

"Is any of this true?"

When you're not where you want to be.

Ask yourself:

"What uncomfortable feelings or actions am I trying to protect myself from?"

"What was going on for my parents when they were at my age or my current milestone?"

"Do I believe I can do this?"

When you're unhappy.

Ask yourself:

"Who am I suffering for?"

"Who am I trying to please?"

"Who am I trying to punish?"

"Can I handle being a happy person? Why or why not?"

"What am I doing to stay comfortable?"
"Are these old ways worth sacrificing my happiness?"

When you're scared of taking a risk.
Ask yourself:
"What am I afraid of?"
"Do I think I'm capable of succeeding? Why or why not?"
"Whose path am I repeating or trying not to repeat?"

SELF-DISCOVERY

Observing old programming and introducing new stories is a great start, but it's not the end. I believe that uncovering the true self is a life-long journey and a way of life rather than a destination. The lifestyle is a combination of learning new things about ourselves and unlearning false truths.

I once had a boyfriend tell me that I was like a book he wanted to keep reading because he found me so fascinating. What a great line, right? Well, after he dumped me, I decided to use that line on myself. I am a great book that is constantly getting better and more interesting. This helps me to release the anxiety of needing to know everything all the time. I also get to live in curiosity, and I am constantly surprised by how I shift and become more of my essence. It's an ongoing love story.

Moving to Los Angeles was definitely the beginning of that story because it was the first time I became aware of myself. While there, I allowed my former self to die. Perhaps the biggest shedding I did was to let go of who I thought I needed to be, and instead, allow who I was to emerge.

As I started to become more soul-led, these are some of the behaviors that changed in me:

How I dressed

I really started to find my sense of style when I moved away from friends and family. In Miami, my wardrobe had been completely influenced by what made me look the "hottest", the most on-trend. I often wore dresses that should have been better categorized as scarves. But In L.A. I discovered vintage clothing, floral patterns, and loose-fitting dresses. It was the first time that I realized that dressing was not for acceptance, but rather for self-expression.

Still, to this day, I pay attention to how I dress, asking myself if it is a true expression of me. This is easy to overlook, but when you're really trying to feel like your true self, try playing with clothes and your appearance. You may find that there is a more authentic hairstyle or color scheme for your wardrobe that feels more honest to who you are becoming.

Feeling the need to be "responsible" all the time

When I was following my head and not my heart, I felt this pressure to stay on that linear path of success, which left really little room for play. I constantly felt like I needed to make the most "adult" decision. I would do too much of that and consequently I would react recklessly at random. There was no place for balanced fun. As I became more authentic, however, I found this really beautiful (safe) playfulness inside of me. Until this day, it's one of my favorite aspects of my soul.

One simple way this was expressed was through movement. I found myself dancing at nightclubs—something I had grown up doing in Miami—using my body for joy. Rather than moving to look cool or sexy, I allowed my awkward, silly joy to be expressed.

And now that I'm *really* adulting as a mother of three, a wife, and a business owner, I dip into my playfulness by getting on the floor with the kids, singing to my husband, and leading impromptu dance parties.

The shame of not fitting in

Like most kids, I always aimed to fit in. But I was also really bad at it. My eccentricities were always pretty obvious, and when they would ooze out of me I always felt really ashamed. If you don't know this already, L.A. is full of strange, eccentric people, "L.A. Weirdos" as my dear friend Mike affectionately calls them (he, himself, being an L.A. weirdo). Shedding that fear of standing out was part of the medicine Hollywood had to offer me.

My relationship with nature

When we're off-path, we're inevitably disconnected from nature. Because I had very little relationship with my natural self, there was no space or use for nature in my life. Sure, I would occasionally go to the beach with my friends, but that was all about being seen and getting some relief from the very hot weather in Miami. In California, I rode a boat wearing a hoodie! I kept looking over my shoulder, waiting for P. Diddy to pour some Cristal in my red solo cup while I stripped down to my tiny bikini. But it never happened. Instead of using nature, I learned to be in a relationship with it. To marvel at it. To listen to it. The love I have for hiking today was seeded in those years spent on the West Coast.

The need to blame

When we acknowledge that we have choices, we empower ourselves. As I began to use my power of choice, I realized that there was no need for blame anymore. In the past, blame was my favorite procrastination tool, and my mother was my favorite victim. I would specifically blame her for my lack of unrealized dreams. As if she wasn't allowing me to accomplish my goals. When the truth is, I myself was too scared to pursue them. Realizing that I always had a choice, and that I was free, was sobering and often hard to reconcile. But it also gave me relief from playing the victim and the opportunity to start healing my wounds.

Realizing my intelligence

Working in the film industry on the West Coast, at some of the biggest companies, meant I was navigating in the big leagues. I was surrounded by extremely talented, driven, and smart people. Being surrounded by these people and simultaneously receiving praise from my bosses made me realize, "Hey, I must be smart too!" It was an opportunity to rework an old childhood lie.

If you're willing to be just a little bit curious about yourself without prematurely forcing yourself to be fully actualized, the book of you can be the greatest page-turner of all time. How about we start today? Grab a journal, and write down some of your most recent self-discoveries.

CHAPTER FIVE

Becoming Your Soul Self

After a few weeks of moving, unpacking, and brunching, I had finally settled in, which meant it was finally time for a night out on the town. Naturally, my nightlife in L.A. began with a quintessential cantina-themed bar, a margarita, and an aspiring film director. It was then that I met Red.

Although I was deeply invested in the hilarious (and degrading) stories my friends were sharing about life as a Hollywood assistant, something on the other side of the room was pulling me like a magnet. I looked up from the conversation, still midway into laughter, and somehow my gaze was in perfect position to accidentally lock eyes with a guy leaning up against the bar. Oops!

I had no business locking eyes with anyone. After all, I had just left an eight-year relationship that had ended in a canceled wedding. But he didn't know that, and as the bar emptied out after last call, he proceeded to walk my way.

"Were you just looking at me?" he asked.

"I'm pretty sure *you* were looking at me," I responded.

Before we could come to an agreement of who was looking at who, my bestie was sweeping me off down the sidewalk and into the parking lot. As I fled the scene, Red handed me his business card and told me to call him. (Because that's what you did in the mid 2000s in L.A. We were *just* getting our first BlackBerry phones and MySpace profiles.) I politely accepted and figured I would never see him again. Famous last words, *right*?

Weeks had passed since that fun night out. Real life was starting to sink in. I was beginning to sober up from all the excitement left over from the life changes I had made. That new-car smell was starting to wear off, and I was starting to face the reality of my choices.

I was now a Hollywood assistant working 12-hour days, sharing a studio apartment with my friend, and crying every day after work. I was completely out of my comfort zone and did not know how to handle it. Everything was new. My emotional muscles were sore and fatigued from all the unfamiliarity. I was not sure I could make it.

This, dear reader, is exactly why we are afraid of change. Although boring and sometimes depressing, doing the same thing every day is predictable and requires less energy. Life on autopilot is energetically efficient.

On the other hand, when we start to make changes, we will be forced to strengthen muscles that have been dormant for quite some time. It will hurt, and you're going to think you can't do it. The same way I feel like kicking my Pilates instructor in the face when she makes me do one more sequence, you will want to punch the Universe in the face when it is training you to become the next version of yourself. This is called resilience building.

STRENGTH TRAINING

How many times have you started something new only to quit a few weeks or months later? I know I have. There are many reasons why we quit. Below I'm going to list a few reasons why I quit at times, and reasons why I've seen others quit.

Your reasons might be the same, but they may also be different. Knowing what leads you to give up on your dreams is perhaps the single most important tool you'll need to reach your dream life. You must know yourself well enough to know what gets in your way. Because sadly, we are our biggest obstacle. This means that we need to know our competitor so well that they cannot trick us into giving up.

ONE: THE INITIAL SIGN FELT STRONGER THAN THE ROAD

Remember that incredible divine moment I had in Rockefeller Center that told me to burn down my life as I knew it? That was such a grand sign from the Universe, which left very little room for self-doubt.

The reason I was now in Los Angeles, living a very different life, was because I had so much trust in that moment. And the more I followed, the more exciting life became. But then I reached a point where that life was so new that it became…hard. So hard that I would come home every day after work with sweat stains on my clothes. Let me explain.

My first job in L.A. was at a huge talent agency. I was an assistant to a crazy busy talent agent who repped all sorts of big Hollywood names. My Bachelor's degree in Public Relations from Florida International University did *not* prepare me for this job. In fact, I think the only thing that could have possibly prepared me for this job was an in-depth study of the book "The Devil Wears Prada" and the movie "Entourage."

I was so out of my league. I had no idea how to keep myself organized, nonetheless my boss, and his 14 high-maintenance clients. All the other assistants were just as stressed out, so no one could help me. I was drowning.

Eventually, I had to quit. When I hit that point, I began to doubt my choices. I even started to doubt the moment in New York City when everything had felt so clear. I thought maybe I had misunderstood the message. Maybe I took the path way too far? Or maybe I just wasn't one of those people who could live their dream life?

In addition to doubting myself, I felt that the Divine had abandoned me. It had given me all these epic signs along the way, but when I found myself sweating like a hog at the talent agency, it was as if my entire divine team had gone on some sort of vacation in the angelic realm. *Where was the Divine now?*

What I didn't understand then was that the road to becoming our true self is innately challenging. We are leaving what is comfortable, in order to become something great. This promise of becoming "great" is always inspiring. But there can be a period where you feel like you've been tricked, like the Divine did a bait-and-switch on you. It sold you an exhilarating dream, but it failed to mention the fine print that explains how damn hard it will be.

When the road gets hard, we begin to feel pain (or in my case, sweaty armpits). And when our body feels pain, we naturally feel the urge to run in the other direction. The pain also makes us feel as if we're doing something wrong, which inevitably causes us to doubt our choices.

In my case, I reacted to this pain by quitting my job. I was so close to calling it quits and moving back to Miami, but thankfully, I decided to just tone down the pain a bit, aiming for something a little less intense. I got the random idea to take an easy job, one that had nothing to do with my career ambitions of being a successful Hollywood executive one day. My nervous system needed a win, so I took a receptionist job at a simple attorney's office. It was the most boring job ever, but it paid my bills, allowing me to stay in California a little longer.

As you follow the road that leads you closer to your true self, you will encounter challenging moments that will cause you to doubt your initial meeting with inspiration. Instead of doubting the initial signs you received, check in with your pain level. How uncomfortable are you feeling? Is it too intense? Can you take a little break instead of throwing all your plans away? Or can you tend to your nervous system, by bringing in some self-care like exercising, massages, time in an infrared sauna, nights out with friends, and so on? Can you activate the supportive inner mother who believes in you, but who can also tend to the pain?

My girlfriend was in labor and showed up a bit late to the hospital. There was no time for an epidural. The nearly 10-pound baby was coming and she was going to have to do it the way our grandmothers did. A few minutes into pushing, the pain was so severe, she was feeling like she wouldn't be able to do it. She even felt faint and told the doctor, "I can't."

Then out of nowhere, this amazing nurse appeared, grabbed my friend's face, bringing her focus back to what was important, and said, "You're going to push this baby out." The nurse coached her with breath exercises and an authoritative stare, not once allowing her to lose focus or turn her gaze elsewhere. Ultimately, my friend did something she thought you couldn't do, which was to get past the pain and birth a vision she had been working toward for so long.

I share this story because it illustrates the insanity that pain causes. When we are in pain, we forget our goals, our purpose, and our focus. In that moment, we're even willing to give up on things we love—like our babies! This does not mean that don't want our baby or that we were wrong in getting pregnant. It just means that our body is reacting to pain in a way that is not serving our vision.

We all react differently to pain, and we don't know what that will look like until the moment comes. This is why some women can follow through with a natural birth, and others need an epidural, so the body can feel safe. When I was experiencing pain at that talent agency, I desperately needed an epidural. The epidural for me ended up being the simple job at the law firm. There have been other times in my life when I was a little more experienced and was able to get myself support (like the nurse), and some techniques to transmute the pain (like the nurse's breathing exercises).

Some anesthesia methods are healthier than others, for sure. And some are just neutral. Healthy methods would be things like exercising, breathwork, creating art, laughing with friends, and so on. Overall, healthy methods tend to be the ones we partake in when we're aware of what we're going through. For example, *I'm going to take the day to binge on this streaming series, because I need one day off from my mind.* Unhealthy would be, I binge watch every day, almost all day, and don't even realize I'm doing it. There's a fine line between healthy soothing and numbing.

Numbing methods can include excessive alcohol, drugs, risky promiscuousness, overindulgent eating, and so on. The key to this is *awareness*. Even if you've found yourself in a situation where you have an unhealthy relationship with drinking, your awareness will birth self-compassion. You can begin to ask your inner child what it needs. When you find yourself in this place, ask the little, scared child inside you these three questions:

What do you need to soothe the pain?
What do you need to feel safe?
What support do you need?

In that time in my life, I needed a break to soothe the pain. To feel safe, I needed an easy job that I couldn't fail at—one that I was overqualified for—so that I could feel secure financially. The support I needed was love and mentorship, from someone who cared for me. I actually found that support in my boss at the law firm. She was an L.A. native, her entire family lived there. And she took me in like a stray cat, inviting me to family dinners, teaching me how to budget my finances, and guiding me in this new place.

When we find ourselves up against pain, we will need to find new techniques (soothing or self-care), safety (a safe place, job, home or person), and a mentor (a coach or a friend we can rely on). Sure, having to bring these three components into our lives may slow us down in our journey. But stopping to gather these essentials is the only way we will have a shot at surviving the journey that will take us to our destination.

Rather than focusing on speed, focus on longevity and stamina. Creating a dream life is a long-view game that requires completely new skills that keep us from giving up. Before you break your promise of living your dream life, commit to upleveling your self-care skills.

TWO: REMAINING GROUNDED CAN BE DIFFICULT

My receptionist job was really boring, but it taught me to ground. Our dreams always require some sort of long-term focus. As we learn skills or move into new stages of life, we are going to be asked to ground deeper and for longer periods of time into something new.

At that job, I was asked to sit at the same desk for eight hours every day. There was something about that daily practice that helped me ground into my new life. It was a quiet office; I was not distracted by any exciting projects or conversations. My tasks were simple and repetitive. In fact, my main job was to be available in case anyone came into the office or called. I had no choice but to stay put.

When we're learning something new, our tendency is to jump

out of the chair. We don't yet have the focus for the new thing. Sitting in it for too long feels uncomfortable, so we try to jump to the next thing and before we know it, we're on to the next project and without having completed the first one. If we do this long enough, we forget what we were working on in the first place.

This doesn't only happen with tasks, it also happens when a new stage of life starts to present itself. When I first met my husband, I was so conditioned to dating men for a few months and then moving on to the next. I had lost the ability to ground into a relationship and work through the challenges. I didn't have the patience or focus to work throughthe nervous energy that would come up in my body, making me think I needed to flee.

Six months into dating Benny, we attended a friend's wedding. As a person in a new relationship, I had forgotten all the polite rules one might follow to be respectful to their partner. I was grinding up on another guy on the dance floor, while Benny watched me from the reception hall bar. In my defense, my dancing partner was a good friend who had absolutely no interest in me. In fact, he had no interest in my entire gender. But, my new boyfriend didn't know this.

As you can imagine, he was embarrassed and upset with me. This was our first fight, and I did not know how to handle it. As an independent (and stubborn) woman, I thought *Forget this guy! There's other fish in the sea!* So I went home that night and started packing up my things from his house. Classic behavior for those of us with a style of avoiding attachment.

The next morning, after the nerves had calmed down, I found myself exhausted. I was too tired to be proud, and I was also just tired from running from one guy to the next. The Divine was telling me I needed to ground in this moment. I needed to dig in. Rather than give into the really, itchy, uncomfortable feeling in my body that was telling me to run, I wanted to see what it would look like if I stayed.

The interesting thing is that I did not know *how* to stay. It had been years since I had been in a long, committed relationship. But all I had to do was decide that I *wanted* to stay. And magically, the steps for staying appeared.

I apologized. I explained that I wasn't perfect. I vulnerably shared that I did not know what the hell I was doing, and that all I could promise was that I would try my best to be better.

As you try something new that requires longer focused time, you're naturally going to want to get up and try the next thing. Because guess what? You're probably going to suck at the new thing at first!

In the early months of my relationship with Benny, I was pretty bad at being a girlfriend. I could have decided that based on my early attempts, I was obviously not girlfriend material. I could have labeled myself as bad and unfit, but a more accurate description was that I was ill-equipped. And all that means is that we do not have the proper equipment for the task at hand. I had yet to acquire the proper skills to be a good girlfriend, specifically a good girlfriend to Benny. I did have some general girlfriend skills from my past experiences, but I did not yet have the specific skills I would need for this new, specific boyfriend.

We typically want to quit, jump to the next thing, or run away from a commitment that seemed pretty amazing at the start. Because we begin to doubt it is our destiny based on the fact that we are not good at it, yet. For some reason, we have a preconceived notion that if something is destined, then it should be easy, flawless, innate, or intuitive. Somehow, because I am meant to write this book, the words should just flow out? And that if they don't, I was wrong about the calling? Remember, this is where we bring in that wise inner mother who knows we can do this hard thing.

Where I see this phenomenon the most is in my intuitive certification program, the Soul Reading Method. Students are pulled in the direction of the program for two reasons: one, they are drawn and intrigued, or two, they are already showing psychic gifts and need help maneuvering them. Once they are officially accepted into the program, they do feel a sense of destiny, knowing that they are meant to be there — even if they don't know why.

But quickly after the first two lessons, my little budding wizards begin to wilt. Why? Because typically, when a piece of our destiny shows up in the path, we are just so excited to have arrived here, we think that arriving was the hard part and the rest will be easy or be taken care of.

I curse the person who came up with the phrase, "Destiny will do the rest." Destiny is not a path. It's a moment. A snapshot of when the stars align. In fact, if we had to give it a timestamp, it would be just one second or less. The second you lay eyes on your future partner. The second you discover your future teacher. The second you conceive of your future child.

Destiny is a moment that changes the trajectory of your current path. It is a window of time — a portal — we climb into, which marks the start of a whole new path. Destiny is an opportunity, not a guarantee.

When my students find the Soul Reading Method, yes, destiny is calling them. Yes, their higher self is reminding them that they are meant to go down this path. But destiny is simply the welcome committee that sells you a train ticket and points you in the right direction. She is not taking the ride with you.

Instead, what comes along for the ride is potential. And potential can be as flaky as a teenager who is trying to find her clique. She may know that the kind, welcoming, smart girl clique is where she is meant to be, but she easily gets distracted by other passengers like Fear, Doubt, Laziness, and Overwhelm.

To add even more pressure, the train ride is a window with an expiration date. It is the window of opportunity. The same way Cinderella only had until midnight to live her dream, when Destiny ushers potential to its window of opportunity, the clock starts ticking.

Unfortunately, we don't always know how long we have to turn potential into realized power. But I do believe that as long as we are dedicated to strengthening our potential, learning new skills, and practicing those new skills, the window will graciously expand for us. It will be there as long as there is consistent commitment toward becoming that realized power.

Realized power is the result of repetitive practice. Destiny is such a good salesperson that she makes us forget that repetition is necessary. No matter how many lifetimes you may have lived as a medicine woman, on this Earth, you will have to practice your craft. No matter how many lifetimes you and a potential partner have lived together, you will have to learn how to create a union and then continuously practice creating a harmonious relationship.

The early stages of new ventures — where destiny greets you — are always easier than the middle stage that requires grounding. It's so easy to buy the equipment for a new podcast and to write down show ideas. But it's hard to find the courage to record, to learn how to make attention-grabbing graphics, and to grow an audience.

It's easy to get a psychic reading where the reader tells you that you'll meet your soulmate in three months. It's hard to get past the awkwardness of going on dates. It's challenging to believe in yourself when dating hasn't worked before.

Taking the ride that destiny calls you to take is challenging, and requires that you constantly show up, even after getting knocked down the day before. It's hard, but fleeing is not the answer. Grounding into the uncomfortable feeling is. Instead of getting up from the situation, get curious about what would happen if you stay. What if you went about it differently next time? What might happen?

THREE: LACK OF FOCUS

I know we just spoke about my husband, but let's travel back in time to L.A. when I was working as the law firm receptionist. After a few months at the most boring job ever, I started to feel comfortable. I even signed up for LSAT classes because I thought it might be easier to get a law degree, graduate, and just get a job as a lawyer. It seemed to be somewhat of a guaranteed track.

Isn't it funny how I moved all the way across the country to get away from predictable roads, only to find myself falling back into old habits, desperately searching for another guaranteed path? These are the moments where we start to forget all about our connection with the Universe. I began to grab the wheel again, because the Universe was feeling like a bit of a reckless driver.

I was deep down this track one afternoon when I found myself in front of the computer faced with a classic admissions essay question: *Why do you want to become a lawyer?*

I could not answer this question. Total writer's block. I searched for an old journal so I could write down some thoughts, one that I remembered stuffing in a purse I hadn't seen since my roommate and had I moved to our new two-bedroom apartment. And out from that purse fell a thin business card, given to me weeks earlier by Red. In a serious need of distraction, instead of answering the essay question, my fingers typed Red's email address into a blank email box.

I wrote a short email that described when and how we met, hoping he would remember. Who knows how many homemade business cards this guy had given out?

To my surprise, he responded almost immediately by saying, "Oh yeah, you were the girl who was looking at me at the bar. Will you go out to dinner with me tonight?"

I'm not sure why I would say yes to such an, um, unpoetic email, but as fate would have it, that dinner was pivotal in my journey.

Over fruity cocktails, he asked me why I had moved to Los Angeles. Now, *this* was a question I could answer. In fact, I could have written an entire essay about it! I decided to just give him the unfiltered version and leave it all on the table.

I shared the story about breaking off the wedding and wanting to pursue a career in film. And by the end of the story, I was telling Red that I wanted to fall deeply in love. I wanted to fall in love with my life, with myself, with my work, and eventually with another person. This probably wasn't the best first-date conversation, but I needed to hear myself say it, because I had forgotten all of it.

I had let that agency job scare me so badly that all I wanted was to feel safe again. Even if it meant forgetting the whole point of the move. I was back in that trance where I wasn't listening to my heart. All I was listening to was my head and my fears.

There was something about Red's energy that was so inviting and heart-based. He gave me the space to dream again. He was so moved by our conversation that at the end of it he said he had a surprise he wanted to show me.

I got in his car as he drove up some sketchy roads, roads that led to the most perfect spot to view the Hollywood sign. I'm sure if I stood in that same spot today it wouldn't be so magical, but there's a certain magic that happens when your heart bursts open, after months of trying to stay safe.

Our sensitivities can be a real distraction from our true path. On one hand, being soul-led means the heart is open, in tune with the energies of the world, which means we feel a lot. But this also means we're susceptible to feeling afraid. If we're scared enough, we're going to look for shelter, like I was by pursuing law school.

I do believe feeling scared and defeated is part of the process. I have yet to find a way to not get distracted by these feelings of fear and setbacks. The trick, though, is to ensure you're not only using your heart to feel the scary things. There has to be enough inspiration coming through as well.

That dinner with Red was inspiring. I didn't plan that relationship. The Universe definitely gave me that win, but I could have gotten in the way. I could have used my sensitivities to feel embarrassed about reaching out, or be afraid of rejection. Instead, I sent that email out with curiosity and feeling unattached to the outcome.

When we find ourselves dipping into fear, we must find our

way back to neutral or uplifting feelings and influences. Neutral energy would be feeling curious, following something interesting or intriguing, or feeling willing to experiment. While uplifting feelings would be feeling excited, eager, and motivated, for example.

If we find ourselves feeling like we can't seem to shake these fearful feelings, we have to get honest with ourselves and ask, *What am I distracting myself from?* For me, the law school track was distracting me from feeling like a failure. I had already made a crazy move and now I couldn't even keep a job. If I could just tell my parents and my friends back home that I wanted to be a lawyer, we wouldn't have to discuss my epic fail as a Hollywood assistant.

Also, it's important to recognize that sometimes we stay in those scary feelings because we like the drama. I mean, who doesn't love a sad, tortured love song? This is why we can get caught up in our own dramatic stories.

Before starting to write this book, I tortured my team and my husband with all my thoughts about how hard writing was, why I couldn't do it, and how I didn't know what to write. I did this for weeks, until one day my husband said, "Enough!" He told me that writers write. And if I was not writing, then I was simply not a writer. *Ouch*!

My dramatic story was so much easier to be in than the reality of sitting down for hours to write. Our dramatic stories are such good distractions from doing the hard work it takes to become the next version of ourselves.

The road is not a straight line, it's normal to zig-zag a little. I needed to quit that agency job, and the receptionist job was a necessary zig-zag. But I was veering completely off path when I lost focus, followed my fear, and started applying for law school.

Thankfully, I heard my dreams out loud that night with Red, so I immediately applied for jobs in the film industry again. And within weeks, I was working in the publicity department at one of the biggest film studios in town. I was prepared this time, knowing that there would be a learning curve, and I promised myself to stay on path.

If you have decided to commit to a soul-led life, ask yourself *Why?* And try to keep it broad. On that first date with Red, I realized that my "why" was because I wanted to fall in love in all areas of life. That was my North Star. Going to law school did not make me feel like being in love. It kind of made me feel safe, but not in love.

What is your North Star? Why are you deciding to live this way?

Let this be your guide. And make sure to say it enough because eventually you will find people in your life who will hold you to it.

SOULMATE GUIDES

When we're the hero (or victim) of our own story, it's easy to overlook all the supporting actors who come into our path along the way. We typically want to decide their role in our lives when they arrive. But living a soul-led life means, soulmates who serve as guides will meet you at different points along the way. And you never have any say in what their role will truly be.

Red was a soulmate guide through and through. But let's be

honest, what I really wanted him to be was a boyfriend. That's the thing about meeting soulmates, right? When our souls recognize one another, our human mind processes it as, *I must be with this person the rest of my life.*

When in fact, soulmates are guides planted in our paths, who are meant to take us to the next journey. They are classmates who remember our soul's contract and the tests we are meant to pass in order to reach the next level.

They will help us study, or distract us so we fail. They can be sherpas, jokesters, sages, villains, and everything in between. How they get us to our next journey can be unique, beautiful, and awful all at the same time.

These soulmate guides inspire us to rise in our strength, at times when we'd rather hand off our power to someone else. The relationship addict in me was dying for Red to make us an official couple. But it was as if his soul would not let me hide in a committed relationship. He was there all throughout my time in California, but at the same time he wasn't there in the way I wanted him to be, which was to fill my every insecurity.

As guides, they will introduce us to new parts of ourselves that we would have otherwise ignored. For starters, Red introduced me to yoga, which was monumental for me. After all, the practice of yoga was the entry drug that led me to spirituality. And just for the record, he never once actually showed up to class. He would just tell me he was going and then would flake a few minutes before. But hey, I kept following his breadcrumbs! He also brought adventure to my life, hippie friends with green diets, and obviously the Grateful Dead.

Soulmate guides always bring better gifts and surprises than the ones we actually hoped for. While I was slightly romantically tortured by Red, I also felt protected by him during my time in L.A. And when it was time to move back to Miami, his soul was the first to let me know.

These souls come in all forms, from romantic relationships, to friends, and pets. Some stages of life can make it easier or harder to stay open to these serendipitous relationships. But I do find it important to leave room for the soulmates that will carry you over to the next road. If you get a random invitation from someone who feels safe, say yes. If you're ever in a group setting, try to engage. If you're always blowing off a person who is trying to build an honest relationship with you, challenge yourself to try.

We have lived many lifetimes with several souls. These souls are here to help us along the way, to bring pieces of our souls back to us, but we have to let them in. And not just let them in, we need to be open to being in a relationship with them, however that may look. We have to recognize the work the relationship is asking us to do in order to really get the soul lesson it came to deliver. Today, set an intention to allow new soulmates into your life who come to support your soul's mission this lifetime.

Dear Divine,

Please help me in opening my heart to the soulmate relationships that come to support me in this lifetime.

Likewise, may I too be a supportive soulmate to others.

Help me to see each relationship as a moment to remember more of my true self.

Amen.

THE PATH AND PURPOSE

After two years of living in California, something truly unexpected happened: I felt a calling to move back home to Miami. I know what you're thinking, *How did you know it was time? What if this was a self-sabotaging move and you were falling off path again?* First of all, I'm very impressed with you, dear reader. Only attentive and dedicated readers ask these kinds of questions.

Here's how I knew it was time. First, the feeling was unexpected. One of the reasons I moved to California in the first place was for my career. Working in the film industry was my dream, so when I started having feelings for another profession, I was shocked. It was as if I had finally scored a relationship with the city's most eligible bachelor, only to then fall in love with the rebel artist. And my new lover was *writing*.

To be honest, throughout the years I had had many career ideas, the same way I had been in many romantic relationships. Considering a career switch to writing was a surprise, but at the same time it wasn't. For as long as I could remember I had been stressed over that definitive question, *What do you want to be when you grow up?*

You see, when we were kids, my older brother had this photo in his room that really left an impression on me. He was about two years old in the photo, holding hands with our father as they both wore green medical scrubs. My mother had made a toddler-sized pair of scrubs for my brother out of my father's medical residency uniform and captured this beautiful moment in their lives.

I was always slightly jealous of this photo. Not because I wanted to be the one holding my father's hand instead of my big brother. But because this photo gave him an undeniable path and identity. The picture served as a childhood vision board, illustrating my brother's destiny: to become a physician.

He had the gifts to match. He was hard-working, an excellent student, and focused on the endgame. I, on the other hand, had no obvious talents or direction. I was involved in a lot of activities, but I was pretty average at everything I did – from school to sports.

I did have some obvious (yet hidden) interests like acting, dancing, and English class. But as a child of immigrants, those interests surely weren't going to add up to anything professional. I eventually entered college, and what led me to my chosen major was my commitment to avoid any additional math classes. That is how I landed in the school of communications.

College and university is a funny thing we humans do. As a society, we coerce 18-year-olds to decide what they're going to do for the rest of their lives. In America, we make this process a serious commitment—one that typically comes with a sizeable loan that often outlasts your career in any given field.

Most of us abide by this process because as new adults, it's the first real shot we get at creating an identity. Once we move into the workforce, we trade in our title of "student" for the title of whatever we're doing to make money — or whatever we're doing on the side that will hopefully make us money one day.

As time passes, we add more identities like wife, partner, parent, business owner, boss, dog mom, homeowner, and so on. They keep us busy for a while, until one glorious day when we look around at our lives and think to ourselves and say, "I'm ok. I'm good. But I'm not fulfilled." We start to wonder if there is something more or… *Is this it?* And at worst, we start to fear that we totally messed it up and maybe even missed our true path all together.

The detour road was coming to an end for me, and I could feel the true path trying to show itself, because I was beginning to think about my purpose in life. Although glamorous and intellectually stimulating most of the time, working in film publicity did not feel meaningful to me. I began to wonder what impact I had on the world and whether or not all these hours I was dedicating to my current job were worth it. I started to ask myself, *Is this it?*

It can be daunting to reach this place in our paths. We may even categorize these moments as "being lost." But as the years have passed, the deeper I go into my path and spiritual process, I have come to understand that these are the moments when we begin to be found. These are the moments when we begin to remember our true path.

A SOUL'S PURPOSE

From a spiritual perspective, living our true path is the search for living our soul's contract. Despite what the name may imply, the soul's contract is not a scary, binding legal document, instead it's more of a blueprint for what our soul expects to complete in this lifetime. Our spiritual awakenings are moments in our human life where we begin to remember parts of the contract. We begin to awaken from the spell of forgetting that hinders us from remembering what we actually signed up to do this lifetime.

Perhaps one of the most well-known aspects of the soul's contract is a soul's purpose. We can thank Millenials for this collective remembering. We were the first generation to really start questioning our careers and what our contribution to the world might be. The question *What is my purpose?* began to trend. As humans, we automatically attach it to our concept of work and career.

In my current practice as an intuitive practitioner, I've had the honor of seeing hundreds of soul contracts and purposes. Based on my findings, I've now come to understand that while work is a portion of the soul's purpose, it isn't the only part. Instead, we might look at the soul's purpose as what the soul has come to accomplish in this lifetime. And that's way bigger than any career!

For some of us, our purpose is most seen in our position within the family lineage. Meaning, we may be here to clean the lineage of old beliefs and ways of being. For others, we are here to seed the New Earth, which will require us to create new systems and live in a way that looks different than the past. Many souls come to Earth as lightworkers here to drench the planet in light so it can ascend past darkness.

There are many different options when it comes to a soul's purpose. And yes, purpose is greater than work. But for now, let's discuss how these two intersect.

Because how we spend the hours of our days ultimately becomes the life we lived, and being more intentional about our careers is a natural instinct for a soul trying to remember its contract and live its true path. Questions like *Why is my work draining me? Should I switch careers?* and *How can I change my work to be more in alignment with the true path?* may start to arise.

Up until this moment in California, career had been an ego

pursuit for me. My entire thought process behind work was, *What job will make me feel the most important?* I was also looking for fun and adventure, which are never bad north stars to follow, but I never gave thought to who or what I was serving while working.

After one too many press junket weekends, I started to question the purpose of my job. And I also started to realize that I didn't like it as much as I thought I did. Still to this day, that is how I qualify what I consider to be a soul-led job. It must meet these two prerequisites: Do you find purpose in it? Do you enjoy it?

Nowadays, I'm happy to report that my work meets both prerequisites. Feeling unfulfilled with my work in film and discovering a spark for writing was the beginning of that journey. A journey that I will share in detail later in this book, in hopes that you too can begin to find your soul-led job or career path.

HEADING TOWARDS ALIGNMENT

Once the detour road drops us off on our true path, the next stage begins: alignment. In the alignment stage, you begin to become very intentional with your choices. You realize that you are the creator of your life and you're willing to start building.

Now, let me be clear. Alignment is not pretty. The process is very similar to reorganizing your closet. You get inspired after binge watching your favorite home organizing show. You order all the pretty clear containers, bins, and baskets. In your mind's eye, you can see the vision of your Pinterest-worthy closet. It's a dream.

You start taking everything out of your closet, and you're feeling strong. You begin to sort. You're not even halfway through sorting when you realize that your room is a mess! And maybe this is not all going to get done in a day.

Aligning your life is the stage in creating your dream life where you will sort, make a mess, and then reorganize by category. Each of us may have slightly different categories, but the most common categories I see are: relationships, career, parenthood (or leadership), and home.

Similar to organizing a closet, as we begin to align, we'll typically start with one category — like shoes — and then move on to the next. While we make headway with the shoes, we may partly start on dresses, but shoes is where the momentum is.

In the alignment process of your life, you may start with the career category, but you may also be working on dating or your current relationship at the same time. One category will have more momentum than the other, and one will take longer than the other to sort. Shoes might have been pretty simple, but purses may turn out to be been daunting.

At this point in my story, I was just about to start aligning my career, but dating was also screaming for attention. A big part of me wanted to be super neat about it and do one category at a time, but to my surprise, career was a much bigger and much more complicated pile than I thought. I realized that the alignment timeline does not care about your schedule. It will take as long as it needs to take. And just like organizing your closet, it always takes longer than we would like!

I don't know how long your alignment process will be. But I do know it's better to start today than tomorrow. And what is needed at first is the commitment to the belief that this is possible — your dream life is completely possible.

Here's what I need from you: I want you to drag out that very stubborn part of you. I know you have it in you! The part of you that will not let go of something because you just can't. The part of you that feels like if you let go, you will die.

Promise yourself that you will not let go of your dream life vision. If you get really stubborn about that vision — with the help of all the divine guidance around you — you will find a way to show up (almost) every day for that vision. Like a painter hell-bent on creating a masterpiece, you will not stop bending life in your favor until it feels aligned, authentic, and soul-led — no matter how long it takes.

CHAPTER SIX

Your Soul's Work

After two life-changing years in California, I packed up my things and headed back to Miami to pursue my new career interest in writing. I knew that I wanted to pivot from publicity to writing, but there was one problem: I needed to make money so that I would be able to live on my own and not be stuck living with my parents.

For some people, living with your parents is a great option as you work on your career pivot. But for me, energetically, living with my parents was very draining. My nervous system was often on high alert when around them, and I knew that my creativity wouldn't be able to flow while living there. So I took on not one, but two, survival jobs.

Monday through Friday, I worked at a local public relations agency, and on the weekends I worked as a bartender at a Miami Beach wine and beer bar. And it needs to be said, I was a horrible bartender. In fact, after a few months on the job, I was fired, mainly because I refused to take holiday shifts, but also because, if I'm being honest, I was just kind of a princess about the whole gig. Even if I had wanted to take on the extra shifts, I couldn't risk my parents noticing that I was working a sketchy nighttime job. I managed to have that job, and keep it a secret, for about three months while living with them. Although, I'm pretty sure my dad had his suspicions—there was that one time when he found a wad of cash in the drawer of my nightstand and started to ask me what kind of friends I was hanging out with.

As soon as I had saved up enough money, I moved to a high-rise condo in downtown Miami. I continued working as a publicist during the day, while submitting my writing work to various publications on the side. My life was shifting at a comfortable pace. After we make a leap of faith, it often feels like the Universe hits an imaginary timer that allows you a certain amount of time to get your bearings. As your allotted time begins to run out, and often without any notice, you'll be pushed out of the safety of its grace and into the real world, like a kindergartener on the first day of school.

My time had come. I sat at my desk, which was more like one very lengthy table fastened up along the longest wall of our tiny public relations office. Let's just say, my boss was more concerned with a trendy zip code than having adequate space for her staff, which forced all of us to sit elbow-to-elbow as we typed away hoping to receive an email stating that we had secured a media placement for one of our clients. Too many days without that email meant that your job was less secure than the day before.

I rarely secured placement. My emotions about the cause always got in the way. If I couldn't get behind the mission of the client, I couldn't pitch with the kind of passion you needed to win the game. Which meant I was constantly on high alert, waiting for my boss to scream my name from her private desk on the opposite wall.

"Who is on the Naples account?" she yelled.

My heart sank into my stomach and I began to feel ill in the way all entry-level employees feel when their boss' stress is pointed in their direction.

"That's my account," I said cheerfully, hoping my tone would calm her down.

My boss immediately called me into the office kitchen. It was the only place with a door that actually separated the rest of the space, which naturally made it "the scolding room."

"Were you just not thinking when you placed the order for these invitations?" she asked in her patronizing voice.

The little girl inside of me was too scared to speak, so I didn't. Instead, I allowed my boss to throw all her baggage on me. The more I allowed, the less the baggage felt like mine. In my silence, I heard the voice again, and this time it said, "This is your chance."

This is *my chance,* I thought.

She's going to fire me, and I will be free to pursue my true calling. Perhaps I telepathically sent her the signal? Or maybe my guides stepped in and whispered in her ear? Within seconds, she uttered the words I had been holding my breath to hear. "You're fired."

"I understand," I responded as I bowed my head, acting as if I was ashamed.

I walked over to my shared desk, took down the picture frames I had decorated with scrapbook stickers, and gave a cheeky wink to my deskmates as I whispered, "I'll call you later."

The Universe did for me what I could not have done for myself. It set me free, so I could pursue what was in my heart. Not only was I being pushed out of the nest in the most loving way, but I felt encouraged by the Universe's belief in me. *It wouldn't let this happen if I wasn't meant to go in the direction of writing,* I thought.

That evening, my closest friend from the agency came over so we could combine stories and recount the day's events complete with the theatrics of two melodramatic narrators. My arms were waving in the air like those inflatable tube guys at a car dealership, as I reenacted the kitchen scene for my friend, when my former boss of just five hours ago rang my phone.

"Hello?" I reluctantly answered, wondering if maybe she did not understand the boundaries that come with being fired.

"Nikki, I was calling to make sure that you understood that I did not fire you early today. You left the office early, and I don't know why. You need to fix the problem, is that clear?" she said.

I wish I could tell you that I was shocked by this behavior, but I wasn't. I mean, I had worked in Hollywood, and I did have a tendency of attracting "Miranda Priestly" type bosses. But without question, my boss had absolutely fired me earlier that day. Everyone in the studio-apartment-size office could attest to that.

It's funny how you can have all the confidence in the world when a sign so grand appears in your path, only to feel completely defeated in a brief moment of confusion. The firing had felt like a sign from the Universe, and now this woman was telling me that it didn't happen? At that moment, all my bottled-up fears of not having a steady paycheck came rushing through my belly. Visions of my parents' faces of disappointment and confusion passed through my third eye.

Was I wrong? Had I overexaggerated the day's events and projected it as the Universe's doing? Did I make this happen because I desperately wanted a writing career to be my truth, or did it really happen because writing was *my truth?*

Taking a leap of faith toward our dreams is a lot like a scene in an action movie where the reluctant hero has accidentally found herself at the top of a mountain or a New York City building and is being pushed to the edge. One more step and she'll fall to her death. Her only other option is to bet on herself and leap to the next rooftop. That kind of character *always* bets on herself, but as soon as she gets to safety, the next challenge arises. Either the building starts crumbling or a fleet of space aliens show up with laser guns pointing straight at her.

Walking out of that public relations agency was me, jumping to the next rooftop. My boss calling me a few hours later was just the next challenge that I needed to overcome. Some like to see these moments that challenge our initial intuitive hit as a test from the Universe. I simply see it as the strength that builds our next evolution. Betting on ourselves isn't only about leaping, it's also about doubling down on our intuition even when others are trying to manipulate our experience. Intuition is like a little pet, the more you feed it by believing in it, the bigger and stronger it gets.

"No," I responded to my definitively former boss. "You did fire me, and I won't be at the office tomorrow."

There was no turning back. After many months of having one foot in the publicity track and another in the writing track, I finally chose the road that felt the most true to me. Even when a seemingly more powerful, more experienced woman was telling me I was making the whole thing up.

Based on this story, it's easy to see her as bad, but I like to see these players in our lives as challengers appointed by the Divine. If we let it go long enough (or if we're too young or powerless to walk away), our challengers become our oppressors. That can be a sticky situation as the constant gaslighting becomes brainwash, keeping us imprisoned by our own mind. If your intuition is going against your environment, but everyone in your environment is making you feel crazy, go outside your circle, and get a second opinion. Allow yourself the opportunity to attract the validation that you need in order to see that your inside feelings are accurate.

Once I decided that my inner feelings were, in fact, accurate, the momentum toward a writing career was obvious. Not only had I just been fired from my job, but I was also starting to receive regular freelance writing work. Within a couple of months, I landed a job as the associate editor of our city's local luxury magazine. My career shift was complete.

Was I lucky? Did I make this happen? Was this all part of my destiny? The answer is: it's a little bit of everything.

Becoming a writer was a destination on my soul's contract. Every time I heard of someone working as a writer or a creative, my heart would flutter. These feelings were the signs leading me toward a shift. It was like a door appeared in my path that I had never seen before. This door was only potential. There was no promise. But the minute I walked through that door by taking some real steps — like pitching stories, learning to be a better writer, and believing in myself — the road started to pave itself. The more I walked the road, the more defined it became. The more it became my reality.

Also, I listened to the Universe to see where I was being asked to go. I had one foot in the publicity track and another in the writing track. Yes, the writing track is what I wanted, but I didn't want to push my way there. Instead, I showed up for it every day and trusted that if I was meant to be there, the momentum would build, which it did.

CHOOSING THE RIGHT ROAD

When you're confused about what road you should be walking, put energy toward each one and see where the momentum begins to build. Momentum can be an external movement, like receiving freelance writing jobs. Or it can be internal movement, like waking up every day feeling the urge to write.

I see momentum as an intelligent life force. Different from our own life force, created by our personal energy. Intelligent life force is an energy that creates on its own. It doesn't need a human to push it in order for it to come into existence. You've heard the expression, "It had a life of its own," before. That's momentum. A human has to start the process — like having intercourse to make a baby — but something divine takes over and uses you to create life. You are simply a vessel for creation.

When we observe momentum and work with intelligent life force, we are allowing our soul's path to come alive in Earth's dimension. Again, we don't clearly remember what was written in our soul's path, but when momentum starts to take place in our life, turning into life force, we can rest easy knowing that our soul's path is speaking to us, guiding us in a direction. It has made contact with us and it is worth our while to follow.

Of course, we need to crank the life force's wheel in order to start its momentum. We do this by feeding the fire, taking action toward our soul's path. Will the fire grow naturally with just a little physical effort, or does it fall flat? This is the experiment we're trying to run.

Your soul's path is synonymous with your true path. Your true path can have several roads of possibilities, similar to a maze having several ways to get to the same exit. In this case, which road you take does not matter. You'll end up in the same place. Like choosing to start a Pilates routine or signing up with a personal trainer, it's not the modality that matters, it's the fact that you're starting a healthy workout routine.

But then sometimes, you're on your true path and roads begin to appear, but some lead back to the default path. This is what we can sometimes refer to as "tests" from the Universe. Giving into my former boss when she asked me to come back, even though all the momentum and signs were leading toward a writing career, would have bumped me off my true path and switched me to a road that led back to my default path.

I know this can sound like way too much pressure for my already indecisive friends. So, I'm going to share a few tools with you. Perhaps you have two roads that you're feeling drawn to (and it's ok if you have more than two). What you want to do is take action steps toward both at the same time. Let's say you're between staying at your corporate job or doing freelance work and starting your own business. You would take steps toward each by sending out your resume to potential employers, and also reaching out to potential clients who might want to commission your services.

When you decide to put energy into two different roads at the same time, try your best to eliminate your judgements, fears, and attachments about the roads. If I were to write articles, but also think I was an awful writer, I would be sabotaging the possibility of a writing career. Instead, see this as an experiment. Let go and allow the life force to show you what direction you're meant to go in.

One road will be more honest to who you are. The actions required for that particular road will feel more natural than the other. It might feel scary or even hard because it's a new road, but at the same time, you'll have a little fire of hope within you. This is internal momentum.

External momentum is created outside of you. For example, clients keep hiring you, yet only a couple of potential employers have called you back. The life outside of you is pointing toward a road.

Sometimes, the build-up momentum is very clear, and you're happy to follow. But what if those corporate employers *do* call you back, because you've been in the industry so long and you're very sought after. Yes, the external momentum is there, but your lack of internal momentum may not allow you to move forward. There is a lack of life force here.

There are other times when the roads ahead are not black and white, but rather a shade of gray. A few years ago, while running my current business, something just wasn't working. Like so many business owners and artists, I had several projects going on at the same time and I wanted all of them to work. Was that too much to ask?

Among those projects, two were showing some promise: my spiritual dating work and my metaphysical work. Being the spasmodic creative that I was, I would sometimes put content into the world about finding your romantic soulmate, and other times, I would share my love for spirit guides with the audience. They were very confused, and so was I.

I knew the dating work was needed, but I loved the metaphysical work. If I could have my way, I would teach about spirit guides and make money. So, I decided to run an experiment. I reached out to 10 dating podcasts and 10 podcasts that would be open to spirit guides to see who would be willing to have me on as a guest. I wanted to see where the momentum was. And guess what? Nine out of the 10 dating podcasts got back to me, and zero of other podcasts returned my emails.

There was no denying it, dating work was calling. You might be thinking, *But isn't living a soul-led life all about getting what you want and only doing what lights you up?* Well, not exactly. Try removing the ego and the forcing out of that belief.

Soul-led living is synonymous with following your soul's true path and purpose. We want to live in a way where we feel we're being guided toward our true path. On the road to that true path, there will be times we need to trust where we're being guided even if it's not exactly what we had in mind. We often need to honor the life force by surrendering to its will.

In my line of business, there are several voices, and it's not always easy to stand out. I believe that to really be a professional artist, you need to have a "hit," in order to claim some space in the market. Just like a musician who has to make a hit album to become noticed, when I watched the external momentum building behind the dating work, I could sense that the Divine was telling me that this work could be my first "hit."

After all, the Divine always has a higher vantage point than us. It can see the big picture when we are stuck on the details. My deepest desire was to make a living sharing my voice and talent, serving people, while being available for my family. That desire was trying to come to life, but there was going to be a journey to get there.

I had my own ideas about how to get there, but again, my human self had a limited vantage point. If I was going to live into this desire, I needed to work with the Divine. I needed to trust.

Although the external momentum was not exactly what I thought I wanted, I did have the internal momentum to make the dating work a success. It would have been a different story if the external momentum had pointed in a direction that was not inspiring for me.

When it was becoming clear that dating work was the road I was supposed to follow, I just felt happy to be in the arena. It's a little like getting a dream job and maybe you're not in the department you wanted, but you're still so happy to be there. That's what it felt like to me. The Divine allowed me to work for the company, but it needed me in another department first. As soon as I did my work there and a position opened up in the metaphysical department, I would be allowed in.

AN EXERCISE FOR ROADS

While you're putting energy toward your different roads, looking for momentum, you can also spend time in meditation seeing what it would feel like to be on each one. All you'll need for this exercise is a pen, paper, and a comfortable place to sit.

Close your eyes and imagine each road. Picture them as streets. See yourself standing in front of each road like an avatar in a video game. Walk down the first road using your imagination, and pay attention to what it feels like or how it looks. Is the road dark or bright? Do you feel excited or upset? Take in all the sensory you can for this road. Without overthinking what you felt and saw, write down on your piece of paper, everything you can remember about that road. Repeat these instructions for each additional road.

If I were back at that time, trying to make a decision between dating work and metaphysical work, I would see that the dating work road was clear and bright. Almost like there would be very few obstacles. No traffic. The metaphysical road feels dark and narrow. It's possible, but a struggle.

This exercise will be a good indicator of where you're meant to go, and even give you some clarity as to why one road might be better than the other right now. Of course, you have free will, which means you can pick whichever road you want. But if we're dedicated to living a soul-led life, we follow our soul's path, which is the path we're being guided to.

FROM SURVIVAL WORK TO CREATIVE WORK

Despite feeling very guided to writing and having the desire to be a paid creative as I was moving back to Miami, it wasn't enough. Unfortunately, desire is never *truly* enough. Our actions and beliefs have to be in alignment with our specific desires. If I wanted to be a professional writer, I had to think and act like one to actually become one.

The greatest mindset I had to overcome was one of survival. People who do what they love for a living are people who are choosing their creative vision over their fear of survival. At some point, someone in our ancestral lineage was trying to survive. It could have been your great, great, great grandmother, or it could have been as close as your father. But, somewhere in that line, the idea that work and money are tied to survival was formed.

For me, the survivalists were my parents. Both my parents and their families were forced out of their home country in light of new communist regime. My father came to the U.S. with his single mother. Not only were they not allowed to bring any money or belongings, but they also had no place to live once they arrived, or a job lined up that would guarantee their survival. Thankfully,

Americans are heart-filled people (despite what the media likes to tell us) and there were charities that helped them get on their feet.

My mother's immigration story is similar. The only difference is she arrived in New Jersey at the age of 17 with her two parents and younger sister. But still, they were only allowed to bring one suitcase with one extra pair of clothes for each of them, everything else had to stay behind. *Can you imagine?*

In Cuba, my maternal grandfather had owned a working farm and several other businesses. Both my grandmothers had secretarial jobs, and my parents were both educated at the best private schools available. But no matter how secure they had felt in Cuba, as soon as they were forced out, my ancestors found themselves in survival mode all over again.

Somewhere in your lineage, someone, somewhere was trying to survive. Literally, trying to make sure that they would not die of starvation. If you're lucky, an ancestor might have worked through that energy and created a feeling of safety in the line. And now you get to stand on a stronger platform. If you do have this position in the lineage, don't waste it! Your ancestors did what they did with future generations in mind, so that those future generations had the privilege to choose.

Or maybe you are that person in the lineage that is tasked with the shift? Maybe you're an immigrant? Maybe a survival mindset has been passed down for generations, and you have the awareness and audacity to break it.

When we're in a survival mode, we pick careers based on what is safe, what will provide us the next-level of status, and what we think will keep us in the good graces of our tribe. Living in survival mode is about following societal rules in order to have a secure position in the food chain.

If you pick a career that your family doesn't endorse, you're at risk of being kicked out of your network, which means that your probability of survival goes down. If you pick a career that doesn't give you social status, then it means you're not getting closer to the top percent that eats first, and presumably, eats best.

We might not be fully aware of this, but many of us are picking careers based on our survival instincts. This is not necessarily a bad thing. I completely support you in doing what you need to do to bring in money and to feel safe. But as you do that, can you consider funding your ultimate dream life? I'm okay with survival jobs, but not survival careers.

LEAVING CAREERS FOR CREATING LIFESTYLES

I've been using the word career, so that we can both get on the same page. But if we're being honest, career is not the right word to represent what you are yearning for. First, we have to recognize that this hypothesis we're trying to materialize where work meets our dream life is a pretty new concept. Therefore, the linear rules of the past do not apply. The word career is limiting and insinuates that we must follow certain guidelines. This causes confusion because our hearts are telling us that we somehow want to have the freedom of time, spend our days feeling productive and energized, express our true selves daily, and have more than enough money and resources to thrive.

What I just described above is not a career. It's a lifestyle. By definition, a lifestyle is a way of living. If you start to realize that you are not trying to find this almighty dream career, but rather are trying to move all your puzzle pieces around to create a truly soul-led lifestyle, you will start to see your possibilities for making money differently. Calling it a career keeps you in the past, rather than creating a new future. Believing that our careers are our one and only purpose feeds the ego and puts us in danger of becoming enslaved to work.

As a collective, we are creating a new soul-led lifestyle that is harmonious and built around our gifts, our values, and our needs. Perhaps the most well-known lifestyle of the past is the American Dream. Built on the philosophy that hard work in school and at your corporate job will guarantee you a comfortable retirement, the American Dream is what so many of us are unconsciously trying to follow. It's ingrained in us, but even as we try following it, there's something about that lifestyle that feels inherently wrong — and we're finally ready to break free from it.

There are many reasons why this conventional lifestyle doesn't work. But if we had to sum it up, it doesn't work because it's an old, linear, one-size-fits-all system that does not serve most. With each new coming generation, we become more and more aware of the limitations of the American Dream and its style of servitude. For this reason, we are collectively dreaming of a new way of life.

I believe we're dreaming of living our lives in devotion to all that matters most to us. Discovering our own unique values, needs, and talents is the first step. Understanding our unique values and living from there is what creates a soul-led life and shields us from the self-abandonment that comes with following someone else's blueprint.

How we make money is one component of our lifestyle. Rather than call it a job or a career, let's call it an offering to the world. As you make your offer to the world, money flows through that offering to then provide for your soul-led life, which is supported by the Divine. The Divine wants you to be utilized to your full capacity, and as a result of you living into your offering to the world, you are then provided for.

HOW TO IDENTIFY YOUR VALUES, NEEDS AND TALENTS

Finding your offering to the world depends on a combination of your values, needs, and talents. Some people discover their talents early on and lead from there, and others have a clear understanding of their values and lead from there. But most of us just wing it and figure it out along the way. Discovering your offering to the world does not happen overnight, but if you pay attention to your values, your needs, and your talents, you will build something special.

Identifying your values, needs, and talents really requires a level of self-acceptance. Because often the three are wrapped up in parts of ourselves that we try to quiet, undervalue, or even hate. The best way to find our values, needs, and talents is to take on the role of an observer. If you were tasked to be a little butterfly fluttering above you while at work, what would you notice about yourself? When we observe, we don't judge, we just state what is with the curiosity of a scientist.

Working in film publicity really helped me identify a little bit of all three. I realized that I valued purpose in my work. I needed to feel connected to the outcome.

As for my needs, I realized that I needed to be in somewhat of a position of influence. The more I observed publicists, the more I noticed that no matter how high you are in your career, you're always catering to someone else, and in the film industry most of the catering was to some pretty big egos. Additionally, after being around so many creatives, it dawned on me that I needed to be creating.

Lastly, signs of my potential talents were just starting to shine through. I was consistently applauded for my technical abilities, leading me to discover my passion for gadgets and anything digital. And since I was constantly being asked to re-write other people's work, I started to think maybe it was a hobby worth paying attention to.

Values are our principles, or standards for life. The reason values can be a little tricky to identify is because sometimes we think we should *all* have the same values. But the truth is, we are all innately driven by different motivators. This is why your oldest child might be motivated to get good grades to please you, while your youngest is just interested in whether or not you're going to pay them $10 for getting an A on their test.

Unfortunately, most of us have been told what we *should* value, which is what threw us into a misaligned life to begin with. But it's ok, undoing those "shoulds" is just a part of the alignment process. All that is important right now is that you understand that your values are your own. They're part of the whole soul package to help you live your soul's true path. Don't fight them and don't look over your shoulder to see if other people approve of them.

As I was trying to start my spiritual business, I was raising two small children and had another one on the way, and I was also running my husband's tree service business. Without really thinking about it, I was automatically prioritizing my children and my husband's company over my dream of having my own spiritual business. To make matters worse, while I was physically with my children all the time, mentally I wasn't. I was beating myself up for not being where I knew I could be in my business, so I couldn't even be present during my time with them.

One day, I was sneaking in a few minutes of work, while the kids were at school and in between my responsibilities for my husband's company. It was almost two o'clock, and I felt defeated knowing I'd have to stop what I was doing and run to start the afterschool hustle. In an effort to quiet my frustration, I heard my inner dialogue say, "The best thing I could do for my kids is be available for them at all times."

I had never noticed this thought before, but when I did, I knew it had been on repeat. Leftover from my mother's guilt about raising her own children, this belief was playing over and over in my mind, causing a lot of discomfort. My belief was clashing with my soul.

Since I already knew that beliefs aren't necessarily truths — truths come from the soul — I decided to rework that thought into something that actually aligned with my values. "The best thing I can do for my children is be a full expression of myself," I said instead.

Even though my actions weren't really adding up, if you had asked me what I really thought kids needed from their mom, I would have told you that they need their moms to follow her intuition and live her full expression. And if that means that she needs to rearrange her schedule to make time for a dream she believes in, then that's more important than being available to the children all the time.

Until that moment, I was following someone else's value, rather than my own value, which is to live guided by my intuition and to live as an authentic expression of myself. My intuition had been telling me for a while that I needed to pursue this business, that it would be important to the future of my family. My life force was begging me to live more authentically. Even though my value would require me to act differently than I had been taught or differently than was expected, I still needed to be true to it.

Take some time to reflect on your own values. There may be some you've known about for a while and maybe others that you have discovered after working a few jobs. Write them down in your journal. And if you need some inspiration, here are a few values I have found among my clients throughout the years.

Example of Values

Authenticity
Freedom
Purposeful, meaningful, or satisfying work
Courage, adventure, and boldness
Creative expression

CONNECTING TO YOUR NEEDS

When it comes to identifying our needs, I find that the inner child is the version of us who knows this best. Listening to and embracing the inner child can be tricky because we are often embarrassed by her needs, and her way of being.

As kids, play is our job. But as we get older, money is introduced into the mix of life, and play is replaced with work. Anything that has to do with play is seen as childish, which can be really threatening to a young person trying to be an adult. Because of this, the inner child is ignored and abandoned — especially when it comes to making money.

I have realized that when I see my inner child and feed her needs, she brings me back so much energy—energy that went missing while trying to become a serious adult. This energy is the fuel I need to make my dreams a reality. After all, dreaming isn't really seen as an "adult" trait. It's the child's expertise. So why are we leaving out our inner children?

Our inner child is so helpful that I often see them as guides when performing readings on clients. People come into my practice hoping I'll see a wise medicine woman as their spirit guide in my meditations when, in fact, the wisdom is coming from a younger self.

Sadly, our culture doesn't always respect the wisdom of child innocence. The patriarchal society praises "intelligence," which is often just indoctrination or programming in disguise. Are we really any smarter as we get older? Or are we just better trained?

There are great therapists out there who can help you reconnect with your inner child, but I'd love to share with you my simple practice. I close my eyes and imagine meeting my inner child in her favorite place. Sometimes I see her among wildflowers and other times on stage. In my vision, I see both my adult self and my younger self. I proceed to ask my inner child what she needs or what she has to say.

Sometimes you won't even have to visit your inner child to know she needs you. Often, when you're living your life, you will find yourself trying to understand an uncomfortable emotion. For me, frustration is the biggest signal that my inner child is unhappy. When I feel an uncomfortable feeling come up, I stop and ask my inner child, "What do you need?"

Other times, it's not an uncomfortable feeling, but rather one of excitement that leads us to our truest needs. During my time working in film publicity, I found that I felt the most excitement when building relationships with writers and journalists. The more I learned about the inner workings of their profession, the more my ears perked up like dog on high alert. I thought, *This is a cool job.* And I quickly began to lust over it.

Admiring a profession from afar, I believe, is an obvious sign pointing us toward our offering to the world. Imagine a stunning woman — dressed in what you would imagine designer clothes looked like, if you actually had an eye for that kind of stuff — interrupts your path. Somehow, when she crosses the road, everything in your life seems to slow down and become muted, just so you can catch the fullness of this mystical being. Her life seems mysterious, glamorous, and adventurous all at the same time. And for just one second, you try to imagine what it might be like to live her life.

Just as you're holding the vision of you wearing the designer clothes and walking with purpose, the fantasy comes to a screeching halt when you realize that you're wearing the same jeans you've had for five years and sneakers that used to be white, but now resemble more of a beige color. Could you *really* ever be that show-stopping woman?

That's how I felt about writers and creatives in general. I was blown away by this concept. Professional creatives, in my mind, were people who were paid to express themselves. I wanted that so deeply. But at the same time, I wasn't sure I could do it. I wasn't sure if I had the skills, the talent, or the gift. I wasn't sure I could make a proper living. And I absolutely wasn't sure if I deserved that kind of space in the world. The inner child in me had her needs, but my young adult self wasn't yet sure if she could provide.

Embracing the inner child can be difficult. Her desires and needs are often our shadow qualities. The reason I often see my inner child on stage when I'm in meditation is because she loves to perform and express herself. A cute quality for a little girl who is seven years old, but it can be a dangerous personality trait as we get older and seek more and more to fit in.

Like most women, I grew up trying to take up the least amount of space possible. I never wanted to upset my mom by stealing her spotlight, and I learned from my brothers that guys often see women as dramatic if we are too expressive. Tucking away my true expression seemed to make me more dateable.

Despite all my concerns about switching careers, my heart was so filled with excitement over the possibility of a writing career that somehow my fears and programming seemed to drown out. Like a relentless guy at a bar pursuing women way out of his league, I began to chase writing, despite having no experience or degree.

Allowing myself to become a writer was me listening to the truth of my inner child. I wish I could tell you that we just have to listen to the inner child once and be done, but unfortunately, her needs and expectations change as you grow.

Take some time to close your eyes and visit with your inner child. Pay attention to where she is, and ask her what she needs. Without judgment, write down what you feel is coming through. Below are also some examples of needs.

Examples of Needs

Living my true expression
Influence
Wealth
Security
Privacy
Steady paychecks
To be seen
To be recognized
To be heard

UNLOCKING UNEXPECTED TALENT

One year had passed since I had moved from L.A. back to my hometown. So much had changed. Just a year before, I had been a misplaced publicist, and now I was the associate editor of Miami's premier luxury magazine. That small slither of desk at the P.R. firm had been replaced with my very own loft office. A large concrete wall that didn't quite touch the ceiling separated me from the rest of the editorial team, giving me my own private space. Sure, my office had no door, but it was a major upgrade from the plastic partitions that the sales team had to endure.

I spent my days exploring the city (and interwebs) for unwritten stories, unexplored cultural eccentricities, and of course, the hottest places to eat, shop, and party in Miami. Not only did I have the coolest job for someone in their mid twenties, but I had also found myself a steady boyfriend who I cared for deeply. Life was looking good.

Finally, my life seemed to be in place. Not everything was completely perfect or settled, but for the first time, I felt like I was intentionally *designing* my life rather than following my programming. Everything about my ife, from the neighborhood I lived in, my current boyfriend, and the writing career I was pursuing felt like things I could be proud of.

Except that every once in a while, I felt this strange feeling in my belly. The uncanny feeling was reminiscent of a sucker punch that your older brother might serve you, leaving you hurt, but also quite confused because your older brother was your hero. There was nothing happening in my life to explain this feeling. No one had hurt me or betrayed me.

I could call it anxiety, a deep fear of losing everything I was so happy to finally have. But the truth is, it didn't feel like worry. To me, worry is consistent, aggressive, an anxious tune on repeat. This was spontaneous, finding me in moments of presence, even joy. It was not hostile, but instead loving and subtle. It would not harass me, but rather, it would visit me. The only other way I would categorize this feeling would be to call it a premonition.

Months had passed since I had felt the "gut punched" feeling, and now another body part was calling my attention. This time it was my right knee, which was experiencing real, physical pain. As mentioned earlier, at at three years old I was diagnosed with Juvenile Rheumatoid Arthritis. My arthritis was like that involuntary summer playmate, the one who is the child of your parents' friends—friends they don't see often, but appear every few summers with very little warning, and before you know it, you're stuck doing barbecues with children you do not know. No matter how odd the children may seem to you, you're stuck playing with them, and there's simply no use in fighting it.

My swollen knee came and went throughout my childhood. Partly because my mother was so good at caring for my condition. It never really bothered me much, except when the swelling would impede me from doing something I wanted to do, like going to Disney World. Whenever this happened, my mother would rush me to my doctor's office, who would promptly remove the fluid from my knee and shoot me up with a steroid. I was good to go!

I hadn't seen a flare-up in years. In fact, this would be the first time ever I would care for it on my own, as an adult. My condition had always forced me be in tune my body. And I could feel the swelling creeping in, a little more each day, but I wanted to ignore it. At the time, my life was a constant string of social events— events where I was expected to show up as a fashionable, well-connected city dweller. Not a hobbling penguin. The possibility of my arthritis paying a visit now was a huge inconvenience.

I was late to meet my boyfriend and some friends at Lincoln Road, so I did that thing you do when you're running late at the airport, where you take on a slight but fashionable jog. You know you're late, but you try to play it down so you don't look like you're in a cheesy romcom scene. The problem with this was that I was wearing six-inch stiletto heels. So by the time I reached the restaurant, my knee was throbbing and bulging out from behind my skinny jeans.

A few days later, I found myself at my doctor's office, where they explained various options for treatment. My options were anti-inflammatory medication, which would cause severe constipation (among other things), for an indefinite period of time; a round of steroids, which would absolutely cause problems in the future like brittle bones and premature cataracts; some infusions that I didn't know much about; or the removal of fluid from my knee, which I had done before, but was very painful.

I thought to myself, *Is this it?* My options felt more like a temporary band aid than a true effort toward healing. Years prior, my father had given me a book on superfoods. It had been my first introduction to the concept that what you put in your body affects its functioning. This book flashed through my mind, and I thought, *Maybe there's a way to heal myself?*

Oh man, sometimes it feels like life was easier when you were in the dark, right? You can't undo what you have seen as a result of your most recent spiritual awakening. This moment in my life was, once again, another spiritual awakening that forced me into even deeper alignment.

That simple question about whether healing myself was possible, brought me down a rabbit hole I didn't even know existed. All of a sudden, I found myself searching for answers in New Age, Self-Help, and Wellness books. A seamlessly harmless Google search for "anti-inflammatory diets" accidentally inducted me into a world of green smoothies and Louise Hay.

At first, finding all this information was fascinating. I could not believe no one had ever taught me that my thoughts created my life, and that most of those thoughts were passed down to me. This all made so much sense! And wait, this spiritual advice-giving thing was *actually* a job?

For someone who was quite content as a lifestyle writer penning articles on the best bikini shops in Miami, stumbling upon self-help writing felt a bit like developing a crush on someone when I was in a committed relationship that, until then, I thought had made me happy. Instead, this tug toward inner and outer healing was dragging me into the darkest corners of Barnes and Noble. In addition to feeling like an adulteress, the bookstore had a way of positioning the Spirituality books right next to the Religious section, as if to intentionally activate my Catholic guilt. My new curiosity was all very confusing to say the least.

The more I read and practiced the tips in the books, the more my knee began to heal. But also, the more my belly began to flutter. The premonition with no words had returned. I still did not know with certainty what the feeling was trying to tell me, but if I had to put it into words, I could feel it telling me that things were about to change — even if I didn't want them to.

Aside from learning so much about healing, my curiosity was leaning toward the voices in these books. *Who were they? Were they making money doing this? Where did they learn this information? How did they have the authority to write on these topics?*

Discovering this type of writing forced me to become honest with myself. Yes, it was fun to write about luxury handbags and award-winning restaurants, but was it feeding my soul? Was this career just a repeat of film publicity, a job that was exciting, but not fulfilling my soul's purpose?

The truth is, I wasn't sure. I wasn't even sure if I had any additional talent. Maybe small fashion stories were all I could muster? Imagine me thinking I could write an entire book! Not only was that a huge undertaking, but I would need to have some sort of expertise, and I had none — other than expertise in the category of changing careers.

Rather than switching careers again, I did the next best thing: I started to blog. Looking back, it was the beginning of my side hustle into spiritual work. In order to understand my confusion, my boyfriend at the time suggested that I find another outlet for my writing, other than the one I was boxed into at my day job. He was right. I needed it. As soon as I started to write freely, I realized that there was a more authentic expression within me. I had thoughts, ideas, and stories that I was not aware I possessed.

This reminds me of my present day as an intuition teacher. In class, my students often feel frustrated because they're not "seeing" any visuals or are not receiving any psychic messages as we meditate. They assume they lack intuitive talent, or worse, they assume they are broken.

I find this to be a misunderstanding of talent. The talent is the expression of an inner gift we must constantly excavate in order to awaken its brilliance and power. It's an inner dragon that lies dormant within the caves of our energetic makeup, looking quite harmless as it sleeps.

Many of us don't want to awaken our talent. We're afraid it might be ordinary or not good enough. Often, we overlook our gifts because it has brought pain to our lives or to the lives of others. My gift lies in my ability to feel deeply. That's a nice way of saying that my gift lies in my drama. Before I understood it, my "talent" was ruining my life by creating uncontrollable emotions and conflict.

Lastly, we fail to notice our gifts because they seem simple, innate, and standard. *You're telling me that not everyone receives visits from their dead loved ones?* Our talents are often such a normal part of how we operate that we don't recognize them as special. We don't recognize *ourselves* as special.

Before the talent is awakened, our understanding of it is all happening within our own heads. *It doesn't make sense to talk about it with anyone*, we think. So it remains asleep.

Until one day, we accidentally wake it up. We do this by feeding it. Feeding our gifts could be as simple as watching a live concert, and dreaming of what it might be like to be able to sing like that. Or we can accidentally do it by reading a book that was just meant to heal our arthritis!

Feeding our gifts may stir up some confusing emotions, but it doesn't create talent. The dedication to expressing a gift is what creates talent. My intuition students begin to see their talent when they allow themselves to express the messages, the feelings, and the visions they are experiencing. This is the infant stage of talent. The more we feed it, the more it grows.

I, unintentionally, began feeding my gift of writing when I started that blog. The more I wrote, the more talent came through. I also had luck working in my favor. Probably the luckiest thing I had going for me was that I was completely unaware of what I was doing. There was no pressure to create something spectacular, because I didn't even know I was creating anything. When it comes to inspiration, there's nothing that will kill your muse faster than pressure to achieve results or expectations of a specific outcome

Discovering your gifts is like retrieving a piece of your soul that went missing before you arrived to this lifetime. If you are determined to live your soul's true path this lifetime, your gifts will be the breadcrumbs that guide you along the way. You won't always remember why you're here and what you're meant to do with this strange life, but if you allow yourself to follow and develop your gifts, they will lead you to exactly where you're meant to be.

Perhaps this section scares you? Because perhaps you fear you have no gifts? I understand. I felt completely ungifted my entire childhood and in my early adult years. This feeling was validated by the strong contrast of my multi-talented older brother, my all-star athlete high school boyfriend, and my more academic and more beautiful girlfriends. Their talents were developed and therefore more obvious and seemingly natural. As a result, I began to believe that I was untalented and not special.

Yes, I'm about to tell you that I wholeheartedly believe that you are talented and special. I say this, not in the way a kindergarten teacher says it to build confidence in those young minds, but to validate your innate feeling that guides you toward believing that your soul has a purpose. Your purpose as a soul lies in your gifts. And while those gifts may be undiscovered, unexpressed, and underdeveloped, that does not mean that they do not exist. A rare creature that lives at the deepest corners of the ocean still exists even if humans have yet to discover it. It is not the creature's job to make itself seen. Instead, it is our job to become better explorers.

Without this understanding of gifts, we begin to identify as consumers rather than creators. A mistaken identity that I believe is making our world and species sick. We have successfully been tricked into believing that our purpose as humans is to consume the creations of a "few chosen geniuses." Somehow, they seem smarter, more talented, and more worthy than we are. When we compare ourselves to them, we feel small and resort to simply consuming what they create for us. This role we take on actually allows them to become even more powerful creators because we have handed off our own power of creation, saying ours is not as good as theirs so they might as well have our power, too. When in reality, they are only powerful because we allow them to be.

There is nothing innately bad about these chosen few. In fact, they are often people we admire, who are doing great things in the world and should serve as inspiration in our lives. The only problem lies in the deception that takes place when we place them on a pedestal, see them as separate from us, and refuse to see their brilliance as a reflection of our inner light.

HOW TO DISCOVER AND DEVELOP YOUR GIFTS

We can learn a lot about discovering our own gifts by observing how our favorite geniuses (or the ones who boil our blood) operate. First off, we must acknowledge that we are already expressing our gifts even if it's in a very small way. The reason they may not look like anything special is simply because they are underdeveloped. An underdeveloped gift is like a cake recipe that you've made only once. Maybe you got lucky, maybe the cake was delicious when you baked it for the first time, but chances are it was mediocre. Your cake can remain mediocre, or you can repeat the recipe over and over again — tweaking it every time to make it just a little bit better — until the recipe is to your liking and standards. Not only does the recipe reach high honors, but the repetition creates a master baker out of you. Your gift has been developed, making you seem talented.

The geniuses we compare ourselves to are specifically skilled in acknowledging their gifts. For some, they had parents, teachers or competitions point out their gifts at a young age. Not only were their gifts identified early, but they had the capacity to receive the compliment and validation. This is where many of us lag.

My high school math liked to begin each class by reading a passage from *Chicken Soup for the Soul*. Eventually, she got tired of those stories and decided to offer extra credit to any student who wrote their own story in the same vein. This was music to my ears, as I knew my gifts did not reside in the math department.

I wrote a story about the time my mother was pregnant with her third child, and she allowed my older brother and I to pick names for the babies. (She was a brave woman). I chose the name Kelley after my imaginary friend, and my older brother chose the name Michael after his real-life friend. Because the baby was a boy, my older brother's name won. My little heart was so disappointed, not just because I'd lost, but because I would never have a sister. Fast forward to middle school, I met my now long-time best friend (and maid of honor at my wedding) whose name was...you guessed it, Kelley.

My story was the teacher's first pick. She did her best to tell me that I had a gift, but I wasn't yet ready to receive it or see it.

In fact, I was oblivious to any signs of literary talent, even though the only honors and AP class I had were in English and Spanish literature. Because I grew up in a world where men were valued more than women, and where Math and Science were superior, I saw my skills as silly and girly.

Take a minute to look back at your life — maybe even your current life — and bring to mind a time where you were being complimented. Even if you brushed it off, what were the last remarks of praise you remember receiving? Journal about these moments. Allow the stories to flow through you without judgment.

As you spot these little special moments in your story, can you allow yourself to receive it? What if when someone compliments you, they're being honest? As you receive these reflections from others, can you allow yourself to see them as signs from your higher self?

Part of being connected to your intuition is to know when you are receiving messages through other people. If we are trying to find our path, we need to learn to attune our ears to the vibration of a divine message that may come through others. These messages are not as obvious as a mentor giving us advice. Instead, messages through others can sound like a song that picks up its tempo toward the middle to bring an emphasis to specific lyrics. In other words, someone might be speaking to you and all of a sudden you hear their voice go up in volume only for a few words. As if that phrase was highlighted among a sea of words. That is the divine speaking to you through others. Receive it.

The next takeaway we can gather from the mirror of our geniuses is that they feel worthy enough to pursue and explore. I do feel it's challenging for us humans to really grasp our worthiness.

We would need to reach some a state of spiritual enlightenment to truly understand what it means to be fully worthy of the Divine's grace.

With that being said, I don't blame you for not feeling worthy enough to take up space with your half-baked gifts. But we also shouldn't sit around waiting for complete spiritual enlightenment. What we do have available to us right now is our perspective, the way we see life.

A genius may seem as if they feel worthy — or maybe even entitled — to expressing their gifts for everyone to see. But really what they possess is perspective that makes expression seem less personal or emotional than it feels to us. Instead, they see it as a game. Just like a child playing pretend, they create, tinker, express and explore as if no adults were watching. It's all a game to the genius.

When seeing the world like a game, the genius makes her own rules. Her rules become her motivation to win in her own invented game. Maybe to start, her rule is just to be the best in her space, or to prove her mom wrong, or to make enough money to leave her toxic relationship. There are no rules about making rules, but I have found that the more playful the rules, the more success a genius will have.

This may feel like a departure from living a soul-led life because it seems as if your human self is making the whole thing up. But instead of seeing it this way, try to see yourself as a parent who is trying to get their child to read. As a parent, you understand that it is important for your child to read because reading is the doorway to many opportunities. But your child is scared and hesitant. He can feel the pressure and expectations on him, so he freezes with overwhelm.

We are all like the child who freezes with overwhelm when it comes to facing our gifts. Deep down inside, we can intellectualize the importance of discovering our talents, but right now that process does not feel fun. In fact, it feels more like death.

Your higher self is the divine inner mother, the soul that peeks through to walk us down our soul's path. A conscious mother faced with a scared child is going to try to reduce the pressure and fear around the task by creating a game. When you see the exploration and expression of your gifts as a game, you are being a supportive inner mother to the talented child within you. Create a game and rules that inspire and motivate you.

Take your favorite social media personality, for example. The one you can't take your eyes off. The one who fascinates you. The one you watch in the way a wildlife photographer studies a cheetah. Now ask yourself, *What game is she playing? How does she see the world?* When you strip away the enchantment of her expressed talent, and you see her as just a little girl playing a game, what rules has she set for herself? Why is she so good at playing the game? Write down what comes through for you.

If you work well with contrast, don't be afraid to explore the figures who frustrate you too, like shady world leaders and greedy businessmen. Study their game as well, sans your personal opinion, and notice how much you'll learn about intrinsic motivation. Take what feels right and leave the rest.

When we don't see the arena of talent expression as a game, we tend to get trapped in the debilitating effects of comparison. If we continue to be mesmerized by our favorite genius, we are at risk of comparing our underdeveloped gifts to their talent. Sometimes the genius we compare ourselves to is close by, like a parent, a sibling, or a best friend who seems to be more talented than us. We are in danger of remaining in their shadow.

What I find to be most hindering about comparison is that we tend to overcompensate with "learned talent" by overdeveloping it. We do this because we are fearful of confronting the curiosity we feel around underdeveloped talent.

My client Emmy is a joy to be around. She so identifies with "being a joy" that she has taken it on as her identity. This started in childhood. The third child in a pack of four, Emmy was "easy" compared to her two older, teenage siblings and "sweet" compared to her aloof younger brother. She was so often praised by this kind behavior that she started to believe it was all she had to offer.

In college, she tried to discover uncharted parts of herself, by signing up for language and art classes. She craved adventure and newness, but because her environment remained the same, the pressure to be a joy was crushing. The thought of trying something new was uncomfortable, embarrassing, and hard because she was going against the flow of her identity web. She eventually silenced the dragon within and continued on a linear path, allowing the promise of a career, marriage, kids, and a home to seduce her, until she forgot about that time where she wanted to discover herself.

As time has passed, she has come to accept her learned talent as her true talent and gift to the world. Chained by the expectations of her, Emmy finds herself climbing the corporate ladder, despite not really wanting to. If she were to slow down and truly be honest with herself, she would give into the pull of working with her hands. She would acknowledge that her life force is begging her to build — or do something — with her hands. But if she were even to entertain this desire, she would be in direct competition with her sister and mother who are both considered the artists of the family. In comparison, Emmy is just a sweet girl with no artistic talent. She is stuck.

What we admire the most about geniuses is that they seem to intentionally develop their chosen gift, rather than a gift appointed to them by someone else. Emmy first needs to have compassion for herself and recognize that she, like so many others, was applauded for agreeable behavior rather than her raw gifts. There will have to be a dismantling of her learned talent, or at least the willingness to see it as an adaptive skill. Second, as a sign of love for herself, she will have to understand that she deserves to follow and develop her interest. Not only is this a kind thing to do, but the survival of her soul depends on it.

It is true that the human experience is expressed through the mind, body, and soul. But we do have free will, we have the choice of turning off the intelligence of any of the three. The less we listen to our desires, the more at risk we are of living this lifetime without a connection to our soul.

Perhaps the most unnoticed strategy of the genius is practice. It's not the sexiest part of the expressed talent, so we tend to overlook it, but we all know it's there. To take an honest look at our schedules and note what we are actually practicing versus what we wish we would be practicing can be both frustrating and sobering.

What is challenging about this exercise is acknowledging that we have a schedule booked with soul-dimming obligations, which is inherently a symptom of misalignment. Rearranging our schedules to a life that is more soul-led requires the same kind of patience needed to detangle a ball of thin-chained necklaces. You have to do a little bit at a time. Add a little time for your interests once a month, increase it to twice a month, and then once a week, until you find yourself regularly practicing your gifts.

Lastly, the genius bets on herself. She enlists herself to play in the biggest arenas, because this is where she is challenged to grow. The same way pets seem to limit their size based on the size of their cage, we limit the development of our talent based on the arena we're in. Often, this is a systemic challenge determined at childhood by the access we had to education and resources growing up. As a teacher of adults, I cannot deny this truth. So many factors play into the development of our gifts, most of which are completely unfair and based on luck and broken systems.

But I do know that as we adult and begin to have these awakenings, we owe ourselves another shot. We owe ourselves some better parenting and talent management. In the words of the great Maya Angelou, "Do the best you can until you know better. Then, when you know better, do better."

To me this means, don't allow yourself to chronically be the "smartest person in the room." Surround yourself around people who challenge you, even intimidate you. Find yourself the best teachers and mentors. Never allow finances to be the reason why you don't have access to growth. And advocate for yourself and your dreams. Train people to respect your pursuits and the time it takes to bring them to life. Let the talent live.

CHAPTER SEVEN

Losing Trust

One month and four blog posts later, I was officially a blogger. Stories about my observations while on jury duty, my thoughts on the self-help books I was currently reading, and musings about childhood populated my amateur website. The blog was a place for me to write freely, without worrying about how many views it would get the company I worked for. It was pure fun, harmless, unimportant even. Until one day when the premonition came to me, turning my leisurely, unimportant blog into my lifeline.

Surrounded by a pile of two-day-old washed but yet to be folded laundry, I sat crisscrossed on my bed, admiring my latest blog post when I heard my apartment door brush across the entryway floor, a sound I had become accustomed to associate with my boyfriend's arrival. Like a dog trained to salivate at the sound of its food pebbles hitting the bowl, I could count the amount of breaths it would take for him to get past the entryway, enter my bedroom, and ease my deeply rooted insecurities. All was well in the world because someone had chosen me, and had granted me worthy of being loved.

Only this time was different. I ran out of the allotted breaths before he could enter my doorway. *Did he stop in the kitchen to get a snack*? I thought. *Or maybe he paused to check his phone? But why wouldn't he just do that in my room?* Something wasn't right.

My stomach dropped. In that moment, I knew the day had arrived—the day where I would meet the phantom face of my premonition. He was breaking up with me.

After a string of unfinished phrases, he was finally able to utter a complete sentence.

"It's not you, it's me," he said, feeling disappointed in himself — probably more because of the lack of originality in his chosen words, and less about leaving our relationship.

It was all over before I could process what had happened.

Being left with a broken heart was an obvious casualty, but what I didn't expect was the trauma it caused to my inner guiding system. Ever since that moment in New York City, when I had received the Divine message to break off my engagement and follow my heart, I had felt connected to my intuition. I didn't know exactly where my life was going at every single turn, but I knew I could trust the longings of my heart. For years now I had been moving through the world with a feeling of being guided. And I followed with very little questioning, because it had yet to steer me in the wrong direction.

Meeting my current boyfriend had been no different. In fact, our relationship felt...well, fated. Not only because he saw me in a way I had never been seen before, but also because of the series of events that led me to him.

One of my first outings with my mom after returning from Los Angeles, was to church—specifically, the Catholic church I had grown up attending. I swear that woman never stopped praying for me, always hoping that the demons that possessed me to be so *wild* would finally leave me. I had been promised dinner after mass, so, reluctantly, I agreed to a one-hour session.

My body folded into its default kneeling position, my butt just ever so lightly resting on the pew bench behind me (a pro tip to save one's knees, learned after years of Catholic schooling). With my head resting on my folded hands, my eyes began to wander amongst the crowd, and I realized that these people were really into this Jesus thing — my mom included.

SPIRITUALITY AND RELIGION

Being that I have now spent several years teaching metaphysical concepts like spirit guides, past lives, and energy readings, people assume I am against Christianity, or any other organized religion for that matter. They assume I have abandoned the religious traditions passed on to me at birth, practiced by the many generations before me. This is an incorrect assumption. In fact, I see my current spiritual practices as an *extension* of the faith I was exposed to growing up.

A rebel by nature, religion always felt very limiting to me. I had many questions that my religion teachers, my mother, and even church priests couldn't answer. Quite frankly, Christianity as I knew it did not have the answers I sought. It's no wonder than when I enrolled in university, the first elective I signed up for was *World Religions*. Before studying spirit guides, I consumed books about Jesus, Mary, and Mary Magdalene written by non-Christians. I studied Judaism and became enamored with the mysticism of the Kabbalah. My most recent religious interests include the study of traditional African and African-derived religions taught by Shantrelle P. Lewis. And as I write this book, my husband and I regularly attend Sunday worship at a local nondenominational church.

As I reflect on my religious curiosity, I believe what drives me the most is a thirst to be connected to the Divine. I feel I'm always reaching, wishing I could touch it. Catholicism never gave me that. In the Catholic church I always felt unworthy, separated from God. As if he was tucked away in that little gold chamber behind the altar, hidden from us down below, who were just resting our lazy bums on the pew bench. The only access we had to the Divine was through a flawed male spiritual figure or through a set of strict prayers.

The day I attended church with my mom posed another opportunity for me to expand my spiritual understanding. I found it interesting to watch everyone kneel down in prayer after receiving the Eucharist. To me, the churchgoers looked like children writing Christmas lists to Santa, asking for toys on their wishlists. I imagined my mother bargaining with God, pleading for him to give me a husband. I imagined her requesting a rare sequence of events that would "unfortunately" cause my brother's current romantic fling to move to Iceland.

For many years I, too, saw praying as a moment to request things from my wishlist, or beg for compassion after committing a sin. But by this time, my understanding had evolved. I was beginning to see Jesus as a spiritual teacher and a guide rather than an authority figure. There was something about being surrounded by all these Jesus believers that made me feel his presence differently for the first time. It felt safe — and actually appropriate — to talk to him about my dating situation. And so, hesitantly, I began to pray.

Dear Jesus,

It feels appropriate to thank you for everything I have.

My mom says great things about you, so I was thinking I would check out your powers and see if they'll work for me.

I'm not sure if you've heard, but I broke off a wedding, burned down my life, moved to L.A. and now I'm back in Miami.

I'm thinking I'm ready for a boyfriend again. It'll give my mom a lot of peace, I could fit in with my friends, and I think I'd feel less empty. Could you help me with this?

Oh, and let's not do this like last time. I would like a cool boyfriend, who is fun, artistic, and who inspires me.

Thank you. Love you. Amen.

Within two weeks I had met my boyfriend. Jesus had come through for his girl! In addition to feeling divinely appointed, this relationship felt very in sync, the result of two people being in the same place in their lives and holding similar visions for the future.

My attachment to the relationship was further augmented by my developing interest in the concept of soulmates. This person felt familiar to me, leading me to believe that he was my soulmate, and destined to be my husband in this lifetime. All of this, coupled with the success of having followed my heart for a few years, granted me the confidence to believe that I knew exactly what this relationship was meant to be.

LOSING TRUST IN YOUR INTUITION

A few years later, all that confidence and self-trust was stolen from me when I was caught off guard by the breakup. If I was wrong about him, had I been wrong about everything else? Losing him was bad, but it wasn't the worst of it. Losing the ability to trust in my intuition, was a far greater loss.

I have heard this same story in many variations told to me by my students and clients. The loss of connection to our intuition can be the result of one sudden moment, like my story, or another type of sudden loss, like death. But this kind of trauma can also happen slowly, over a long period of time, like being unknowingly trapped in a relationship with a narcissist. And sometimes it's subtle, like losing ourselves to motherhood or a life-sucking job. The common thread is that we have lost the ability to trust ourselves.

At first, we may blame ourselves. *I should have seen this coming,* we think. *I can't believe I fell for that.* We later follow with self-punishment. After being dumped, I isolated myself from all my close friends who were in committed relationships. As if I didn't deserve support during such a hard time in my life because I had brought this upon myself.

Eventually, we may seek answers from others, hoping that their inner knowing is infallible, unlike our own. You'll start off with a few online searches or videos made by online gurus, but ultimately we seek someone who seems to be closest to the source of divinity. It was this way of thinking that led me to my quest to find the best psychic in town.

Just like any great streaming series about a reluctant heroine just starting her journey, a wiser, way more hip girlfriend inevitably enters the storyline to save her new best friend from drowning in her own self-pity. Lilly's upbringing ran parallel to mine. Raised by Cuban parents, her father was a doctor like mine, and although we attended the same Catholic high school growing up, we didn't become friends until early adulthood.

When I met Lilly, something about her made me feel like she was more mature than me. Although younger than me in age, it was immediately clear that she was more seasoned at life than I was. She gave me the same feeling that many parents try to vocalize when describing their child who is obviously an old soul.

I do see a fair share of old souls in my practice. Despite all the regular trauma and awakenings that humans go through, there is a natural wisdom that peeks through an old soul, giving off the vibe that they have some sort of expertise in the human department. They are the Seniors of Earth High School. In the simplest terms, old souls possess an unexplainable spiritual swagger.

After just a few weeks of knowing Lilly, she already felt like the kind of friend who might be able to help me with a request that I was too embarrassed to ask anyone else. She looked like a person who might know a psychic — or could at least find one through her contacts.

Before I knew it, we were driving a BMW through the shadiest parts of town at 9 p.m. to meet with a psychic who had been recommended by a friend of a friend. I felt like I was in the middle of a drug deal, but really it was just my Catholic guilt that was feeding my nerves.

The psychic welcomed us into her home each at individual times to keep our readings private. Lilly entered the living room first, while I waited in the car. A short while later, as soon as I saw the townhouse door open, I jumped out of the car to switch spots with Lilly.

The room was completely dark, lit only by three candles, setting the stage for either a ghost story or a sacrificial ceremony. The woman asked me what I had come for, so I began to tell her about my unexpected breakup. She nodded her head, listened compassionately, as she shuffled what I now recognize as Tarot cards.

After throwing the cards on the table, her compassionate face quickly turned to concern. "I'm sorry to tell you this, but you will never be happy again unless you marry this man," referring to my *very* ex-boyfriend. She could barely finish the sentence, my eyes began to well up, and I felt myself starting to cry.

This psychic had just validated my deepest fear, that my ex would become "the one that got away." After weeks of blaming my faulty intuition, instead I started to blame myself for ruining my "soulmate" relationship. I must have done something to screw up the divine plan, and now this stranger was legitimizing my fears.

"But have no fear, my love," she said gently. "For just $675, I can reverse the spell and heal you."

As if being snapped out of hypnotic trance, I immediately stood up, turned around, and walked out the door. It turns out the psychic did heal me. She healed my intuition problem — and at no additional cost. Because without a doubt, I knew that everything I had just experienced in that dark room had been completely false. My soul came forward, and even though it was just a flicker, it took over my hurting body and said, "Hey girl. We got this. Just wait and see."

FALSE PREDICTIONS

I don't mean to vilify this woman. Obviously, I truly believe in the power of a psychic reading. But when it comes to intuitives, there's an endless spectrum where one might pull their psychic information. Not all intuitives understand their gifts and therefore can unintentionally connect with lower vibrational beings. And most mysteriously, sometimes a "false" reading is exactly what the soul ordered.

At the time, I cataloged that psychic reading as a scam. It was exactly what my mother had warned me against. Despite knowing deep down that the information was not true, I cried to Lilly the whole way home, asking her to invalidate the psychic's prediction and validate my feelings instead. Remember, the knowingness I had felt was only a flicker. My energy was still so low because of the breakup, that I could only hold the high vibration of knowing long enough to walk out the door and back into the car.

After years of intuitive development and spiritual study, I can tell you why my intuition was wrong about my ex, and why I had that experience with the psychic.

When I met my ex-boyfriend, my intuition had told me to date this person. I was guided and pulled into his direction. Where I went wrong was when I decided to arbitrarily level that up. My intuition had only said, "Date this person." It was my own ego that added, *because he will be your husband.* My intuitive hit was hijacked by my own ego, so what I heard was, "Date this person, because he will be your husband."

Looking back, dating this person was an extremely important step in my spiritual development. He encouraged me to start blogging, which was the beginning of the work I do today. The breakup catapulted me into a world of psychics, which led me to study the metaphysics. It was all meant to be. It just wasn't how *I* wanted it to be at the time.

As for the psychic, she gave me a prediction. She predicted that I would never really be happy unless I found my way back to that guy. A prediction is like a road of possibility, projecting from a person's energy. Both your true path and your default path can have several roads within them, as we have discussed in earlier chapters.

Because my intuition had been injured by the breakup, I was at risk of getting off my true path and defaulting to my default path. It was like my human self was contemplating whether it had the energy to recover from this, and ultimately get back online with my soul. Because of the pain I felt, I was no longer identifying with my spiritual truth, but instead with my physical reality.

When we talk about someone being "low vibe," what we're saying is that they are vibrating at a more dense point on the scale of energy. If the scale of energy was from zero to 10, zero would be closest to the feeling and vibration of total despair, and 10 would be similar to the feeling of bliss. The lower we go, the heavier or denser the energy. The higher we go on the scale, the lighter the energy. When we are lighter, we can rise above our everyday situations. We can see life through a spiritual lens.

I was hanging out in a lot of low vibrations at the time, which was creating these roads that were leading toward my default path. The default path can be considered a lower vibrational path, because it is created by our lower vibrational thoughts, which ultimately create our energy.

The psychic was reading one road. It might have even been the strongest road for me at that moment in time. She saw the possibility of me never getting over the breakup, maybe picking a future partner strictly on emotional security, or not marrying at all.

Her prediction was not wrong. It's just that when she connected to that road, I did too, and that feeling was enough to break me out of the dark haze I was in, so that my soul could once again come through, and remind me what it feels like to be on my true path. That divine intervention helped me disconnect from the road I was unintentionally creating, and just barely hold on to a road of my true path.

That was the healing the psychic was referring to. A soul heals when the block that keeps you from your true path is removed.

Oftentimes the block need not be fully removed. The truth is, we're usually not ready to have it completely removed. It does serve a purpose, it keeps us safe from the vulnerability that comes with living open-heartedly. Most of the time, all we need is a small opening, just enough to get a glimpse of what's true and possible for us. Similar to a sky filled with clouds, if you look for it, you'll eventually find a little blue corner, reminding you that the clear sky is still there, despite the obstructed view.

For this reason, a "false" prediction can sometimes be exactly what we need. I was reading a client one day, and I saw a road where she embraced her body weight, although at the time she wasn't happy with it. A few months later, I saw her at an event and she was significantly thinner. Before I could even celebrate her shift, she told me, "Nikki, I didn't want you to be right. I couldn't accept your prediction." She didn't like the road I saw, so like me, she clawed her way over the mountain of doubt, away from the default path, and landed on her true path.

This is why default paths are never a bad thing. They often give us the contrast that fuels our inner fire toward what is really aligned for us. This is also why some moments in life catch us off guard, like my breakup. It took me down a path that would have never existed without that experience. We might call this a catalyst, being catapulted toward our truth, or an event that caused a spiritual awakening. In the moment, it feels painful, as if something in you is dying. It feels that way, because something in you *is* dying: a part of the ego.

EGO DEATH

There are many definitions for the ego. In this book, I am going to define the ego as the false self. You can imagine it as the version of you that thought the default path was just fine. Think about the time when you went through something horrible and came out of it realizing what *really* matters in life.

My client, Marianna, unexpectedly lost her husband. She came to me a few weeks after his death. And when I read her energy, it looked completely different than when I had read her just a few months prior. She was someone who was always worried about what others thought, constantly drawing in the need to please. After her husband passed, though, all of that went away. She simply did not have the energy to worry anymore. It's as if when her husband left his body, he took all her worry with him, because she had just faced one of her biggest fears.

Her worry was part of her ego, and it had become such a huge part of her personality that she had started to believe that it was a component of her true essence. But it wasn't, which is why it was ready to die. This next journey she was about to take needed more of her true essence and less of her ego.

Not all of us embrace ego death as gracefully as Marianna did. Especially when it's our first conscious moment. Looking back now, I understand what that breakup was, but at the time I was so angry about being shoved into a life I did not want. Since then, I have experienced several ego deaths: the birth of my sons, the discovery of my husband's addiction, changes in my business, and so on. Now, I know to welcome these deaths, to fall into the arms of the angel of death, and to surrender to the inevitable.

This surrendering so many gurus speak of only happens after going through a few ego death experiences, so don't be too hard on yourself if you work hard to control your path. You must first learn to trust death, before learning not to fight it. Ego death and these unexpected experiences appear on our path to create greater alignment. Once we start to acknowledge this, then we can begin to welcome death with open arms every time it comes for us.

HOW TO WELCOME EGO DEATH

First, we must identify what ego death is and what the signs are. In the simplest terms, ego death is when an aspect of our personality is trying to leave us. This aspect of our personality is an adaptation and not our true essence. We have developed this trait in response to something in our environment.

A physical example of an adaptation can be best described through a story that my neighbor told me, about his friend who worked in our local paper mill. In his job, his friend was responsible for repeatedly pressing a critical button. He held this position for so long that his fingers ultimately adapted to the shape of the button, leaving large craters in each finger. His body adapted to the environment to the point that his fingers no longer looked human. His fingers weren't born looking that way, they became that way to be in harmony with his environment.

This is an example of a physical adaptation, but we make intangible adaptations all the time. In Marianna's case, she learned to worry because in her family, when you love someone, you worry about them. Her true essence is not a worrier, but with time, she adapted to her environment.

At some point these adaptations clash with our true path, and to continue forward, a part of the ego must die. Now, Marianna's husband did not pass because she needed to let go of her ego. His passing had to do with his own soul's path, but it affected Marianna's soul too. Could she have let go of worrying without her husband passing? Of course. This is just how it worked out for her. And there is a lot of mystery as to why it had to come as the result of such a difficult experience. As humans with limited access to our soul, there will always be questions and mystery.

I, too, had many questions after my break up, and all the other ego deaths I experienced since then. But in the midst of all these unanswered questions, there is also the truth of what is trying to leave us. We may not know why, but it's obvious that we cannot continue forward with parts of us that belong to the false self.

Ego death can come from surprise events, like losing a job, but they can also come from happenings that we instigate. When we first moved from Miami to North Carolina, we lived at the bottom of our property in a small guest house, as we built our permanent home higher up on the mountain. My whole family was excited about moving to a bigger house, but getting there was a journey.

The weeks leading up to the move, I was asked to shed so much old emotional baggage. Our permanent home is nestled among huge, old trees that vibrate at a high energetic level. It felt like in order to live amongst these trees, we also needed to vibrate at their level, or at least close to it. It was hard to work through my inner turmoil, but at the same time, I had called this upon myself, because *I* wanted to live amongst these trees and be in harmony with their energy.

When we think about living a soul-led life, we're imagining a future version of ourselves who is happy, whole and authentic. Which means, she holds a different energy than our current self. She didn't get to that future place by continuing to be the same person. We often think that to get to these future visions, all we need to do is push harder and faster. When the truth is, what we need to do is make an energetic shift instead.

Pushing means I'm dragging my body with me through time. Energetic shift means I carry a whole new energy, thereby attracting new experiences. Pushing takes time. Energetic shifts can happen as quickly as we are ready for it.

The house we were building higher up on the mountain is a modular home. It was built in a factory, brought to our property in pieces, and then put together on the land, like building a Lego set. The day the pieces came in was surreal. There was no house on the land in the morning, and by the end of the day there was a full two-story house with a basement. Even the kitchen and bathrooms were already completed inside the house.

It was incredible to watch, but at the same time it was extremely shocking to my nervous system. In my mind, I thought I was ready for it. But when I saw it built, my energy was not yet attuned to someone who could have such a nice house and land.

At the end of the building day, my nervous system was bringing me back to a time in my childhood when my father's business had started to crumble. As a child, the deterioration of his business had felt so sudden. One day, I was riding in my mom's luxury car and the next day I was being told I couldn't buy a new dress for the Homecoming dance. We were at the peak of success for just a few months and then it all crumbled, leaving us worse off than when we started.

When I saw this house completed, the memory in my body started to tell me that everything was about to crumble. My ego had taught me to brace myself when I reached a peak of success, because it was possible that I'd lose it all very soon. In order to be the woman who could live in that house with inner peace, I needed to let that go. I needed to care for my body and the inner child as we transitioned to this higher vibration. The higher vibration was that of a woman who could embody and hold all these blessings. A woman who felt worthy of the house and who could trust that it would be safe to receive all the good that was happening to her. I needed to make an energetic shift toward my future, aligned self.

Ego death comes in many forms, but one sign that all have in common is a strong feeling of not being able to move forward. Sometimes we are very aware that we are trying to move forward, like when you're trying to reach a goal but feel very blocked. And sometimes, life itself is trying to move us forward and we just can't seem to go with it. Instead, we end up in a loop, in a replay of similar experiences, or in a depressive funk. These are signs that something within us is trying to leave.

The next step? We must let it leave and die. This may sound easy, because obviously we want to let go of anything that is blocking us. But in truth, its difficult, because our adaptations have kept us safe for so long. In my life, I'd learned to not go "too big" or be too greedy in order to stay safe from losing everything. This was a very helpful adaptation for many years, keeping me honest and in check with my values.

But while it was helpful, it wasn't completely true. Not all people who are "going big" are doing it irresponsibly. Building our family a nice house doesn't make us greedy. There are a lot of blind spots in the ego's perspective. It doesn't always see the whole picture. For this reason, it will cause friction when we're trying to move forward.

When these moments show up for us, we need to ask ourselves what this block is about. When you think about the block or where you're trying to go, notice any thoughts or beliefs running through your head? Write them down.

Next, ask yourself what kind of character is saying these beliefs. Can you give this character a name? For example, when I thought about writing this book, Prestigious Penny showed up for me. She's a part of my ego who looks for mainstream success and approval from industry leaders (whatever that means). She's annoying, but she's also here to help me survive by receiving a gold star from some imaginary gatekeepers. When I identify her, though, I laugh a little and realize how silly she is. And I also can recognize how she's been in my lineage for many generations. It's easier to let her go when I understand her a little better. What character is with you as you try to move forward?

Also, when feeling blocked or noticing an ego death, it's helpful to perform an energetic body scan to spot the discomfort. An energetic body scan is done by closing your eyes, and imagining that you are a little light that is inspecting your body from head to toe. As you scan your body, you want to feel each part and notice where the block might be hiding. Once you find yourself stopping, ask that body part what it has to say.

For example, maybe as you scan, you find yourself stopping at your right shoulder. Hold your attention there and see if it has anything to say. Or notice if any memories come up for you. Sometimes poking the body part can help. One of my somatic healing teachers, Dr. Paul Canali, taught me to push a light-weighted medicine ball into the discomfort and speak out the pain or memory. This kind of body work can be life changing. Write down any information that is coming through from your body.

When ego death presents itself, we don't need to feel pressured to leave the adaptation completely behind. That might not always be possible. What is most important is that we are aware that it is there and that we understand it. We need to recognize that these are parts of the false self.

I am aware that Prestigious Penny is there. I love her because she helped my ancestors survive and rise in the ranks for many generations. But I'm also aware that she is an old technology, she cannot help me write a heart-centered book. She can hang out if she likes, but she can't make any writing decisions for me. Since she's pretty vain, she *can* help me pick out my wardrobe from time to time (if she's still around).

Other times, the ego death can be more aggressive and the adaptation is swiftly taken from us, much like a toddler losing his pacifier when the time is appropriate. These more aggressive deaths typically come with a tangible change to our lives. We don't have much of a choice when it comes to letting go. We are being asked to surrender.

CONTROLLING VS CREATING

I feel that surrender can be a very hard concept, especially for us high-achieving, manifesting, dream-makers. We can use all the spiritual words we like, but deep down, we're a bit controlling. In our defense, there is a thin line between trying to control our experience and trying to create it. Allow me to do my best at defining the difference.

Controlling is synonymous with being attached to a plan that leads to an outcome, and being attached to the specific outcome itself. Let's say you have a goal of owning a house in a specific type of neighborhood. In order to get that house, maybe you've created a plan that includes saving money, keeping your credit score high, and receiving a few promotions.

As you follow that plan, maybe most of it works out, but the industry you're in starts to tank and you lose your job. You did not plan for this. If we're controlling, we may start to get angry that our house dream is never going to materialize. Or we might start aggressively looking for a job in the same industry, although no employer is calling back.

The controlling person misses the signs from the Divine, who is trying to guide them toward a higher path. The Divine never said you weren't going to get the house, it's simply trying to tell you is that there is a better way, with an even better outcome.

The controlling person not only misses the signs, they also mistakenly direct anger towards them, and view them as unfair. They stomp their feet about their terrible luck. They worry that they'll never have their house. Overall, they see everything that is happening — which is out of their control — as a direct attack against their plan.

The creator also has her plan and works to follow it, but when the tide begins to change, she takes notice. Rather than fight the tide, she observes it first. Asking herself, *What is this trying to tell me?* Different from someone who might just go with the flow, a creator is more intentional. She stops to observe the signs, as if she was in conversation with the Divine. She rearranges her plan accordingly, still moving, but trusting that there is a better route being paved.

In my practice, I see these new routes as upgrades. Often, the upgrade happens because of the collective's evolution. Similar to when you use a map app on your phone, and the path starts to change due to an accident or updated traffic patterns in the area. The app tries to find you a better way. Not only are we constantly evolving, but so is the greater collective, which affects the routes we try to take.

Additionally, sometimes our routes upgrade because our souls make more progress than expected. This is similar to being in high school and deciding to take the honors level class rather than stay in the mainstream English class. Based on the readings I've performed, it seems that souls have these options as well, and sometimes they will upgrade in the middle of a lifetime.

Maybe you've felt this before in your own life? Perhaps you were so excited about a specific career path, climbing the ladder, only to get to a certain point and feel… empty? What happened? You were so certain, and even excited. Well, what happened is you upgraded. And the collective upgraded too, which gave you more possibilities.

An upgrade can be confusing while you're in it, but if you take the perspective of a creator, with time you will realize that it is in your highest and greatest good. And listen, if you can't find that perspective while you're in it, don't be so hard on yourself! During my breakup, I couldn't see the bigger picture. It wasn't until I experienced several ego deaths, that I was able to have the wisdom to meet them with grace.

THE SEARCH FOR ANSWERS

Obviously, I wasn't satisfied with my first psychic experience. I was determined to find a guide to help me make sense of everything that was happening in my life, and so I continued on my quest to find the perfect reading. I spoke about my pursuit endlessly, and it finally paid off one day while having dinner with two of my girlfriends. We laughed about my most recent traumatic psychic event, and brainstormed ways in which we could find a good intuitive.

With no promising leads, we walked back to our car, parked in a 5-level parking garage about half a mile from the restaurant. And would you believe it, tucked inside the passenger side door handle was a tacky business card promoting angel readings! Now remember, this was way before phones had started listening to our conversations, and the parking garage was nowhere near the restaurant. This was no coincidence, it was just pure divine intervention.

My two girlfriends booked a session immediately, while I waited to hear about their experience. I didn't want to further traumatize myself! To my surprise, the reviews were great, so I booked my session too.

The experience was a far cry from the last. For starters, I drove during the day to her beachfront condo, where the sun lit up the entire room. The fact that she performed *angel* readings put me at ease. After all, there are plenty of angels in the Bible, so how bad could this be?

She was kind and gentle, and her information was spot-on. She even predicted my husband a year and a half before I met him! That day, I was converted to a believer. *There's really something magical and helpful about these readings*, I thought.

Perhaps the strangest thing that happened that day came, not from the psychic, but from me. At the end of the reading, I looked straight into her blue eyes and asked, "Do you think I can do what you do?" I'm not sure how those words escaped my mouth. I went from being terrified of readings, to wanting to know if I had any psychic gifts myself. Talk about being afraid of your own power!

She was so kind, and responded to me with encouragement and a list of books to read. I quickly began to study about angels, past lives, anything metaphysical. Like so many of my students and clients, I was guided deeper and deeper into this spiritual world that until then, I had known very little about.

There was a part of me that wanted to stop learning, because this stuff was making me weird! I was afraid that if I kept going, I wouldn't be able to relate to anyone. I was afraid of being judged, being unlovable, and — to be honest — I was afraid of not being marriage material.

Fortunately, my curiosity was stronger than my fear. I continued to present as the lifestyle editor, the friend, and the family member everyone expected by day, but at night I would lock my door — hiding even from my roommates — and study as much as I could. I was enamored with it all.

My curiosity led me to become certified in hypnotherapy, theta healing, and Reiki. At the time, I was studying simply for my own healing. Simultaneously, I was keeping up with my blog, which had now become a dating blog, filled with my new spiritual observations. My life had taken a strange twist, but somehow I knew to ride the wave in order to prevent myself from drowning.

It wasn't until I met my husband, Benny, that I started to realize my current work wasn't quite what I was meant to do. Actually, if I'm being honest, his daughter, Aly, was the person who gave me the courage to change. Seeing her in my life made it very clear what I would have to do.

CHAPTER EIGHT

Manifesting Your Dream Life

I met my husband Benny at my best friend's engagement party. Benny and I had been at the same party many times before but had never met.

Despite being the Maid of Honor, I was partially dreading the engagement party. After being friends since middle school, I was pretty sure I would know *everyone* at the party, meaning there'd be no dating prospects for me. Plus, my parents and all my friends' parents would also be there, making my singledom feel even worse.

I was having a conversation with a guy was trying to hit on me, by making fun of me. You know that guy, right? The guy who is still using his kindergarten dating skills of pulling a girl's hair to get her attention? Well, I was stuck in that conversation with that guy, and was honestly quite confused.

My confusion led me to look away from the man-child for a moment, thinking *Maybe I'll get some sort of sign from the night's sky*. Instead, I spotted Benny. *Who is this handsome, tall man?* I thought. And secondly, *Why the hell hasn't my best friend introduced me to him yet?*

He was talking to my friend's boyfriend. I'm not sure if it was the soulmate connection or my desperate attempt to get out of the conversation I was in, but without thinking, I walked over and interrupted their conversation. My friend's boyfriend quickly got the hint and left Benny and me alone for a brief moment before my Maid of Honor duties took me elsewhere.

Later that night, at the after party, an acquaintance of mine (who happened to be a good friend of Benny's) began pulling my arm and dragging me to the balcony of the high-rise condo. "I have someone I think you should meet," she insisted. "I've been wanting to introduce you guys ever since I met you."

Wouldn't you know it, her "someone" was Benny. The two had been in school together since kindergarten. Maria and Benny had played Mary and Joseph together in the first grade nativity play, a coincidence that makes me smile every time I think about the role she has played in our lives.

Following Maria's insistence, Benny and I sat together and began to get to know each other. Ten minutes into our conversation, he pulled out his phone and casually showed me a picture of his daughter. *Slick move, Benny.* He was feeling me out to see how I felt about the fact that he had a kid.

Three months later, I met his four-year-old daughter, Aly. Benny and I had a rocky first few months, mostly due to the commitment phobia I had developed since my last relationship. But after a few months of hot and cold, we decided to commit to each other — and that included a commitment to Aly. We were a threesome from the start.

After a few months of driving from my office in Downtown Miami to the suburbs where Benny and Aly lived, trying to make it in time for dinner, I just knew I couldn't keep this up. Benny was a single dad, he needed help, and Aly deserved a structured home. Showing up at 7:30 p.m. just didn't feel right for me.

I was raised by a really resentful mother. She was an incredibly sharp, talented, and ambitious woman, yet she also wanted to be a mother. She raised three children in the 80s and 90s, a time when you had to choose between staying home with your children or working all day at an office. Those had been her only choices.

I was raised on that resentment. I swam in the energy of an angry woman, every day, who was forced to choose between her ambitions and her children — two desires that shouldn't be mutually exclusive, but often are.

Behind every passive aggressive response from my mother, all this sensitive child could feel was the pain of an unjust choice. All I could hear was the frustration of an unseen need and unquenched desire. It was heartbreaking to experience, but her anger birthed a new dream that was encoded in me, one I didn't know I had until I met Aly. I wanted both. I wanted a career I loved *and* a family. And I wanted those two aspects of my life to somehow harmoniously intertwine.

I thought I would have a little more time to figure out a synergetic lifestyle that would include my passions, motherhood, and financial security, but Aly was my bonus baby who forced me to figure out this puzzle sooner than expected. My beloved magazine job was no longer a fit, so I started to look for online editorial jobs I could do from home. I already had a few online side gigs (because an editor's salary is never enough), but I needed a full-time income. This desire ultimately manifested in the form of a dream job. I was offered a job as the Miami editor of a well-known online publication based out of New York.

The only downside was that it would take time away from my blog, which at the time was transitioning from dating to general self-help. I was still keeping my metaphysical interests on the down low — practicing meditation in the early morning when everyone was still asleep — but I figured self-help talk was safe to write about. I saw my fashion blogger friends beginning to make money, and the wellness and modern spirituality pioneers were starting to make noise online and in books. All of this made me secretly believe that, perhaps, my blog could be more than just a creative outlet.

The dream job quickly became the job from hell: low pay, demanding deadlines, and 24-hour accessibility. I was in charge of launching the Miami section of a very popular website. Sure, it was glamorous, but I could see that I was building someone else's brand and that once I left, I would have nothing to show for all my efforts. It just didn't seem like a good use of my time or my effort.

By this time, I had already moved into Benny's home. When I needed a break from my new job, I would emerge from my home office and walk into the kitchen to find Benny's company papers sprawled all over the counters. At first I didn't want to overstep, but based on the mess of papers I saw, I was getting the feeling that Benny's lawn and tree business was kind of disorganized and in need of help. A lightbulb went off in my head.

After working for several large companies throughout my career, I was well trained in online marketing and really anything digital. I looked at Benny's company and thought, *What if I could bring this thing into the digital age?* I started small, just helping him get organized and building him a website that didn't look like a Microsoft clipart party. But what I really wanted — and what I knew would be best for our family — was to work with him full-time.

This idea had been swirling around in my head for months, but I was scared. Scared of not having income, leaving my identity as an editor, and putting strain on our relationship at the start of our marriage. It all became clear to me when two days into our honeymoon vacation, my company was reaching out asking for assignments even though everyone knew I was on my honeymoon. It just didn't make sense to me anymore. The glitz, glam, and stress were no longer worth it.

On that trip, I asked Benny what he thought about me leaving my job to work full-time with him. I told him I could run his business, organize it, get him a proper online scheduling system, and increase his sales in a big way through online marketing. In return, I wanted some time to work on my blog and my personal brand. Despite having only $3,000 in our bank account at the time, Benny agreed. We had just become not only husband and wife, but also business partners.

DREAMING IN PARTNERSHIP

What came after were years of grit, sacrifice, courage, and imagination. I had always been a dreamer, but never had I dreamt in partnership. Even in my past relationships, whether romantic or not, I had always prided myself on being independent, always figuring out everything on my own. But as my dream began to grow — encompassing lifestyle, purpose, and family — anytime I tried to create my dream life on my own, I would hit a wall. Benny could always spot (and later vocalize) this habit I had, of doing life as a lone wolf. He taught me how to be a team player, which for us meant putting our hearts and minds together to manifest our dream life.

I introduced the word manifesting to Benny, pointing out that he was a natural talent. Somehow, anything the guy needed or wanted would eventually find him. It was a gift he didn't know he had, and now he refers to himself as a master manifestor. I know, I know, I've created a monster.

Sharing my dreams with Benny, listening to his visions, and working together to make them happen was a crucial skill we developed early on in our relationship. Believe me, I tried to keep my dreams separate. I tried doing my little magic rituals at night, away from his sight, but they never worked as well as when I would loop him in. There's a sort of supercharge power that comes from dreaming in a group, a phenomenon I continue to experience with Benny and one I see every day while working with my current team in my business. I've even learned to include the kids.

Manifesting in partnership or in group takes a certain level of vulnerability that most of us are not naturally comfortable with. I remember before I even met Benny, a girlfriend of mine sharing with me how she and her husband would make spreadsheets that detailed how they spent their money, and that's how they would make their dreams happen. When I heard this, I felt pretty nauseous, I was sure I would never be successful at partnership. For starters, I had way too much money shame to create a budget spreadsheet, much less share it with another human. And secondly, I wasn't sure I could trust anyone with my dreams other than me. Either they weren't going to believe it or they were going to try to change it. Those were always my fears. Sharing and doing it together just felt like way too much exposure for me.

Despite my hesitation, life somehow faced me with my greatest fear. The dreamer in me was still alive, but I also had this man and these small little humans watching me. Throughout the years, I've had to share my dreams, fight for my dreams, and convince my partner to trust me, too. No matter what kind of mess you may find yourself in, trust that there is a way to your vision. It starts by planting seeds that will ultimately create the change you dream of. Here's what I find works.

GET HONEST

First, you must do your own soul searching and find what it is that you really want to create. This requires self-honesty and no judgment. I find this to be a stage in our lives where it's very helpful to surround ourselves with people who are open-minded, nonjudgmental, and who dream big. If you don't have these kinds of people in your life, listen to a podcast, read a book, or watch a movie that has this type of energy.

Also in this stage, you will need a level of self-honesty that might be greater than you've ever allowed yourself. My time in California exposed a hidden desire within me that I never knew was there. Experiencing land, mountains, hiking, and nature in California was like meeting a lover I never knew existed. I moved back to Miami because I knew it was the next step in my path, but my longing for a deep connection to nature never left me. It was buried deep within me, because it was the only way to survive in Miami and fulfill the cultural expectations of staying close to family. But that didn't make the yearning disappear.

A few years before I moved from Miami to the mountains, I received a reading from a colleague and former student of mine who saw my ache for land. Using the Soul Reading Method technique, she went into my heart chakra and was able to see and then express a love for nature that, up until then, I had been too afraid to acknowledge. She saw me, and her ability to convey my desire so clearly, made me see it too. Now that she had shown me what was in my heart, I couldn't just unsee it.

Getting clear on what you want might sound simple, but the truth is that we often hide our true desires as a form of self-protection. I did not want to acknowledge my love for nature because I knew that it would mean moving my entire family away from our hometown. It would mean having to tell my parents that I was moving their grandchildren to another state. And it would mean having to explain to my friends why I was, once again, the complicated friend who couldn't just be happy with what made everyone else happy.

Our desires can be beyond inconvenient, they can also feel impossible. If what we want seems like it's never going to happen, then why even bother acknowledging the desire? Let's say you want to move somewhere that is more aligned with your soul, but your partner's job keeps you where you are. In this case, you may think it's better to not entertain the dream at all. But burying our dreams deep within us, simply because we can't see them becoming reality, creates dishonesty within ourselves. This dishonesty ultimately creates resentment, and a misaligned life.

Even if we could get past how unattainable our dream is, the longing for it can cause so much discomfort and frustration that we'd rather not think about it. I once had a client, Amanda, tell me that she had unsubscribed from all the home decor magazines she once loved so much. She explained that seeing all the beautiful photos of homes and furniture was making her extremely frustrated with her current situation. Amanda longed for an soul-filled home that reflected her heart and inner creativity. But she had a fixed income, two children in expensive private schools, and a husband who just wouldn't budge on the budget. She was stuck, she didn't see the point of acknowledging her dream of having a beautiful home because there was no way it was going to happen (at least not any time soon). Thinking about it was taking a toll on her mental health.

This decision to reduce her exposure to home decor was a move made by her inner mother. Amanda needed to take care of herself, which I applaud. But instead of telling her inner child, "Hey, it looks like reading these magazines is frustrating you, let's talk about it," she said, "You're never going to have this life, so you should just stop dreaming."

As Amanda's coach, there were two red flags that stood out to me. First, I could tell Amanda was blaming herself for where she was. She was embarrassed to admit it, but she was feeling like maybe she had married the wrong person. Her father had always told her to marry someone "well-off"—someone that could provide her with a good life. And she tried, but ultimately felt that the man she had first met had completely changed as the years went by. It was as if she was experiencing a bait-and-switch. How many of us can relate?

Secondly, she felt like a failure for not having followed her father's advice. She hadn't even followed the back-up plan properly, which was to maintain lucrative career, no matter how much it would take her away from her children, in order to guarantee her a financially comfortable life. The shame surrounding this made her believe that she wasn't worthy of nice things. *She was bad. This was all her fault. How dare she want anything else? She did this to herself.*

Shame takes up so much of our vital creative energy. It stores our deepest guilt in hidden pockets within the body. Anytime we get close to creating a soul-led life, the pocket of shame is activated, causing a deep discomfort in the body, a sensation best described as a feeling that our inevitable death is near.

Shame is what keeps us from being honest about our desires, which blocks us from ever being able to pursue them. I have found that working around shame only leads to creating a life that circles around your desires, but never actually brings them to life. Instead, we must go toward, in, and through shame in order to manifest our deepest dreams.

Shame is our greatest roadblock. When we delve into it, the illusion that shame creates (in Amanda's case, that she was a bad person) explodes, just as an enormous rock would explode after being filled with dynamite. The rock is no longer in the way. We can now continue on our path.

The best way to explore shame is by feeling it and expressing it. When you are heading toward a dream and feel blocked, you may notice your body react. In Amanda's case, it was anger and disappointment, the mesh of emotions that appeared just before her decision to cancel the magazine subscriptions.

Sometimes the feeling is subtle, like not being able to sit down and finish the project you know you should finish because it's going to lead to so much. Sit with that uncomfortable feeling that makes you get up from the chair. Can you describe that feeling? Can you give it a voice? There is so much wisdom in that feeling. It's a key to the next journey.

Other times, the feeling is debilitating, like a panic attack or a dissociation from the body. It can feel scary and very unsafe to go into it. If this is the case, get yourself the support of a therapist or healer that you trust. Call up the feeling when you're with your trusted guide and begin your exploration.

We tend to fear delving into shame because it can feel like falling into a well with no bottom. *How deep is this wound? How far will I fall? Where is the ground, and will it catch me?*

I don't know how deep your fall will be, but I do know it's less painful than carrying around the pocket of shame for years. Carrying it around with you means hours and years dedicated to producing enough energy to keep us safe from a fall that will often last just a few weeks and sometimes only a few minutes. The fall frees us, while working around shame keeps us in an endless loop.

Like Brene Brown has taught us, the medicine to shame is vulnerability. For "strong" people out there, vulnerability can be foreign. To me, it was. I always thought I was an emotionally vulnerable person. In fact, my husband will tell you that living with me is like being on an emotional rollercoaster all the time. But vulnerability is more than just the presence or awareness of emotions. I see vulnerability as an act of bravery—one that leads us to no longer hold our pain in solitude. We must identify the pain, give it words, and safely share it with someone we can trust.

Some time ago, I found myself dealing with unexpected waves of anxiety that would find me at the most inconvenient times. After a few months, I decided to go in. As I would focus my attention on the pain in my stomach and heart, I would receive flashes from high school. Like most teenagers, I craved independence and exploration. But following these desires meant my mother's expectations of being a "good" young woman. I acted on my desires anyway, and since then, I've been faced with the juxtaposition that following my heart means being bad. The further I go into my heart, the more I feel that I am disappointing others.

Naturally, the more I moved into my dreams, the more aggressive the pocket of shame became. But once I went in, cried some big teenage tears, the breakthrough began and a soft angelic voice came through my ears to assure me that I was not bad at all. Not only did I hear the message, but for the first time, I saw what it felt like to *not* see myself as bad.

This healing experience was followed by vulnerable conversations with my brother, my best friend, and one very special interaction with my daughter. Because I was releasing this belief and stored memory of being bad, I felt the need to talk to my daughter about my feelings of being a bad mom, specifically to her.

You see, I came into Aly's life when she was four years old. We both instantly knew that I was meant to be her mother and her, my daughter. The only problem was that I really didn't know how to be a mother. I hadn't experienced those hard first three years of a child's life, which is when moms are usually born. I was late to the party, and as a result, I had always felt "behind" as her mother. Like the time I sent her off to her first dance recital, without a single ounce of makeup on. Thankfully, my "mom tribe" quickly dolled her up, she went on stage looking beautiful, and I was left feeling like a terrible mom.

You see, in addition to feeling behind, I felt unfit. I was raised by the kind of woman who upholds the patriarchy, with its endless "perfect female" rules and its trademark training of being less than boys. There have been many times in Aly's upbringing that this woman has come through my voice and undoubtedly hurt her. Rather than speak my guilt and stop the cycle, I kept it to myself. Because that's what strong leaders do, right?

It wasn't until I went into my shame about being bad that I felt ready to tell Aly how I had felt unfit to be her mother. I apologized for any hurt I may have caused in the past and told her I would do better. This conversation furthered the healing of my shame pocket.

The more we work through our shame, the more we feel worthy of a bright future. We also begin to feel safe enough to be honest about what it is we want. The next step is the stage where we work to believe in the dream.

DEVELOP A NORTH STAR

Since we are speaking of being honest, I must admit something. I never really understood the whole "believe in yourself" thing. It just never made sense to me. We are sensitive beings, meaning every new and unknown thing feels painfully hard. It's part of being us! How does one have time to believe in themselves through such a debilitating fear of the unknown?

Also, most dreams seem impossible and come with no roadmap, leaving our practical minds with a lot of questions. By definition, our dreams have not been accomplished before. We have never done the thing that made that dream come true. So naturally, we lack confidence, because you can only become confident in something you have done before. Doing it is what gives us confidence.

Instead of trying to believe in yourself, I encourage you to envision your final destination. Amanda would envision a beautifully furnished house. She may not know how to get there, especially considering all the real obstacles she had in her way, like her husband and fixed income. But she can most likely envision the finished product, and that's all that matters.

Bring to mind the dream you became honest about while reading the last section. I want you to close your eyes and imagine that you are standing at the start of a life-sized maze. You have an aerial view of yourself standing at the beginning. All the way at the end of the maze is the future version of yourself who has accomplished the dream. As you see this future version of yourself, allow yourself to feel how real this version is, and how real the accomplishment is.

Now, take a look at the maze. Notice all the routes and all the dead ends. These are all the unknown paths that will begin to appear to you as you move forward. It's not your job to know how or which route to take, your job is just to know that the end, the future version of yourself, the accomplishment, is real. You can open your eyes.

The end of the maze is what I like to call the North Star. I know very little about the journey, but I do know that there is this one, very real, bright star that I'm trying to reach. It exists, therefore there must be a path to it. What we need to believe in is the actuality of destination and refer to it as our North Star. Hold on to that North Star, but there's no need to become obsessed with it. Come back to the present moment and observe the various routes.

There were many times in the early years of our relationship that Benny and I didn't see eye-to-eye on our collective dream. A few months into running his business together, the growth had been incredible, and he quickly realized that I, too, had some sort of special sauce. But we didn't always agree on what I should be *doing* with my talent. For many years, he felt that my pursuit of becoming a spiritual blogger (I didn't have the word for it yet) was selfish and unrealistic. It only looked like that because I didn't have a clear understanding of where I was going, and I was swimming in so much doubt that I was often obsessed with my own process.

Although I was constantly confused by my direction, I still believed in my North Star. Which, honestly, was Benny's North Star too, he was just still dealing with some doubt. Your North Star is your big vision for your life. For me, it was to live creatively and abundantly, while fostering a loving family. Benny wasn't yet convinced on the "creative" part. His vision at the time was more like: survive, make money, and provide for family. But if you think about it, we both wanted the same thing, mine was just a little bit of a higher vibration, appearing dreamy and unrealistic to my very masculine counterpart.

One of the reasons I was so stuck on making my business work— though Benny's was doing well and showing so much potential—was because my work could be done anywhere. Also, Benny's service-based business was complicated, and even dangerous. It required a lot of employees, insurance, and money to make it work.

Because Benny had not known anything other than hard work (we can thank our immigrant ancestors for that), my dream of a simple, online business seemed idealistic to him, silly even. He constantly asked me to start an online marketing business, where I could use my digital skills for other people's businesses and in return have a few lofty retainers as income. Although this was tempting, I really had to stand my ground and dig deeper into what my heart was calling me to do. I needed to hold that vision even while knowing that my husband didn't agree, and knowing that he didn't believe in me...yet.

To be fair, no one around me believed in my abstract idea of becoming a spiritual coach, who wrote books and sold online courses. The idea seemed so foreign to my science-froward family and my straight-arrow friends. If you're dealing with the same kind of doubt and naysayers, listen to me: don't back down just because the people around you don't share your imagination.

Creating the life we are trying to create takes imagination, we are literally trying to make something that has not existed before us. It's a new trail that comes with no blueprint. The only way to get through the trail is with our own instincts. If we listen to anyone else, we will inevitably become lost.

PROTECT YOUR DREAMS WHILE YOU BUILD CONFIDENCE

We must protect our new idea, like a mother protects a newborn. A kangaroo gives birth to a joey as early as 21 days after conceiving. The baby is so vulnerable, born no bigger than the size of a bee, that she keeps the new life in her pouch for another ten months.

Your new business idea — or any new dream for that matter — is a joey. This means you're not telling too many people what you're creating. Sometimes you're even keeping the idea safe from those closest to you. You're also working on the idea, allowing it to grow while in your pouch, and not showing it to the world until it is strong enough to stand on its own two feet.

This was the case when I first started my business. Even if I had wanted to share my idea with others, I could barely articulate it, because not even I knew the specifics of what it was. I was constantly rewriting my email signature and social media descriptions because I had no idea who I was (in business) or what I was doing. One day, I would describe myself as a writer. The next, a coach. And on the third day, I would crumble and label myself something esoteric like "intuitive dreamweaver."

Even though I was shifting and making visible moves, no one was really noticing. Now, if I would have reported back to my husband every time I changed my online title, his concern for me would have quickly extinguished any hope I had inside. The same way the mama kangaroo has to continue existing in the wild while she carries her young, your idea will have some level of outside exposure, but there needs to be a way to keep it from the predators—those who can hurt it the most. In most cases, predators are people we care about and whose opinions can affect us.

FIND YOUR PEOPLE

This does not mean that we are meant to care for our new idea on our own. On the contrary, you will absolutely need a community and support in order to raise this young idea. I found my support, and a community of likeminded female entrepreneurs, by hiring my first assistant Danika (who is now the president of my company). In my current business, I have the honor of observing my students blossom in their intuitive gifts when they *finally* find their people within our program, the Soul Reading Method. Our students are from all over the world, from all sorts of backgrounds and ethnicities, but in class, soulmates tend to find each other. And through the protection of the community, the intuitive feels safe enough to grow into her true self. Witnessing this is one of the great joys in my life.

It's completely okay if you need to seek support outside of your usual community. In fact, based on my own experience, and watching my students become their true self, I have found that leaving the tribe to find those who truly understand you tends to be pretty typical. Just like any great hero's journey, once you become strong within your new identity, you will return back to the tribe to share your newly discovered gifts and path.

When you're in the process, though, you may feel misunderstood. Almost as if you're being banished from your community. But instead, let's think of it as a rebirth. As if the mother energy of your community is birthing you out through a portal that will take you to a new world that you are meant to discover — for both your own growth and the growth of your community. We are meant to expand, but not all of us are brave enough to do so. Only the strongest are asked to venture beyond the four walls they know best. The only reason you are being called to the beyond is because you are the most fit candidate for the job. You are the hope of the tribe.

Your community of origin does not know that they are hoping for your success. After all, they are stuck in their own heavy doubt and fear. But their souls know that as you expand, you will then bring that expansion home. Whether that's by teaching your children and family your new soul-led ways, or by leaving codependent relationships altogether, which eventually invites and initiates healing.

We seek to live a soul-led life because we are souls who are called to seed the New Earth with light, new structures, and enlightened consciousness. We are visionaries, although we struggle through the journey. Remember visionaries are only given this special title after the fact. Only once their dreams become reality, are they recognized as visionaries. Before and during the creation process, they are referred to as so many other things: insane, phonies, crazy people, delusional artists, and—my personal favorite—witches. I know this, because I've been called them all — plus a few extras spoken in the Spanish language.

Early on in my business, I remember seeking out guidance from my childhood friend Janet Jones, founder of the wildly successful VXN Workout. I was expressing my fears about starting a business based on intuition and metaphysics. "Isn't that crazy," I asked her. I'll never forget her response.

"Yeah Nikki, everyone thought I was crazy when I was texting people to come to my new workout dance class. It wasn't until the business took off that people started applauding my idea, as if they had never doubted me," she shared.

I admired her so much for that. I started to think *If people are calling me weird, perhaps it's because I'm on to something?* In the meantime, I would surround myself with other visionaries, like Janet, who would carry me through as I birthed this new business. When you begin to seek these people, you'll be surprised how many of them are out there! It's actually quite exciting. You begin to create your own special coven of misfits, weirdos, and risk takers who think like you and inspire you further.

Visionaries like you and me are, by nature, black sheep. We stray from the herd, searching for more expansive spaces. We challenge the rules, the people who made them, and the people who uphold them. And by default, these tendencies can isolate us.

The isolation can feel personal, causing us to believe that something is wrong with us, or that we're too high maintenance for wanting something outside of the norm.

I believe we have lost so many talented dreamers to the fear of "not fitting in". People who could have made beautifully eccentric lives, but instead succumbed to the lies that "isolation from the herd" propagates. Yes, we are a herd species, but what if you're just stuck in the wrong one? What if you're a zebra hanging out with a bunch of horses?

My client Nabina came into our session already in tears. Together with her husband and another male partner, she owned a chain of restaurants. She loved her work, but she was worried that the stress was getting to her. She felt depressed and anxious all the time, and no matter what she did, she continued to gain weight without any real explanation. Nabina feared that for the sake of her health, she would have to leave the family business.

The more we spoke and the deeper into her challenges we went, I started to realize that these weren't just symptoms of stress. These were the symptoms of loneliness. Her husband was her go-to person for pretty much everything in life. They were great life partners in general. But as the business expanded, Nabina's vision began to look quite different from her husband's and the other partner's visions. And although she had a team of over 100 people, she still felt alone.

Together, we discovered her loneliness. I told her I wanted to introduce her to two other clients of mine who were both seasoned female entrepreneurs, with large companies just like her, who lived in her city. Our next session, Nabina showed up in tears again, but this time with happy ones. She had found her people, she told me. She could not believe how much she had in common with these women, including how many of the same challenges they shared. After a few months of consistent lunches with her new friends, she began to feel more at ease and energized. She had people to bounce ideas off of and get inspired by, so by the time she got back to her husband and business partner, she felt more confident and clear on her ideas, making it easier for her to get them onboard with her visions for the business.

What if Nabina had never met these women? What if she would have quit the business? Just another business run by two dudes! No offense, but Nabina was valuable, she was bringing a vision to the city that mattered. We would have lost her contributions, all because she lacked support from people who really saw her and understood her. This is why it's so important that we each find our people.

If you are lacking in this department, there are a few steps you can take. First, you must recognize the value in finding your community. I get it, I'm a former lone wolf, and in the past I thought adding more people to my life felt like a chore. I was physically surrounded by a lot of people: childhood friends, family, a husband, and clients. But even ten people who can't resonate with you, don't outweigh just one person who is on your same journey.

Bringing these people into your life is going to greatly expand you and increase your efforts. Just a few hangouts and brainstorming sessions with them, you'll be moving so quickly toward your dreams that you'll feel like you're cheating the system.

Once you recognize the value, you can simply set the intention. Say a little prayer to the divine, stating that you're ready for your people to find you. Place your hand in your heart as you say it (or write in your journal), so you know it's coming from the purity of your heart.

After you set the intention, look out for signs toward your next steps in finding these people. Often, they will just show up. But other times, you'll be guided to a class, stumble upon an online community, or have an urge to be more talkative at a party. When you're out and about having conversations, avoid censoring yourself too much. Instead, challenge yourself to talk about your interests. When we mention our interests, people will either give a thumbs up or thumbs down. Thumbs up are your people. Thumbs down means, next!

A month before I was due to give birth to our first son, Benny and I realized that we might need some extra office help for the business. I put the word out, and to my delight, an old acquaintance replied. While in college, I had worked for a production company that taught acting classes to high school students. One of my students was now an adult, and she was looking for an office job.

One morning, about three months into working together, she decided to confide in me by sharing a dream that she couldn't quite understand. You should know that although at the time I was secretly practicing meditation with my spirit guide, I was certainly not out of the spiritual closet. So when she asked for help with her dream, she was asking in the way that a close co-worker or a friend might ask.

"I had this dream where this huge blue angel with wings showed up," she explained.

"Are you referring to the Archangel Michael," I asked?

"You know Archangel Michael?" she eagerly replied.

If you're not a metaphysical geek like myself, Archangel Michael might as well be a code for people who are trying to hide their witchy selves. He's like the gateway drug to metaphysics. It seems as though somehow most people's spiritual awakenings involve some cameos by Michael at one point or another.

In this casual conversation about dreams, the mention of one Archangel led us to connect over a shared interest. We were so excited to find this link that we began to play using our lunch hour to practice our intuition. She would practice tarot spreads on me, and I would connect with my spirit guide as I asked for messages.

After a few years of keeping my intuition skills quiet, it was beyond freeing to have Stephanie in my life. In those few months of playing together, my intuition skyrocketed. As a result, the few coaching clients had at the time, started to receive psychic readings, by accident. This one of the first signs of where my career, business, and soul's purpose was headed.

Benny and I continued to talk about our joint dream of building something and creating financial freedom for our family. And my secret ingredient: to live creatively. We were on the same page; we just had different ideas as to how to get there. Benny insisted that I commit further to his company, while I fought for more freedom to grow my own business. For a while, we agreed to disagree.

During that season of our lives, I kept up with the bare minimum of my responsibilities with his company, played the rold of primary parent to our children, and struggled to grow my own business. It was tough. Not only was I physically exhausted, but I was also emotionally exhausted by the misalignment my life was displaying.

After hiding my dreams and interests for so long, I began

feeling like I was going to explode. I felt like I couldn't live one more day in this life—one that was beginning to feel completely unfair. Because I had done the work of getting honest about my dream, protecting it (and working on it), and finding my people, I had gained the confidence that I had lacked in the beginning stages. My mind began to shift and I started to see that I was worth the investment. In fact, I started to realize that the best thing we could do as a family was to get behind *my* vision. I knew where I was going, and it was going to work. I started to realize that I deserved support. The problem was that I had no support, and I was beginning to become really mad about it.

CONNECT TO THE ENERGY OF SUPPORT

The problem with gaining confidence is that, from one day to the next, you'll look around at your life and find yourself really upset. It's as if yesterday this life didn't bother you much, but something happened overnight and you are now just really damn mad. Don't be frightened by this shift in emotion. This is a sign of upleveling and healing.

As mentioned in a previous chapter, the tolerable becomes intolerable. You're no longer available for the B.S. that you used to entertain. The person who used to entertain it, is not you anymore. And this behavior is not an energetic match for who you are becoming. This is a good thing. This is the moment when you begin to rise. *Picture a phoenix here, rising from the flames, wings wide open for a dramatic effect.*

It was the end of a very typical day. I stood in our kitchen washing dishes from dinner, while my kids, still unbathed, watched T.V. My husband? Relaxing in bed, because after all, *he* had had a really long day working outside the house. Not like me. The one who was miraculously performing the invisible chores of motherhood: getting kids to school with the proper themed outfit and perfect project, laundry, defrosting meat in the morning to later cook said meat at night, picking up that specific granola bar so that the second child doesn't have a fit when he gets home, paying every bill and saving enough for summer camp (so that you don't become the summer camp), buying birthday gifts, planning birthday parties, stocking the fridge, all while being emotionally stable enough to not cause childhood trauma in these tiny little humans. In addition to those chores, there were my job responsibilities with Benny's company and the readings I would perform somewhere in between it all.

I saw myself, standing in that kitchen at the end of the night and thought: *"Girl, you are the miracle worker. You're the true hero here. You are worth the investment. You deserve and need support in order to get to the place you know this family must go."*

The people I knew who were thriving had support. This lie that I kept telling myself about needing to prove my worth in order to get the support I needed began to feel stale. And the thought that my idea was silly compared to others was starting to annoy me.

I knew I needed to start demanding support. Not from others, but from my life. The truth is that I created an unsupportive environment. A collection of my inner beliefs had created that scenario. Typically, when we look for change, we try to talk people into treating us differently. That works only sometimes, depending on who you're communicating with. What really works is feeling and acting out the change yourself.

I decided to hold an energy in my body that demanded support. It would be the norm that I am a supported person. Beginning with that evening in my kitchen, I started to tell myself, "You are supported." I carried myself the way a supported person would. I had fun imagining my life with a babysitter, a full-time assistant, and enough time to do what I knew needed to be done. I started to think and act this way.

People who are supported understand what it means to invest in themselves and in their dreams. They are calculated risk takers. At a certain point, after enough experimentation, and when they see that their visions start to get legs, they know it's time to ask for an investment. That investment is usually money, time, and/or help. At this stage, I needed all three.

But first, I needed time. I needed more hours to work. I had clients coming to me for my unique spiritual perspective on dating, and I also had a book that wanted to be born. I needed some solid hours, outside of just nap time, to write.

In order to get that time, I needed money to pay for babysitting. I didn't have the money, so I needed to "raise" the funds. Naturally, I asked my husband first. This wasn't the first time I had asked him for money, but it was the first time that I saw it as an investment— one that he would be silly to miss out on.

Despite being the support system that allowed him to make money, I had always felt that using some of that money to pay for a business coach, a website, or a simple life-saving massage was frivolous. But over time, I started to realize that I was the best investment worth making. I knew this because I had started to see something in Benny's eyes that truly scared me. He wasn't going to be able to hold on much longer. I knew that his work was killing him, and that our family would not be able to depend on him for much longer. My work, on the other hand, was much more sustainable.

We were two months away from expecting our third child when I looked at Benny and said, "I have an idea for that money in your savings account." He was intrigued, but definitely not expecting what I was about to present. "Let's use that money to get a full-time babysitter. My business is getting some traction and I don't want to abandon it when the baby comes."

He agreed, because who can say no to a woman who was 7 months pregnant, with another two kids in tow. But also, he could see the conviction in my eyes. I was going to make this happen.

Well, it's safe to say that investing in me was one of the best investments he ever made. As I write this book Benny has been able to take off three years from work, due to his wife's business success. Can I get a high five, sister?

There will come a time that you believe in your vision enough to ask for support. Not only is this important so that you can move forward, but also because support is the energy of abundance. When we feel supported, we are in the receiving mode. Things are flowing our way, and we feel worthy enough to receive it. The energy of support is an expression of deep self-love. You love yourself enough to give yourself what you need, you are proclaiming you are worthy. This ultimately translates into feeling worthy of your dream life.

Connecting to the energy of support isn't only beneficial to those receiving support, it also helps when you are the one providing the support. For the first six years of our marriage, I was very much in a supportive role. I struggled with it because deep down, I wanted to be the star, but as I grew and started to understand that our family was a team, I trusted that being the support was what I was being called to do at the time.

Benny was really taking off, while I was going through the dying stages that come with transitioning from maiden to mother. In those years of death, being the supporter was a great role for me. The more I embraced it, the more I benefited from being connected to the energy of support. It was a very sacred gift to be able to grow in my power behind the scenes. We'll talk more about motherhood in the coming chapters, but for now I want you to know that you have a very important purpose even when you're in a supportive role. Understanding these roles is part of dreaming in partnership.

Feeling supported by the humans in our lives ultimately translates into feeling supported by the Divine — and that is where the real magic lies. Remember if living your soul-led life is part of your soul's contract, then the Divine wants you to have that life. When we understand that, we begin to feel worthy of divine support. When we receive divine support, magical things begin to happen, things like finding the right help at the right time, receiving the money you need right when you need it, and so on. When we know that we are supported by the Divine, we leave space for magic.

CALL IN DIVINE SUPPORT

Feeling this level of support also means you can begin to involve your ancestors, spirit guides, ascended masters, and higher self into your everyday life and spiritual practices. At this point in your creation process, your dream is becoming a must. It's no longer just something you wish for, but instead it begins to feel like something you need. This is usually when we begin to realize that we need some divine help.

Currently, divine guidance is a part of my everyday life. But when I first started to build my spiritual connection and realized that I wasn't creating on my own, but rather co-creating, I began to understand the magic that comes once you surrender to divine help. I would get down on my knees, next to my bed, and admit that I had no idea what to do to get to where I wanted to go. *Help, please.*

Jesus was always my first phone call. After all, he was the O.G. miracle worker. The reason this process of surrendering to divine guidance and support was so helpful was because it allowed me to get out of my own way. Until this point in the creation process, you're building the strength to believe. You're getting your heart on board, you're taking action, and you're asking for help. You're doing everything you physically can. The physical steps ultimately run out, and that is when you start to hear, see, and feel the presence of something greater.

When you see a dream come to life, what you just witnessed is a miracle. Dreams becoming reality are miracles because the natural progression of an average path does not produce such wonder. The default path is what most people walk because they are asleep to the soul's true path. They are asleep to the soul in general. Someone living a soul-led life is always reaching to connect to the soul. This awareness in itself is a miracle.

Without the awareness of the spiritual parts of our being, we are living a very physical life, moving at the speed of our body and to the default programming of our brains. But when we reach for the spiritual, we break free of the body's default settings and begin to work with energy, shifting it and manipulating it until it aligns with our soul's truth.

Doing can only get us so far. Shifting is what creates miracles. The miracle is unexpected, and previously seen as impossible. But as you begin to work with divine guidance, you will be mentored through this process. Allow me to explain some of the divine guidance you will work with at this stage and how to connect.

ANCESTORS

Ancestors are the people in our human lineage to have lived before us. Many ancestors that guide us are people so deep in the lineage that we may not even know their names. Ancestors come to support us in our creation process because our dreams matter to them. In a lineage, every generation is connected, whether we like it or not. And every generation does its part in moving the next forward.

Some generations are more fruitful than others, and often there is the opportunity for a great leap forward. I believe you are that opportunity. And because of this, your ancestors are invested in you, and in your dreams.

Naturally, they want to be your cheerleader, but your healing and growth is also their healing and growth. As you move forward in your soul-led life, you will undoubtedly be faced with reviewing your family's past. As you begin to heal the past, by understanding it differently and therefore acting differently, you set the generations before you free.

For these reasons, they are eager to help. While they do have their limitations — after all, you most likely are the more advanced soul — they are wonderful aides in helping you remember your strength. They love to sprinkle some luck along your path wherever they can. And they offer clues for the next step in your path through music, unexpected gifts, and coincidences.

To connect with your ancestors, consider creating a visiting space. For example, on our land we have a small rock garden, decorated with Benny's grandmother's favorite angel sculptures. Her presence is always there. Ancestors will also meet you with music and love to dance with the sounds of your culture. Lastly, an altar with photos, candles, and other memorabilia is always a great activator for connection.

Whether you're in a space they love or are setting the tone with music, close your eyes, and just begin to talk to them. Have a journal with you and write down what you feel that they are saying. Or if the conversation is flowing, just talk.

Sometimes, they will visit you in a more organic way. When you're in a hard place in your journey, feel their presence and allow them to help remind you who you are. You are their living dream come true.

SPIRIT GUIDES

Spirit Guides are beings that serve as our spiritual coaches. Their job is to make sure we live out our soul's purpose. Many people sense a guardian angel at some point in their lives. Or perhaps the religion you come from has saints. I believe these are synonyms for spirit guides, but overall, the feeling is one of being watched over or guided.

Spirit guides come in a wide range of forms. Some are our spiritual ancestors, meaning they have lived other lifetimes with us. They could be our mother from another lifetime. Some spirit guides are animals, mythical creatures, goddesses, wizards, or medicine people. In my program The Soul Reading Method, I map out each category, but for now, just know they are with you to support your purpose and spiritual growth. And know that you can have more than one.

To connect with your spirit guide, you want to prepare yourself for a relationship. Each spirit guide has a different personality and therefore has a different way of communicating. It can take some time to understand them, so don't be too hard on yourself if you can't seem to connect the first few times.

Connecting with a spirit guide is done through meditation. They like to meet in what I call "a place of nature." When you close your eyes, imagine any place of nature. It can be the tree in your backyard or the lake you grew up visiting. Once you have that visual, ask the guide to come forward. Depending on your unique psychic abilities, you may see, hear, or feel something. Try not to have expectations and just start by writing down what your guide looks or feels like.

When you're getting to know your spirit guide, I would suggest meditating with them two to three times a week. Your meditation sessions will probably be about 10 to 15 minutes long and will increase over time. In each session, try to get to know them even more by asking a question. Come with questions like:

What is your name?
What do you want to work on together?
Do I know you from another lifetime?
What is my next step toward my dreams?

For extra support, use my free guided meditation for meeting your Spirit Guide found at **nikkinovo/soul-led-book.com.**

With time, you will get to know your spirit guide so well that you will feel them on a regular basis.

ASCENDED MASTERS

Ascended masters are perhaps what you feel most familiar with already. Mary Magdalene, Hathor, Jesus, and Buddha are in this category. Some teachers consider an ascended master to be a human who once lived on Earth and later became enlightened. My definition is a little wider than that. I see ascended masters as the "famous" guides who are assigned to many souls — different from our spirit guides who feel a little more custom to us — and hold a themed medicine. I even include the archangels in this category.

If you grew up with a religion, you may already have a relationship with a particular spirit guide. Feel free to work with them even deeper, through dedicated meditation time with them. Ascended masters serve as divine messengers, channeling messages and teachings through us as we write.

I have also found that their ability to divinely intervene is greater than what an ancestor or spirit guide can achieve. This is why connecting with them often feels like a humble prayer. Rather than the partnership you ultimately will feel with your spirit guide, there is more of a jedi master and jedi student feel to this relationship.

To connect with ascended masters, nature and deep meditation are helpful. You want to humbly invite them into your space. Do your best to listen. Sometimes you will receive a message at that moment, and other times, within a few days, you will receive a healing, a message, or even a miracle.

At times, you may call in a specific ascended master, and in other situations, the ascended master may come to you. Like the time I was reading a client and saw the Hindu goddess Kali around her while in my meditation. My client was entering a time of great change that felt very destructive. Kali was there supporting the process. My client had never heard of Kali before, but ultimately studied Kali through text and mediation, leading to a very transformative season in her life.

HIGHER SELF

If everything above sounded too woo-woo for you or too much like pagan worship, allow me to present your Higher Self. The truth is, we are all one, a segment of the Divine. The same goes for ancestors, spirit guides, and ascended masters. They are simply messengers from the Divine, who help us understand such a grand concept.

Imagine that you just started your first job as a cashier at a large retailer. If you were receiving all your guidance from the CEO of a global retail company, you would probably be very confused. Having supervisors and experts in H.R. will be much more helpful than trying to get all your information from the CEO.

This is why working with ancestors, spirit guides, and ascended masters can be helpful — and honestly more fun, and colorful. But if you're not really feeling connected to these reflections of the Divine, then consider working with your higher self.

The higher self is the soul version of you who knows what's going on. The way I see my higher self is the version of me that placed me in this game called life. As a human, I am a fraction of her. I have a limited vantage point because I'm so low to the ground, but she is higher up and can see the whole plan.

In meditation, I can connect with her and become her. As I merge my energy with hers, I start to remember my true essence. The higher self is our true essence.

The beauty of working with the higher self is that she has a lot less identity issues than we do. As we have already learned, our identities are often false. We create these personalities built off our upbringing and our adaptations. When we connect with the Higher Self, we feel a bit more limitless.

In my readings, I often look for my client's true essence, especially if they're on a default path. If they're on a default path, then naturally they are disconnected from their true essence—who they really are at a soul level. It's fun to describe what the Higher

Self is showing because although the client might be disconnected, deep within them, they remember this part of themselves as I start to share. Connecting with the Higher Self activates us into remembering who we really are.

I feel it's important to mention the role that astrology or human design may have when it comes to understanding our true essence. I find our personal astrology and human design to be aspects of our human personality that our higher self chose. Like picking out an outfit for a doll, the higher self wanted these aspects in order to complete our mission this lifetime. Our true identity is more expansive than our personal astrology and human design, but these are helpful aspects of our human personality that help us understand our purpose this lifetime.

Connecting with the higher self is more like merging rather than communicating. The goal in connection is feeling one with the higher self, as if you were allowing her to come through you and be. It's a type of channeling.

You'll want to close your eyes and imagine you're viewing your Higher Self in some far away land. You'll ask her to come down and merge into your body. Hold your focus on your heart, and just let yourself speak her words. Or, you can write what is coming through if that is more comfortable.

You may already be merging with her from time to time as you access your intuition. You may hear her calling you from her faraway land. A sign that it's your Higher Self and not an ancestor, spirit guide, or ascended master is that it just feels like a part of you. Or like someone is calling you from your home. Or like your heart has just received a bolt of powerful energy.

Merging with the Higher Self requires quiet, focus, and presence. A regular meditation practice will help you get there. Also, regularly emptying your mind through mindfulness techniques is helpful.

No matter which divine guidance you choose to work with, you will find your physical efforts receive a spiritual boost. When you're feeling stuck and lost, you can receive guidance and an overall loving feeling that will give you the strength to continue on your true path. Combine these relationships with some manifesting techniques, and you will begin to experience the shift.

MANIFESTING TECHNIQUES

Now that we've discussed the process for planting seeds to create the change, throughout the process you'll want to arm yourself with manifesting techniques. These techniques should be used throughout your alignment process. They will support the heavy lifting that change tends to require.

For example, if you're trying to change your home and move into a more soul-led home, you'll have to do some heavy lifting when it comes to finances, getting papers together, and building your credit. Those are the physical steps you will take, but there are energetic steps to take that will shift your reality in a way that the physical cannot. What can often appear as luck is caused by energetic shifts. We can initiate energetic shifts through manifesting techniques. Here are some of my go-to techniques.

Visualization Combined with Movement and Feeling

Most of us have heard the benefits of visualization, but sometimes, what we're dreaming about feels very foreign and distant. Seeing it won't do anything if we can't *feel* it. This is why adding movement to your visualization will help you shift from "Imagine if I could have this," to "It feels amazing to have this."

How you do this is by adding some theatrical production to your visualization. Once you know what you want your future to look like, pick a song that embodies that energy. For example, when I want to manifest more money, my go-to songs are "Bitch, Better have my Money," by Rihanna and "Money in the Grave" by Drake and Rick Ross.

Interesting choice in music, I know, but it gives me the money vibes. I'll put this music on, dance, hike, or ride my bike, and visualize whatever "more money" looks like for me. What this does is help me in getting past any fears I have in my body about money. I'm becoming more comfortable with holding the energy of more money. My goal is to make this feeling of having more money be my default state. Once this energy is my default state, I am now vibrating at a new level, which attracts new opportunities for money. Yes, I will have to follow through with any inspired action that comes my way, but before that comes my way, I need to vibrate at a new energy level.

Once you pick your song, bring in some sort of movement. Close your eyes, visualize something that reminds you of your dream, and move your body in a way that makes you feel the future.

Surround Yourself with Visual Reminders

Surrounding yourself with visual reminders of your future is like living in a real-life vision board. I like to intentionally place items in my space that act as reminders of where I am going. Looking around my office, I have herbs that hold the energy of the strength of Mother Earth, quartz from the top of our mountain, a piece of art my best friend bought me that says "Write your own story," and written messages from my meditations.

There are so many visual reminders of where I am headed in my office and home, it would take a few pages list them all. The point is to fill the spaces you exist in the most, with visual reminders of how you want to feel and where you are headed in life. As a mom of three, I know that we can't always take full control of our living spaces, but even small reminders work.

There's a window over the sink in our kitchen, a spot I frequent often when washing dishes and preparing meals. On the windowsill, I have a flower from a sacred land I visited and a rock I found during a very healing moment. These two items do not necessarily remind me of my future, but rather who I am at a soul level. And as long as I am reminded of her daily, she will guide me to my true path.

Mantras and Journaling

I believe there is a special type of magic that comes with writing down your dreams. They have a way of finding you when you decide to declare them as real by writing them on paper. This is why I like to write down the beliefs I need to hold as I move forward.

This takes a little digging. If you're trying to bring something into your life and it's feeling a little hard or sticky, get curious with yourself. Write down questions that help you find the belief that is holding you back. Some examples of questions are:

Why don't I have this in my life already?
If I get it, what is something bad that might happen?
What do I fear when it comes to having (insert your desire)?
If I wasn't afraid, what does it feel like to have (insert your desire)?

As you curiously question yourself, you'll find blocks in how you're thinking about your desire. You may find a fear that is holding you back, but isn't really real. Through questioning yourself, create new beliefs that help carry you over based off what you discovered about yourself.

For example, let's say I'm trying to create a life where I'm making money doing something I love, but I don't even know what it is yet. And maybe as I'm asking myself questions, I realize that I have a fear of not being around for my children, leaving them to feel abandoned. After I find that fear, I'll ask myself if that is ultimately true. Is being around all the time the true definition of a good mother? Instead, I may find that what my children really need is for me to feel happy and fulfilled. That is what makes me the best me. So, my new mantra would be "The best thing I can do for my children is live life doing what I love."

Fill your journal with new beliefs and repeat them often. Repetition is what makes them mantras. The idea is that you hold focus while you repeat them so that your brain starts to believe this as truth. Once your brain believes it, the block is lifted.

MANIFESTING TECHNIQUES FOR PARTNERS

Lastly, I want to give you some techniques for manifesting in partnership. Again, I know that you may not feel safe enough yet to manifest in your partnership (specifically your romantic one), because some healing is needed. But if you're feeling ready to try out a few, here are mine and Benny's favorite group manifesting techniques.

Get on the Same Page

Like I mentioned earlier in the chapter, sometimes you have to get your partner on board. This doesn't only happen in romantic relationships, but also with work relationships. When I have a new, crazy idea, I usually present it to my team in a meeting. If I'm feeling like I really need to sell it, I'll make a little presentation that maps out my idea. Because ultimately I know that if they don't like it, or believe in it, it's just not going to work.

Benny and I have learned to go back and forth on an idea, until we both feel comfortable about pursuing it. We do this through conversations, showing each other videos or other research, spreadsheets, or really whatever it takes. Sometimes we're not even trying to convince each other, we're just trying to explain how we each envision the outcome.

Don't be afraid of a little confrontation. Learn to debate with your partner and have some evidence to back up your idea. If they don't like your idea, try not to take it personally. It's your job to think of creative ways to get through. And if you need to bribe your partner in some other "physical" ways, I won't judge you. You do what you need to do.

After we come to some sort of joint visualization, we split tasks. After ten years of manifesting together, we know each other's strengths and what we have to offer. We don't try to overstep.

Although Benny still insists on telling me how to design and decorate our properties. Cue: eye rolling emoji face here.

Once the roles are very clear, you just start knocking out the tasks. Its important not to resent your roles, even though it is sometimes warranted. For example, I don't love paying bills, but Benny is even worse at it than I am, so I take it on. He has a lot of other strenghts. It's not worth fighting over it, as long as we both feel like teammates working toward a joint venture.

Unfortunately, when working in partnership, it's never really apples-to-apples. This can be so hard to experience. Like when a mother bears the majority of child rearing in the first few years of life, while dad is trying to contribute in other areas. Sometimes we feel very disconnected from our partners because we don't have enough conversations to remind us about our team efforts.

I remember constantly feeling alone when the children were babies and Benny was off working. When I would share with Benny, he would remind me that what he was doing, work-wise, was for us. It didn't make my work any easier, but constantly reminding each other that we were in it together, helped us focus on seeing each other as partners rather than feeling like we were in competition with each other. I had to consistently remind myself that we were on the same team, working toward a common goal.

Don't underestimate regular conversations about your joint projects. After a few conversations, you will find the best way to attack the goal. It may even take a change in roles. For example, since the beginning of our marriage, Benny was always the financial provider, and I was the support and main caretaker of the children. There came a time in our relationship, that a reversal of roles was needed. It's important to be aware when roles may need to be redefined or shifted in order to reach the common goal.

Sketch it Out

When you manifest in partnership, you each have slightly different visions. For this reason, Benny and I like to sketch out our visions, so we can merge our creation power in a deeper way. Sometimes sketching it out means drawing, like when Benny draws me his plans for the backyard. Other times, this means creating a list of materials with prices, so we understand what the project entails. And often it just entails a to-do list that maps out the steps we can actually see.

Grab some paper and colored pens. If you're artistically challenged like me, give them to your partner so they can draw the vision. Or get online and start creating a digital representation of what you envision. Keep your final product somewhere you can both see it. It will be nearly impossible not to make it happen when it's staring at you each day.

Get Physical

Not that kind of physical (although that might be a nice reward for resistant partners). Once Benny and I decide what we want to manifest into reality, we visit the future. This usually involves Benny driving me to some sketchy property, where he will then ask me to trespass.

All kidding aside, Benny and I always like to visit some sort of visual representation of our future. When we were in our first house together, we were dreaming of a house with a large lot of land so we could raise some animals and let the kids run around with more freedom. There was a neighborhood in Miami that had this criteria. It was a little further west than we would like to live, and most of the homes were outside our budget, but it did have the vibe we were dreaming about, so on Sundays, we would throw the kids in the car with some electronics so that we could have a little time to drive around the neighborhood, and dream a little.

We also used this technique five years before we bought our land in North Carolina. Despite still working to feel secure enough to pay our mortgage back in Miami, we were already dreaming of farm land in North Carolina. So for our wedding anniversary, we booked a weekend trip to the area and asked a realtor to show us a few properties.

Something happened on that trip, as if the land activated us. Because the five years between seeing those properties and actually buying our property was filled with deep, deep healing –both on a relationship level and as a family. Looking back, my belief is that we had the desire to live the way we do today, but we were not at equivalent vibrational levels. We had absolutely no idea how it would happen, but we somehow committed to the land that day. In return, the land committed to us, and brought us down a wild roller coaster ride that eventually guided us to the soul-led life we live today.

CHAPTER NINE

Learning to Lead

Soul-led living is for leaders. If you're reading this book, then you are a trailblazer. You're trying to not follow anyone else's path, but you're own. And by default, that makes you a leader.

In this chapter, I will discuss my experience with motherhood, because it was my role as a mother and wife that birthed — and continues to birth — the leader within me. Yes, I've worked for many large corporations, but becoming the matriarch of my family was what inspired me to learn how to be a soul-led leader and embody queen energy.

Whether you are a mother, will be a mother, have no desire to be a mother, or are currently experiencing challenges to become one, I believe you will find something for you in this chapter. To be a mother, you do not need to birth another human from within you. Because to mother is to lead with divine feminine energy. I have a feeling you have mothered many things, and will continue to do so throughout your lifetime.

This chapter has found you because you have been called to lead or will be called to lead soon. Alongside other mothers, who together with their children and partners, are seeding the New Earth, you will create new standards and blueprints for soul-led motherhood, family, and community. May this chapter help us build this new vision together.

It was the first time I had ever pushed a baby out of my body, and quite frankly, I nailed it. The year I gave birth to Oliver, I was pregnant alongside seven of my closest friends. Oliver was the last of the 2013 babies, which I found to be an advantage. I didn't have to make a baby registry from scratch, or be surprised by the weird goop the doctor wanted to put on Oliver's eyes when he was born. That entire year, I was learning the do's and don'ts from the seven soldiers who went before me. I was ready for battle.

In addition to my field research, I was also a meditation ninja, whose morning ritual was all about prepping for a peaceful birth. I used hypnobirthing techniques to help me prep for the big day, consulted with doulas, and made a game plan with my friend who was a pro at home births. Although I knew I wasn't going to have a home birth (growing up visiting the NICU with a neonatologist for a father had made the hospital feel like a second home to me), I wanted the best of both worlds. I planned to labor at home until

I could no longer, then rush to the hospital, and push.

This was my plan and, miraculously, it worked. I felt contractions early in the morning, sat on my bouncy ball to meditate and pray, washed and blow dried my hair, made breakfast for Aly, sent her off to school with the neighbors, and then in a slightly demonic tone demanded that Benny take me to the hospital immediately. Within 30 minutes of arriving at the hospital, I was ready to push. My breath and the pain guided me, and somehow my body knew what to do. On the final push, I reached for Oliver's small chest and pulled him out myself. I felt so empowered.

Three days later, we arrived home with our new son. After a tortuous car ride home with Oliver's nonstop crying, I went straight to his nursery to change his diaper. I imagined the crying must mean that he was wet, right? I figured if I changed him, he would be comfortable and stop screaming.

Alone in his room, I stood over the changing table, trying to undress him and not break his tiny arm in the process. His diaper was completely dry. Just as I started to wonder what he needed, a little trickle of liquid hit my face. It took me a few seconds to understand what was happening. *Is there a leak in the roof?* I thought. Nope, this child was peeing in my face. I screamed, and quickly grabbed whatever I could find to cover him so it would stop, but I was too late because now his butt was in on the fun. Waste coming from all angles, I began to sob.

My parents rushed in. "Nicole, Nicole, que paso" they asked with worry? Through my tears, I managed to tell them what had just happened. I needed a hug, but instead what I got were two new grandparents bursting into laughter at the sight of their daughter covered in their grandson's pee and poop. In their defense, it was pretty damn funny. And now knowing Oliver's personality, this welcome into motherhood makes so much sense. That child is here on Earth for a good time.

It was funny, but at that moment I was so scared. Somehow within those three days, I had slowly begun to lose myself. The woman who had meditated her way to a five-star birth was not the same person who had come back home. *What happened? Where did she go?*

I did my best to pull myself together, wiped the pee and poop off of me, and walked into the living room with my new child. My parents, my husband, and my two brothers were in the kitchen, enjoying some *pan con bistec* (Cuban steak sandwiches) for lunch. They conversed, laughed, and shared stories. The scene was very familiar. This is how we had always gathered, and if it had been just one week prior, I would have been in there with them, serving food and exchanging jokes.

Yet, this day was strikingly different in my mind. As I watched them interact, I no longer felt a part of them. It was as if the room had split in two. I was on the side of the room for people who had the very serious responsibility of caring for another human life. It was for those of us drowning in worry. They were on the side for people who were free and alive. These people who in the past had known how to love me and care for me, could no longer see or understand me. I was alone in this new journey.

The weeks to follow were filled with ups and downs. One moment, I would be in bed with my adorable new little love and Benny, feeling completely full. As if I needed nothing else in life, but these two loves. And then the next moment, I was exhausted, overwhelmed, and on the verge of tears.

Before I knew it, life began to find a new routine. Benny went back to working 10-hour days and the check-in calls from family and friends stopped coming. Everyone was going back to life as usual — except me.

At the time, I really could not understand what I was going through. Why I felt happy but also deeply sad and unsettled at the same time. Taking care of Oliver wasn't really what was bothering me. I loved playing with him, dressing him in cute little outfits, singing to him while I wiped his booty. He brought me so much joy.

People always tell you it's hard when you become a new mother, and I just assumed they were referring to the part where you have to care for the baby. When Benny saw me struggling, he also thought it was the burden of caring for a newborn. So when Oliver was about two months old, Benny came home for lunch one day with someone I had never met before. She was a small, gentle-looking woman who looked like she might be related to one of Benny's long-time employees.

"Who is this," I asked? "She's here to help with Oliver," he said. She was, in fact, his employee's sister, and she was looking for work as a nanny. Benny took the news as a sign, hired her on the spot upon meeting her, and brought her to my house as if he was the hero saving me from all my motherhood woes. And let's be honest, he was also trying to insure that he wouldn't have to get his hands dirty with the child care.

She was loving, helpful, and having her in my home for a few hours a day did give me breathing room. But her help didn't solve my problem. Because my problem wasn't really about time. It was about the silent death I did not know I was experiencing.

Birth is a portal, where life and death intersect. One life is swapped out for another, like a relay race. Just as the child takes their first breath of life, death sweeps in with no mercy for the new mom. The child brings new life, while the woman who is about to become a mother dies. Everyone is celebrating the new life, which often leaves very little space to grieve the dead.

While some moms might have taken advantage of these babysitting hours by taking a full, uninterrupted shower or squeezing in a nap, I did not. Instead, I worked.

I worked because I had to. Benny and I were both self-employed, and I hadn't really thought through maternity leave. But I mostly worked to stay alive.

You see, so much of my self expression and independence was wrapped up in my work. It was this little space I carved out for myself, where I didn't have to be what my parents, friends, or husband wanted me to be. When you're stuck in so many identity webs, work can be the only place for true authentic expression.

"If I could just write a book, like I always said I would, I could hold on to myself."

"If I could just hit the goals I wanted to hit before I became a mom, I could be free."

"If I could just experience my true self through my creative expression, maybe I won't drown."

I was dying, and so afraid.

In my family, motherhood and marriage were presented as the ultimate sacrifices. From my perspective, it seemed like most of the women I knew gave up on their dreams and individuality because they had the responsibility of marriage and motherhood. Somehow a woman's dream was secondary to any marital and parenting responsibilities. And let's also now throw in the responsibilities of being a financial provider. We have come so far as women, but somehow this very ancient programming is still in our collective subconscious.

This cannot be my fate, I thought. I would fight for my space, my voice, my truth, and my expression. Not only was I going to fight for my own individuality, but also that of my children and husband. Somewhere in my heart, I believed we could all be individual expressions, while also being members of a united family. A powerful family, created of self-expressed members, where no one's power takes from another.

Still, until this day, I fight this fight. I call it a fight, because we're still in a place as a society where this way of thinking feels like going against the grain. Everywhere we turn, we are tempted to follow old blueprints. In fact, the stream flows towards these blueprints. The most well-meaning loving people are going to tempt you that way. The teacher at school is going to advise you down the blueprint path. Corporate life will offer you golden handcuffs in exchange for the silencing of your individual expression. Consumerism will tell you what you *really* want. And social media will remind you that your partner isn't enough.

As leaders of our families (and future families), we must be ready to swim against the current, in order to create new paths for mothers, fathers, marriages, children, and families. This is the way of the New Earth Family. You have been chosen to lead within this movement, and I will share with you what I have learned so far to win this battle.

GET COMFORTABLE WITH GRIEVING

It's hard to be the leader of your family when grief is stuck in your body. It was difficult to be Oliver's mom those first few years when I wasn't able to process and accept how much I was saying goodbye to by assuming this new role. When we don't grieve, we can't be present. Our eyes are seeing and experiencing one thing, but our body is swimming in what could have been.

We tend to think that we just can't get over the past. We had a hard childhood, a bad breakup, the death of a loved one, and now we're stuck with that past. To survive, we tell ourselves that it's okay, we soothe ourselves in unhealthy ways, or we just stay stuck in victimhood.

When the truth is, we are not stuck. The pain is stuck. The memory is stuck. And if we can just express it, the cycle can end (or at least lessen enough) for us to move forward.

I must admit that I am a bit of a complainer. No one in my family really knew how to grieve, so they complained instead. If you find yourself complaining, this is actually a good thing, because just below this complaint is an opportunity to grieve something, accept your current stage, and ultimately move some stuck energy.

To me, grieving is letting out an emotion we have been trying to control. It's the very uncomfortable feeling of crying, screaming, sobbing, yelling, shaking in a way that we cannot control. It just comes out, and we let it.

An example of grieving would be when you share a story from your childhood to your therapist, she says nothing, and you start to realize how messed up that past experience was, how your younger self deserved more, and now you will cry about it as a form of grieving.

Maybe you've had these conversations with your therapist or a friend, but haven't been able to cry. Try closing your eyes while you tell the story from the past. Let yourself go back to the experience, connect with your former self, and speak to her. The pain might be too great, so you may have the tendency to disconnect from the memory. But just like in meditation you do your best to remain focused on the breath or a mantra, and you return to the breath or mantra when you lose focus, do the same with the pain of this memory. The pain is your point of focus. Once there and still with your eyes closed, express it. Let your body do what it wants to do. Maybe this means crying, screaming, shaking, etc.

After the birth of our second son, Ethan, I found myself talking a lot about how I was disappointed by my birthing experience. I had had such a powerful experience with my first birth. This time it felt like something had been stolen from me, but I couldn't quite put my finger on it.

I knew Ethan would be my last birth and I was a little sad that he wasn't a girl. I was very aware that this was a selfish thought, because I already had Aly and Ethan was a healthy child, but I had always imagined myself giving birth to a girl. In addition to that, I thought maybe this time I'd get lucky and be able to deliver with my female OBGYN doctor, who also happened to be my friend. *How cool would it be to have a friend and a woman help me deliver this child?* I thought.

I was attached to an outcome, and none of it went my way. Instead, an old male doctor delivered me in a room with my husband, my father, and a young female nurse who was treated as a second-class citizen. My mother had never really learned how to soothe or support me growing up, so she had learned to keep her distance from me, especially in moments of stress. I don't have sisters, and I just didn't know how much I needed a female presence at the time.

Somehow, the male-dominated delivery room seemed to trigger my perfectionist tendencies. My subconscious was playing out this thought I had about men not being able to handle me or my emotions. I had to be the strongest one in the room, so I asked the nurse for her hand, used my breath through each contraction while the guys talked about who knows what, and I labored without making a sound.

The male doctor applauded me for the most quiet and controlled delivery he had ever experienced in all his years of practice. I was so proud. I followed this gold star by asking the nurse to get me nail polish remover because I couldn't stand how my nails were chipping. I was being sewn up by the doctor and removing nail polish at the same time. Benny knew something was wrong, but I told him I was good. This was not a big deal. I'm a pro, and my nails were bothering me. What?

Although the birth felt disappointing, everything after felt so much easier than the first time. We even convinced the hospital to let us go home a day early, because we felt confident as parents and were ready to get back to our other two children.

This time, everything felt different in the best way. I was an experienced mom, I knew what kind of support I needed, I understood how to let myself die once again, and my work was becoming more defined. So really I just thought I had been disappointed by the birthing experience, but not sad, or traumatized. It wasn't until seven months later, when I went to Asheville, NC for a retreat with the sister circle I had joined earlier in the year, that the birth came back to haunt me.

We were sitting on this beautiful wooden deck when a female healer from the area came to be with us. We were all dressed in white sitting in a circle, and the healer was explaining how she performed her energetic healings. She went one by one, releasing stuck energy in each of us. Finally, it was my turn, and I was scared. *What is going to leave me*? I thought. *I'm all good here. Plus, um, how embarrassing to release the demons in front of other people. No thanks!*

I stood up and she started to cradle me, rocking me in a circular motion. I was getting dizzy and felt the need to get down on all fours, like I was going to vomit. Ethan's birth started to come into my memory and I started to realize how angry I was about it all. It was as if I'd lost my voice in that moment and it was ready to come back among these sisters. I screamed and moved as if I was delivering another child. Everything I couldn't express in the delivery room was said amongst these women. Not only did I get to release, but the vulnerability I experienced met by the support of a sister circle opened my heart in a way I had never felt. And just like that, I grieved what I felt I had lost.

That was probably the most dramatic example of grieving I've experienced, but there can be small ways to grieve, too. You can walk through nature, alone, play music that helps you reach your grief, and release it into the wild. Mother Earth can take it from you. Dancing, jumping, kicking, crying, screaming, it all helps, so don't be shy.

We grieve not only when we move into new stages, like Maiden to Mother, but really when anything is changing and affecting us. Like when your children go off to college or kindergarten. Or when your marriage turns out to be a little different than what you thought it was going to be. And even when your life changes in the way you want it to, there is often a sadness for paths that never came to be.

As much as I was excited to leave the city for life on the land, after about a year of being here, I had to mourn the death of a life in Miami that I never got to have. For many years, I had worked hard to fit into the city blueprint. Get your kids into the best school, keep the perfect house, squeeze in expensive vacations, and smile for the camera (preferably in matching clothes). I had tried that life, and while it didn't make me happy, there was still grieving to be done after we moved. First, I had to grieve the loss of that old dream — even though it wasn't authentically my dream, it was still unborn. I also had to work through the feelings of failure for not accomplishing what I once sought out to do.

Grieving is often not a one-and-done moment, but the awareness followed by processing it through and out of the body will set you free. There are many griefs that we will carry with us for the rest of our lives, but when we honor them, we can become present again and allow new stories to unfold. We can honor our grieving by making physical and emotional space for it. Like having an altar for a past love or starting a foundation following the death of a friend.

Grief of a loved one can be more acceptable for our society, but what about the silent grieving? Like the loss of an unborn child, or a relationship that ended too soon, or the sadness of losing our younger self? How can we honor these silent losses?

For this kind of grief, I love to make discreet shrines. Meaning, you might pass by it and not even know what it is. For example, if you're mourning an unjust childhood, place a picture of your younger self in your home with a symbol of what was lost. Maybe she needed attention? Put a ceramic star next to her. Or maybe she needed more play? Place a small vase of flowers to represent an open field. You can take it a step further, by tending to your shrine by changing out the flowers and sending love every time you pass by the photo.

Some losses may need a ceremony to be set free. For example, if you're grieving a relationship, find a rock, draw on it in whatever way feels right, and leave it in a nearby park. Give a eulogy and mark a small gravesite. Even if the relationship wasn't "good," it's completely okay if you need a proper sendoff for its death.

Learning to grieve, I believe, is a leadership quality. Leaders are constantly being asked to be one step ahead, but also to stay very focused on the present. If we don't know how to mourn all the transitions and losses of our lives, we can become stuck, ungrounded, and unable to lead. We grieve not only for ourselves, but for all those we have been called to lead.

Grab your journal and allow yourself to answer the following questions. Closing your eyes and placing your hand on your heart—so you can feel your body—can help you go deeper.

Is there a transition that you need to grieve? (New mom, student to professional, single to married, married to single, etc.)

What past event do you find yourself complaining about often? What needs to be grieved there? What was lost?

Is there a recurring pain in your body? Is there anything in the pain that needs to be grieved?

Is there any past experience that needs to be tended to with a shrine or set free with a ceremony?

DEVELOP YOUR INTUITION

A leader's compass is their intuition. Without intuition, a leader may get confused, exhausted, or rigid and, by default, may end up following an old pattern. Or sometimes we're aware of our intuition, but it's only working randomly and by chance.

At first, as a young mom, random and unreliable intuition was all I had. I was taught that I would just *know* what to do when I became a mother. That some magic motherly instinct was supposed to kick in after the birth of a child. *Well, mine must be broken because my kid just peed in my face,* I thought.

I became a mother and a boss around the same time. And neither of those positions came naturally to me at first. My heart was open, but I was scared and too afraid to ask for help, so worry was the energy I led with for a long time. It wasn't until my business became more intuitive and metaphysical that I started to trust and understand my intuition enough to follow it regularly.

By now you have learned that my interest in intuition began in my early twenties after a sudden breakup. At first, the only reason I was interested in intuition was because I wanted answers. And I didn't want just any old answer — I wanted accurate ones.

My search for truth was like a dangling carrot held in front of me by the Divine. And I could not resist following it. The more

I studied and meditated, the more answers I received — but also, the more questions I had.

Following the breadcrumbs led me to hours of intuitive practice, which ultimately built the business I have today. I was not born psychic, but I did train myself to be the intuitive I am today. To the point that my waitlist for readings is nearly 1,000 people long. I am humbled and honored by how so many want to spend time with me and my intuition. While I am grateful to have developed this gift that created my business, I am most thankful for the mother and leader that my intuition has guided me to become.

Every quarter, budding intuitives join my certification program, Soul Reading Method. Most of them think they're coming to add a new professional skill to their business. Yet all of them leave realizing that developing their intuition is the greatest personal gift anyone can have.

Throughout this book, I have sprinkled intuition tips, but let's now talk about how you can develop and use it in your day-to-day life — especially as a leadership skill to lead your soul-led family.

The New Oxford American Dictionary defines intuition as *the ability to understand something immediately, without the need for conscious reasoning.* Sounds like magic, right? When our intuition is underdeveloped and we're depending on randomly occurring downloads it does kind of feel like magic. Because we have no idea how the message came through and when it might come again.

Our intuition does not need to be that unpredictable. In fact, it should be something we can call upon, on-demand, when we need it for guidance. It should be trustworthy and reliable, so that we can make informed decisions as we lead. Let me teach you how.

First, I'd like to define intuition a little differently than the dictionary does. To me, intuition is the expression of information that comes from reading energy that is unseen, but is very much present. Basically, there are times when you are reading energy, receiving information, and then are able to express it. It seems like magic, because the energy that you are using to receive the information is not visible to the human eye, nor does it come in physical form.

If intuition could be put into words, it would say something like, "I feel like I should go this way, but I don't know why." The only reason we "don't know why" is because we can't see, physically hear, or touch the energy that holds this information that was just given to us. Instead, we need to learn to hold focus on the unseen energy, receive information, and then express it.

LEARN TO HOLD FOCUS

Receiving intuitive information comes by focusing on energy. Throughout this book, I have encouraged you to hold focus on pain and body parts. When you do that, you're being intuitive! You are reading energy, even though there are no words.

The best way to increase our focus is through meditation. Closing our eyes for 10 minutes a day and focusing on your breath will increase your intuitive gifts tremendously. The goal of this exercise is to bring your mind back to focusing on your breath every time it tries to drift off onto something else.

When trying to receive intuitive information, you are going to place your focus on some sort of energy. If you're reading a person, you'll put your focus on their energy (in Soul Reading Method we focus on a person's chakras). If you're reading a future possibility, you'll hold focus on a road.

The options for point of focus are truly endless. For now, just know that what you're trying to do is hold focus and allow information to come into your mind or body without filtering the information through your logical brain. Approach this work with curiosity, and playfulness. Don't focus on being right, but rather on seeing what comes through.

WHERE IS YOUR INTUITIVE GIFT?

The next step in developing your intuition is understanding how you as an individual receive intuitive information. Historically, we have been taught the seven psychic clair's: clairvoyance, clairaudience, clairempathy, clairsentience, clairalience, clairgustance, and clairtangency. I don't like to get too caught up in the titles, they tend to overwhelm people. But if you're curious, a quick online search will provide you with loads of information. Instead, I'd like to go over how I like to categorize the rainbow of talent that has come through my online classrooms.

Seers

Possibly the most desired intuitive gift of them all is the ability to see (clairvoyance). This means that when you close your eyes, you can see visuals — like in a dream — that give you a message. The visual is usually symbolic and needs to be translated as a metaphor. For example, you might see an apple, but what the apple really means is that you are meant to be a teacher.

Clairvoyance can also mean, visually seeing a being, an aura, or energy in general with your physical eyes. Like the time I saw my great grandmother and the Angel of Death standing next to my grandmother's bed, just days before she passed.

When I first started developing my intuition, I was actually quite afraid to see things. At the time, I thought that seeing things meant ghosts standing next to my bed while I was sleeping. So I made sure to tell the angels that I was working with at the time not to visit me. You can talk to me through my sense of hearing, but don't show yourself. No thanks!

Although I had no sense of visually seeing at first, the more comfortable I became, the more I allowed myself to see. I say this so you know that you can develop any of these skills, but it's important to lean into what is feeling most natural at first.

Signs you have the Gift of Seeing: People who are creative or visual learners, typically have the gift of seeing. If I tell you to visualize the street of the neighborhood you grew up in and it was easy for you to see it, that's a sign you will be more inclined to intuitively see.

How to Develop Seeing: Guided meditations, like the ones I provide with this book, will be helpful. Also, allowing yourself to unleash your imagination is important. If you were (or still are) someone who had a wild imagination as a child, you might have been told that it was silly, so you learned to turn it off. Well, consider this your calling to bring that back. All your wild adventures are welcome here. They just need to be interpreted into messages.

How to Interpret Visual Messages: Visual messages are meant to be interpreted in the same way that pretentious guy you once dated, interpreted art at the museum. He may have been annoying, but he was on to something! When the visual comes forward, ask yourself, "If this was a riddle, what would it mean?"

You also want to develop your own intuitive language. For example, when you see colors, what does that mean for you? For me, I work a lot with chakras and each chakra has a color, so if I see a color on someone while in meditation, I know that it has something to do with a chakra. That may not be true for everyone, but this has become part of my intuitive language.

Maybe you're really into animals, flowers, or tarot. When you close your eyes and receive a message, you may see one of these. What does that animal, flower or tarot card mean to you? This is your intuitive language. You and I may see the same exact visual, but interpret it differently. That is okay, because who ever received the message is the one who is meant to interpret it.

Lastly, literature and film are riddled with metaphors. Even Jesus' parables are all about interpreting a deeper meaning. My father (the OG intuitive in my life) loves literature and film, and growing up as a kid he would bore me with all his explanations of the hidden metaphors in movies like "Star Wars." Today, I am grateful for those lessons, because it's what made me a quick and accurate intuitive.

Feelers

Perhaps the most overlooked and misunderstood (and therefore often despised) intuitive gift is the ability to feel or sense energy. These are my empaths, the people who can walk into a room and feel that something is off. The developed healer has learned to feel what is coming through her body and express it. In the expression is the intuitive message.

The problem with feelers is that because we did not know that sensing energy is part of our intuitive gift, we have learned to absorb energy into our bodies and mistake it for our own. Most feelers never learn that their sensitivity is a superpower. Instead, we suffer through life with ups and downs, taking on everyone's energy and never knowing where our center really is. This is why intuition development and understanding energy is so important to the feeler.

Signs You Have the Gift of Feeling: Eventually, a feeler will learn to express herself through a creative outlet. Feelers are usually beautiful artists, writers, actors, and musicians. Once a feeler learns to channel her feelings through art, she is free. But she might not know that her art is a physical interpretation of her intuitive gifts. Feelers often tend to assume that they are "too much" or "a lot to handle" and, in response, tone down their feelings in an attempt to keep those around them comfortable (like the story I shared with you about Ethan's birth).

How to Develop the Gift of Feeling: When feelers enter my programs, they tend to feel intuitively ungifted. Because they have learned to understand their ability to sense the energy around them as just who they are. *Doesn't everyone feel every drop of energy?* they think. The answer is no, not everyone does.

So the first step in developing the gift of intuitive feeling is to recognize that it is a gift in the first place. Also, you'll need to reverse energy in yourself a little bit, so that you can begin to realize the difference between your own energy and that of others.

I recommend starting each morning with a little energy check in by asking yourself, "How do I feel today?" And then go through your day and notice if you sense any extreme changes in your mood. This is not a perfect exercise because it can trigger old trauma or unprocessed emotions throughout the day, causing a change in emotion. But try to see if any switch in energy feels surprising and ask yourself if maybe it's not yours. Could it be your co-worker's, your boss, or your stressed out friend who you just hung up the phone with?

In class when we're learning how to read energy, my feelers tend to think they're not getting any information. They compare themselves to seers and start to believe they are duds, because they're not getting enough information to share. But the trick is, the feeler needs to learn how to put words to what they are feeling. They must learn to interpret what they're feeling in their bodies.

When a student tells me "I'm not getting anything," I'll ask them to tell me what they're feeling. Often they'll say, "Well, I just feel nervous. Like I'm going to be wrong." When I turn to ask our volunteer (the person whose energy we are reading) what their feelings are at the moment, she'll say, "I'm feeling really nervous because the whole class is reading my energy."

The feeler needs to learn to ask herself, "Is this energy mine?" when it comes to what her body is feeling. And if it's not hers, whose is it? What is it trying to say?

Another tip for the feeler is to take the emotion out of her body and put it out in front of her to read. Imagine you're feeling nervous and the feeling is in your stomach. Close your eyes, focus on your stomach, see a ball of nerves, and now imagine out from your body to in front of you, like a TV screen. Now watch and observe the energy from the screen. What is is trying to say? Write it down.

Lastly, the feeler will tend to be very good at using their hands to feel energy — even if it's not physically infront of her. Place your hands over your loved one or animal. Without touching them, feel what you are picking up. Do they feel calm? Is their energy electric and fast? Notice anything that is coming through.

How to Interpret Intuitive Feelings: Because the feeler is mostly bringing energy into their body to understand it, their job is to give words to what they are feeling. It's easy to get overwhelmed by the feeling (which is when you want to take it outside of you), but if you could let that feeling talk, what would it say?

Give the feeling a voice. Imagine it as a person who is trying to talk to you. What story does it have to tell you? If you close your eyes and focus on that nervous feeling in your stomach, maybe it wants to tell you that you are nervous about the future and you're not sure how to get to where you want to go, but that you will learn along the way.

Hearers

Possibly my most natural intuitive gift is the ability to hear intuitive messages. I have trained myself in all other categories, but hearing was my first skill. Hearers receive words, through their ears. That moment in New York I told you about in Chapter Two is an example of hearing. When the mind is empty a calm voice that isn't your own comes through and shares a message.

The challenge of a hearer is to learn to understand the difference between their inner chatter and divine messages. Through a meditation practice, the hearer begins to learn the difference between the different voices that come through. Hearers also deal with fearing that they may be slightly crazy. *Voices in my head? Shouldn't we be diagnosed with something?*

Signs You are a Hearer: Most hearers are really sensitive to sound. I am constantly asking my family to lower the volume on the TV and their devices. We also tend to sympathize with people by saying "I hear you," rather than saying "I understand" or "I feel you."

At some point, a hearer remembers hearing a voice or a sound that was not physically there. It's an experience that is hard to explain, so they often don't share it.

Hearers have a connection to music, sound, and the vibration of certain words. They can often act as an amateur DJ at any gathering—picking the perfect playlist, they love concerts, and they are attracted by sound experiences like a sound bath.

How to Develop the Gift of Hearing: A hearer must be a skilled observer, always listening for different tones. For example, when people talk to me, certain words often "stick out," the volume turns up when certain words are said. When this happens, I know to observe those words and ask myself, "What message is coming through?"

Maybe the most important thing a hearer needs to learn to do is slow down and bring moments of silence into her life. When holding focus on energy to receive messages, the hearer should sense her ears and pay attention to what is coming through.

An untrained hearer may often receive a high-pitched buzzing or wringing through the ear. This only means that the vibration that is coming through our ears, we are not yet trained to decipher. When this happens to me, I ask the energy to please change its tone so that I can understand the message.

A great exercise for those interested in developing the skill of hearing is to set a timer for five minutes. During those five minutes, walk around your space (maybe your home, your backyard, or your office) and focus only on what you hear. After five minutes, write down what you learned about the space you were in — and about yourself.

Knowers

Knowers have the gift of just, well, knowing. Different from a hearer, the information just drops into their brain. They don't even know how it got there. Whereas the hearer has a phrase come through like a ribbon of tape going through the ears.

Undeveloped knowers are often labeled as "know-it-alls" or judgmental people. So when I meet them in class, there's a lot of reframing to do. You're not a judgmental a-hole, you just know stuff.

The difference between being judgmental and being a knower is in the energy. A judgemental person feels tense when delivering their opinion, while a knower feels unattached, curious, and at times even confused by what they know. "I don't know why I get this sense that we should stay away from that person," are cautions they often receive.

Signs You are a Knower: You knew something before it happened. Someone has told you in the past, "You think you know everything!" You often start sentences by saying, " I don't know why, but..." And you feel like you've received a "download," which is a word that describes how a knower receives their information.

How to Develop the Gift of Knowing: The best knowers are actually non-judgmental people with an open heart. First and foremost, they have learned to stop judging themselves. With a non-judgmental mind, they have learned the art of being unattached to thoughts, leading them to understand what are thoughts of the ego versus of those of a divine source.

To develop knowing, allow yourself to go through your day observing your thoughts, but not judging them. As you observe, you will find that most of them are from your anxious, inner chatter. And every once in a while, a calm, matter-of-fact thought will come through. This is different from the norm. Ask if there is a message here for you.

MEDIUMSHIP

Now that you have perhaps identified where your natural intuitive gifts might lie, next we're going to learn about where the messages are coming from. There are all sorts of energy sources that we can receive information from. Like we learned in earlier chapters, we can receive information from Spirit Guides, Ancestors, the Higher Self, the Divine, Souls, and so on.

But you can also read energy off of the auras of people, places, and things. You want to think of auras as the energetic thumbprint of a person, place, or thing. You can also think of it as a person's vibe. It's the energy people give off, even when they're not saying anything.

You can also read the energy of possibilities. Like how we learned to feel into different future paths in earlier chapters. The moment has not happened to you yet, but when you learn to read energy, you can travel to a future time to read the energy of a certain possibility. Cool, right?

I started off by receiving information from spiritual beings (spirit guides, ancestors, the higher self, loved ones who have passed, etc.) because it felt familiar to me. Growing up Catholic and being Latina meant I was often praying to saints, making offerings to the many renditions of the Virgin Mary, or talking to loved ones who had passed.

Actually, in high school a close friend of mine passed away in a horrible car accident. After his death, his soul would often come visit me, and we would chat. I never told anyone, but it also didn't feel weird. Now I know that what I was doing was practicing mediumship.

Mediumship is the practice of translating information from one spiritual being to a human language. I know the word medium has been associated with people who have the ability to speak to the dead, but I want you to think about it more as a translator for spiritual beings.

If you like the idea of working with spiritual beings, pick one and start arranging "meetings." Set aside time to meet them in meditation. It's important that you *actually* set aside time, if you don't, you're not really developing your intuition but rather training it to come as it pleases. You're also telling spiritual beings that you have an open door policy.

Early in my intuitive studies, one of the first spiritual beings that came my way was that of my best friend's mom. Her mother had passed away from cancer when my friend was 21. I never knew her mother in the physical plane, but I got to know her very well on the other side.

The first night I went out to dinner with my friend, we were new co-workers and just getting to know each other. I went to the bathroom for a moment, and while I was alone in a stall, I heard this voice say, "I'm a mother, but I am not your mother." I thought maybe I had drank too much wine, so I let it go, and left the bathroom in a rush.

I sat down with my new friend as she started to explain how her mother had passed a few years earlier. *Ohmygod,* I thought. *Her mother just visited me in the bathroom! I'm not drunk after all!*

I didn't say anything at first because I knew my friend wouldn't be open to it, but as our relationship progressed, we eventually became roommates and best friends, so it was time to tell her about these visitations. I told my friend that her mother felt a little overbearing and she was always interrupting to offer her advice. "Sounds exactly like my mom," my friend replied.

She was getting so intrusive that one day I was driving down the highway at 60 miles per hour, and she was trying to get my attention so I would give my friend a message. "I'm driving here," I said out loud in my car. "I'll get back to you when I actually pay attention to you and not kill myself in the process!"

This experience taught me the importance of "meetings" and

energetic boundaries. I was already meeting regularly with my first spirit guide — about three to four times a week in meditation for 20 minutes — but then I learned to hear the "ping" of a spiritual being, and made a habit of setting aside time to hear their message for me if I wanted to.

If you want to work with spiritual beings, pick one and start making time for meetings. To start, 15 minutes, three times a week, will give you a solid foundation. You'll work up the time and eventually find yourself sitting in meditation for an hour.

When you meet with them, remember to bring a notebook and a pen. Intuition needs to be expressed in order to understand the full meaning of the message. When you write, don't worry if you don't understand the message yet. Just write. Once it's on the paper and you read it back, you will decipher its meaning. If you prefer speaking, record your voice with your phone and speak what you believe is coming through.

READING ENERGY

Another way to actively use your intuition is to read energy. I believe that when people speak of psychics, what they're referring to is a person who can read energy. In my experience, the difference between a psychic and medium is simply whether they are reading energy or translating energy. Nowadays, most of us combine the two, which is why you see more people refer to themselves as intuitives. To be intuitive is to be practicing a mix of the two.

I learned to read energy by accident. I'm so happy I did, because it is still one of my favorite things to do. This accidental discovery changed my life.

Oliver was three years old, Aly was eight, and I was finally getting out of the "new mom" fog. I signed up for a Reiki certification, because I wanted to learn about chakras. I was curious about these colorful energy wheels I kept seeing on posters hung at my local yoga studio.

For those who don't know, Reiki is a Japanese modality for energy healing where divine healing comes through the practitioner's hands. Reiki is taught to a practitioner in three levels. In each level, you receive an activation, and the last level is when you become a Reiki Master.

I did not understand what an activation was, so I didn't know what to expect. At the end of Reiki Level 1, my teacher placed his hands over my hands, passed the activation, and then class was over. It didn't feel like much, until a few weeks later when something weird started to happen in my meditations.

Although it was hard to keep a regular meditation practice with two young children, I managed to find some pockets of time to connect with my spirit guide. I was being taught a lot in my meditations, so I was always eager to come back for more. Typically, I would come to my meditations to ask my spirit guide's for help with some coaching clients that I just couldn't seem to help.

It was a regular day just like any other, I had come with a client question that had me puzzled, but this time instead of giving a metaphor, I began to see my client's chakras and the outline of her body. My spirit guide instructed me to start reading my client's chakras to find out what was blocking her.

As I held my focus on one chakra at a time, they each became animated, sharing messages, and tips for healing what was blocked in my client. I quickly transferred what I was receiving in meditation to my piece of paper, labeling the paper in the order of my client's chakra. The next time I met with my client, I shared what I had received, and she was in total shock. "How do you know all of this," she asked me?

This was the beginning of how I developed the Soul Reading Method. People would come to me feeling stuck, not sure why they couldn't move forward in life, and I could find answers hidden in their energy. After a while, the information didn't feel hidden at all. It's amazing how much can be seen in our energy!

After I learned to read chakras, I taught myself to read anything with energy, which is, well, everything. Today, I still start students off by reading chakras, because they are energy forms that were discovered in India as early as 1500 B.C. There is a lot of information on these energy centers, so they give us something to work with when we're trying to read energy.

Reading chakras also gives us a point of focus. I can tell you to read the energy of your dog or I can tell you to read the root chakra of your dog. Reading your dog's overall energy can be overwhelming, but reading a small part of it helps you be more precise.

Reading energy requires focus. When you focus on energy, it's as if you become it. Feeling completely present with the energy, for a moment you forget that you are in a physical body. Once in that presence, you're able to receive the information hidden in energetic form.

If you would like to try to read energy, practice on a pet, a plant, or a tree. Close your eyes and imagine you see a blue circle on the pet, plant, or tree. If practicing on a pet, the blue circle will be found on the pet's throat. The blue chakra is the throat chakra. Now ask the blue circle a question that pertains to the pet, plant, or tree. If practicing on a pet, you might ask "Why are you whining all the time?" Or if working with the plant, try something like "Is there a way that I can take better care of you?" And if reading a tree, ask it if it's happy where it is. Write down what you receive.

MEDIUMSHIP AND ENERGY READING FOR EVERYDAY LIFE

Besides being a super cool party trick, mediumship and reading energy are very valuable skills for leaders because they helps build confidence. When you receive a random intuitive hit or a gut feeling, it might be hard to trust at first, but as you become more skilled in translating energy, you will then have more information at your disposal.

As a mother and a leader, there are several uses for your developed intuition. You'll learn to read the energy of the schools you're considering for children. You'll know what job is best for your partner and family, and which one isn't. If you have a business, you can learn to communicate with its energy and listen to its guidance. And if you have some loud animals, like we do, you'll better know what they need.

One of my all-time favorite stories about using my intuition for the benefit of my family was the day we met Ethan's nanny. Ethan, our third child, had just turned one and it was finally time for me to go back to work full-time. After discovering how to read energy, word about my readings was spreading like wildfire. My latest dating book, "The Final Swipe" had been released a few months prior, and my business was starting to see the momentum I had been dreaming of for so long.

I needed full-time help, but like most moms, I was afraid of making the wrong decision and traumatizing my child for life. Although I was afraid, I also knew that Ethan was more than just a one-year-old baby. He was a soul — a very old one, actually. I knew he had his own soulmates and perhaps one might come in to be his nanny?

After speaking to a nanny agency, we were booked for three interviews scheduled with three highly qualified caretakers. That morning, as I changed Ethan out of his pajamas and into his play clothes for the day, I spoke to him and said, "Hey little guy. I know there's a really old soul inside your little body who can help me pick the right person for you. But since you can't talk, you'll have to give me a sign when we meet the one for you. Got it?"

I dressed him in soft black joggers and a gray tee with an American flag on it, handed down to me by a friend. A quick styling of his hair, and he was looking handsome for his interviews.

After two great interviews, I was already feeling a little confused. They were both great, but I hadn't received a sign from Ethan. I kept waiting for him to give me a thumbs up or something, even though I knew that was impossible considering his age.

Finally the third candidate arrived. The three of us sat down on the couch together, and Ethan maneuvered his way next to her. Although he wasn't showing any sort of special attention toward her, I looked at the two of them and realized that they were wearing the *exact* same outfit. She was dressed in black jeans and a gray shirt with the American flag on it.

I was so taken back by this that I even asked her if I could take a picture of the two of them. By then, she must have known she had the job. And although we have moved and outgrown the need for full-time help, she is still a part of our lives and our families became quick friends.

You just can't make this stuff up! Sure, intuition is magical, but it's even more magical when you develop it and learn to direct it.

SEE YOUR CHILDREN AND FAMILY MEMBERS AS SOULS

I gave you a little glimpse of what it means to see your child as a soul, rather than just a human, but let me explain why I believe this to be another invaluable leadership skill.

I had been putting off pregnancy for a long time before I conceived Ethan. Oliver was a really sensitive baby and Aly still needed a lot of my attention those first few years after I married her dad. And I was trying to fight for my new business all at the same time. It was a lot for me to handle. Adding another baby to the mix just sounded insane.

During that time period, every intuitive I would meet with would tell me that there was a female baby that was trying to come through me. "I know, I know. Tell her to wait," I would say.

Comfortable with my intuitive gifts at this point, I knew I had a spirit baby with me. A spirit baby is a soul that hangs around someone, waiting to come through. I've seen spirit babies be around women and men who are not even in partnership. They often come to guide the new parent and prepare them for the baby's arrival.

You may have felt this, yourself. Maybe you were given a baby name way before you conceived, like I did. In my early 20's, while living in L.A., I met a guy at a party whose name was Oliver. I knew then and there that I would have a boy, and name him Oliver. When the time came, my Cuban parents were confused by the British name I picked. But it all made sense when Oliver started to speak, because he somehow had a British accent. Everyone would ask me why he spoke in a British accent, to which I would respond by saying, "I don't know, it's either too much Peppa Pig or he was British in a past life."

Just like Oliver, Ethan was a persistent spirit baby. The day before he was conceived, I had a reading with a psychic who came highly recommended. She told me that I was meant to have another child and it needed to be soon. She continued the reading by drawing a picture of a plant that was dying, which was supposed to symbolize my two children. "Without this baby, your other two children will not bloom," she said.

Oh jeez! Ok, I get the point, spirit baby. That night I told Benny we needed to try for one more. It was important to the health of our family. So we did, just before bed. And when I closed my eyes to go to sleep that night, I saw a flash of a baby's face appear. "Are you kidding me," I said out loud? A few weeks later, I found out that I was pregnant.

What I missed in the details of that message — or what I refused to see — was that Ethan was a boy. The flash was clearly a boy, but I blocked it out of my memory, because having another child was scary enough. My thought process was that if maybe it were a girl, it would at least be a little more fun.

When the time came, we decided to host a little gender reveal party for our third child. Two days before, I had taken the envelope given to me by my doctor's office with the gender results, handed it to my favorite cupcake shop, and asked the baker to make me cupcakes filled with pink or blue filling, based on the results in the envelope.

Confidently dressed in pink at the gender reveal party, Benny took a bite of the cupcake and it was blue. "No," I said. "Give me the envelope." Sure enough under *Sex*, the doctor's report said *Male*. I tried to hold back my tears, hoping no one would notice, but my family had already caught my tears on camera.

Although I managed to snap out of it at the party, I was still processing it later in the week. My ego was bruised, because by this point my intuition was very developed. I predicted the genders of babies all the time. *How could I get my own wrong?*

I quickly understood that this was my ego speaking. I grieved the baby girl I thought I was going to have, and immediately embraced the baby boy that was coming. As the weeks passed, and Ethan grew in my stomach, his energy was so potent and strong. Different than what I had felt with Oliver, who was more playful and fun.

Being that we thought he would be a girl, Benny and I did not have any boy names in mind. We searched online for names, but nothing stuck. Until one day, I was visiting an embroidery store and saw the name Ethan embroidered in blue on a blanket hanging on the wall. "Ethan Essig," I thought.

I came home to ask Benny what he thought about the name Ethan. He suggested that we look up the meaning online before we decided. The name means strong and wise, which was exactly the energy I was feeling as he grew inside me.

Like Oliver, I believe Ethan gave us his name. He is the living embodiment of "strong" and "wise." And a Capricorn to top it off!

Before Ethan, I could intellectualize that our children are souls with their own purpose and true path. But it wasn't until he showed me that his birth was not about me, that I really started to fully understand and live like a parent who saw her children as souls. The sobering experience at his gender reveal party activated this knowing within me.

Our children are souls with their own purpose and path. It's easy to get caught up with what we want for them, how we think their lives should be, and even what gender they should be. Even worrying about whether we're being a good parent to them or not (my favorite pastime) is actually entirely our business. They came here to experience whatever they're meant to experience.

Besides understanding that they have a greater purpose in life than just being our child, remembering to connect with them at a soul level is important. That story I shared about Ethan and his nanny, that was me meeting him at the soul level. The brain of a child is developing, so their communication and expression may be limited, but that doesn't mean they are not wise.

The truth is many children being born in recent years are the most advanced souls we've seen in a long time. Children of the sun is what I like to call them, after reading the term in Rebecca Campbell's book, "Letters to a Starseed."

As we begin to see our children as souls, we'll start to understand what they're *really* trying to say to us. Have you ever been with a dog, a cat, or any pet, and feel like they're trying to tell you something? Like somehow the two of you might be actually communicating telepathically? They may not have the verbal skills to communicate with you, but energetically something is happening.

This is how we want to look at our children. Maybe when your child asks you to play and not so much because they need it, but because they know *you* need to play. Or maybe you struggle with one child more than the other because there is a past life pattern between the two of you that persists.

Once when Oliver was a toddler, I was meditating to experience a past life having to do with motherhood. All of a sudden, I saw myself with 7 children, Oliver being the youngest. He was small and weak, and the entire family had pity on him and had learned to treat him differently. I never shared this experience with him, considering he was young and it didn't really mean much to me at the time.

Fast forward, Oliver was eight years old, and we were hiking on our land in North Carolina, and I was showing him this cool formation a few trees were making. It felt like a portal to me, and every time I stepped in it during my hikes, I would be brought to a past life. I told Oliver that I thought these trees were creating a past life vortex.

He stepped in and closed his eyes. I asked him if anything was coming through for him. "I'm very small and not very strong. I'm in a wheelchair. You're with me and you feel bad for me."

I could barely believe what he had just shared. (Although I shouldn't have been surprised, children are amazingly quick at all things intuitive). He was explaining the past life I had experienced years before, but didn't really understand its meaning. That day, I understood that I needed to stop seeing Oliver as weak. Somehow in my subconscious, I thought he wasn't strong enough to overcome adversary and I protected him more than our other kids. His soul spoke to me that day, and I now knew that he needed me to break that pattern.

Not only are our children souls, but our partners are too. When someone comes into my practice, complaining about their partnership, the first action I take is to connect with the souls. The couple is human, but within those bodies are two souls playing out roles. Before coming to this lifetime, you and your partner got together and said, "Hey, I'll act like this in our relationship and it's going to help you grow into this. And you act like this to me, so that I can learn this. Deal?"

On the human level, how your partner is acting might be really annoying, but on the soul level, something else is happening. There's a reason for the annoying behavior. If you're in a situation where you can't figure out what is happening between the two of you, ask yourself, "What am I supposed to learn here? What action is my soul trying to ask me to take?"

And just as a side note: this is not permission to spiritually bypass any abuse that may be happening in your life. Even if the person is an amazing soul, it's not an excuse to be a horrible human.

In situations that are not dangerous, consider observing how the two of you interact. Rather than judge, look for patterns and get curious about what is making you two stuck. Ask yourself, "What is this soul trying to tell you?"

Another exercise that can be helpful is closing your eyes and imagining that you can see everyone in your house from above, as if the roof were removed, and you're now looking at a toy version of your home. See everyone in the house, moving around, and going about their day. Imagine that they are all actors. What role is your partner trying to play? What about your children? And how about your pet?

Write down each family member's "role" in your journal. How do their roles interact with yours? Write that down, too.

Seeing our family members as souls is translated as taking a higher perspective. Seeing the situation from above. As humans, we tend to constantly zoom in, and by doing so, we miss so much. Practice zooming out often, and you will find creative solutions you never knew were there.

UNDERSTAND SEASONS

To be a great leader requires a keen sense of seasons. Growing up in Miami, the only seasons I knew were hot and hotter. Living in perpetual sunlight and heat trained me to believe that life was either permanently good or permanently bad. If something bad was happening, I would automatically assume that my life was ruined and that I was doing something wrong.

Now, I understand that life is constantly contracting and expanding. Meaning, things in our life will die, forcing us to go inward, so that we can later expand. This doesn't only happen within us, but to everything around us. Our families, economies, our relationships, our businesses and so on, are constantly changing. To be in flux and changing, is to be living.

If we don't understand seasons, we won't be able to guide ourselves, or others, through the storms of life. Storms always end. It would be unnatural for them to remain permanent. But we can perpetuate them by resisting what is.

Self-trust is strengthened when we begin to trust the world around us, by understanding its natural rhythms. When I was a sleep-deprived mother to my first newborn, I had an experienced mother of five grown children remind me that although I was in a hard season, these first few years were actually a very small part of my life. What I did not know because of my inexperience was explained by an elder who understood the season I was in. With this information, I was able to settle into the present a little more.

All of us understand some sort of season. In Hollywood, there is a season in the film industry. Every year, the same awards come and go. Employees stay in their jobs through the end of the year to collect holiday bonuses and then jump to the next best opportunity sometime in January. Projects are put on hold from November until about March of the following year. You may notice a similar season in your career, where you live, or in the flow of your life.

When we are new to a particular season, the most helpful tool will be a mentor or an expert who intimately knows these particular winds of change. Someone who is well versed in the season we are currently in. To receive guidance on a season is different from receiving instructions on how to walk our path. Our paths may be unique, but the season will have some predictability.

If for whatever reason you don't have access to a mentor, the seasons of nature can always serve as a guide. I like to start with Fall, because it's the season where everything is about to go inward. It's the end of a former life. Nature is going back to its source. Winter is death. It's about being lost, grieving, and getting to our deepest core. After surrendering to death, life surprises us with Spring. In Winter we receive little signs to have faith, that a light is coming at the end of this tunnel, if we could just allow ourselves to decompose. This light is Spring, when life begins to bloom. Summer is the full expression of the hard work of a full season. It is time to harvest what we have sown.

If we want to stick with the new mother metaphor, Fall would be right before she gives birth. She's excited for what's to come, but has no idea that she is actually walking the plank to her inevitable death. For her, Winter would be after the baby is born. She can feel confused as she loses the identity she once had. But as she allows herself to grieve and accept this new season, she will be carried over to Spring. In Spring, she begins to explore new parts of herself, by studying new interests and discovering new inner strengths. Ultimately, Summer comes as she lives fully embodied as the next version of herself.

Naturally, when something in our life turns into winter, it's easy to believe that it's the end. Our fear of being stuck in this season will cause us to resist. Instead of flipping on our backs to float, we frantically doggie-paddle to shore. To float in this season, is to trust.

Other seasons, like Summer, will ask us to take major action, and if we don't notice these signs, we may miss a lot of opportunities. Our first Summer with a vegetable garden was mostly a loss, because we were completely unprepared for all the harvesting. We had become accustomed to the slow pace of winter and the planning of Spring. We had no idea how much we needed to pick up the pace in Summer!

Understanding the seasons of our lives not only tells us how to weather through them, but it also tells what kind of action to take in the moment. My clients often want to detox from their masculine, aggressive tendencies and move into a more feminine approach to life. They often think that to be intuitive and spiritual, means constantly being flowy, slow paced, and soft. What ends up happening is that they commit to no action, out of fear of being too aggressive, and therefore turn off their intuition to the natural rhythm of their life.

No matter what gender we are, we hold both feminine and masculine energies. Feminine is creative, flowy, intuitive, emotional, nurturing, and web-like. The masculine is action-oriented, protective, strategic, and linear. We want to look at these energies not as who we are and therefore how we must act, but instead as tools. Our understanding of the season will tell us which tool to use. We no longer need to be afraid of being too much of one or the other. We simply must listen to the direction of the season's wind.

The challenge here can be that we exist in several ecosystems at the same time. Your inner season can be different from the season of your business. An accountant might be in the middle of tax season, when she finds herself going through a divorce. The season of her business may be Summer, while the season of her marriage might be Winter.

Also, seasons of life, unfortunately, are not broken into perfect three-month segments. We can, personally, be in Winter for years. In these times, what is most important is to follow the natural rhythms of the times. Here's a chart of what those rhythms may look like and what action can follow.

Fall	**Rhythm**	**Action**
The end of a cycle	Busy	Celebrate
	Joyful	Gather
	Exciting	Say Yes

Winter	**Rhythm**	**Action**
Death	Lost	Float
	Confused	Surrender
	Tired	Rest
	Sad	Heal
		Reflect
		Grieve

Spring	**Rhythm**	**Action**
New beginnings	Hope	Explore
	Possibility	Learn
		Try
		Make Asks
		Plan
		Dream

Summer	**Rhythm**	**Action**
Full blossom	Clarity	Push
	Reward	Move Forward
	Fast Paced	Harvest
		Take Risks
		Save/Store

Today tap into your inner season. Close your eyes, zoom out, and look at your life from above. See the last few years, your current year, and the next few to come. Based on what you just saw happen in your life, and knowing how seasons work, where are you currently?

Write down your season in your journal. Next, look at the actions that coincide with your personal season. What action do you feel inspired to take? Write that down, and make a plan to take some action!

CHAPTER TEN

Healing Foundations

I knew that my husband was sick, but I had no proof to back up my unexplainable feeling. And quite frankly, it was the first time I wanted my intuition to be wrong.

He walked into our home office one afternoon, dressed in his dirty work clothes and muddy boots, to update me on a business matter. He spoke about a client and assigned me a task that he needed me to complete. Yet, I couldn't truly hear him. I was too engrossed in his lifeless eyes.

While I held focus on the death in his face, I heard the voice of my intuition once again. "He is not well, and he will not be able to provide for the family much longer," it said in a matter-of-fact tone. Although it was probably one of the scariest premonitions I had received to date, the voice was peaceful. It somehow made me feel that everything would be okay — just like that time years ago in New York City. There was no time to panic. All I could do was move forward.

Right away, I felt two paths present themselves to me. I could either address my husband's health, or I could work on making my own money, so that I would have some power in the situation. I chose the latter. Here's why.

I knew that my husband could not fathom focusing on his own health and healing unless his family was taken care of. At the time, we were living paycheck-to-paycheck, trying to provide for a mortgage, private schools, childcare, and everything else a family of five needs. Benny was the center of our operation. Our foundation — and survival — was built on him. If he could not perform his role each day, everything else would surely crumble.

So many of our families are built this way, right? It's painful to think about it. Historically, our men have often been treated like racehorses, forced to go out each day to perform, win and provide. In return, women have had to look the other way and ignore the unacceptable habits that men create as a result of their position in our lives. Subconsciously, they become our survival, so we overlook what may seem small in the moment, but with time can grow to be the destruction of our joint foundation.

In a patriarchal society, women are deceived into believing that they are less than their male counterparts. As a result, we wait with great expectation for our kings. And if you're a woman who has waited long enough, you inevitably have found yourself disappointed. For women in a patriarchal mindset, the men they have waited for so long ultimately become the greatest disappointment of their lives. It's not until a woman realizes that she is a queen that divine balance will finally bless her kingdom.

Benny and I were no exception to this outdated, codependent, patriarchal pattern. Here's what this looked like for us: I was the primary parent and Benny was the primary provider. He had zero responsibility when it came to the children or the house. We had that thing going on where I would have to ask him to watch the kids when I needed help. As long as he provided, he could do what he pleased. And on the flip side, I did not believe in myself enough to financially provide in a way that felt in alignment with my values, so I would watch him suffer at work day after day, and do nothing about it.

To save our foundation, my instinct was to become financially independent. I needed to break the loop we were in, and since I did not have control of him, I could only work on myself. I decided to lean into my business, placing less attention on Benny and his business. In the past, I had tried putting my efforts into his space, but that was no longer working, because I could not physically make the healing changes for him. I knew he was drowning, but I needed to swim to shore first in order to try and save us all.

This was the beginning of a real expansion in my business. Somehow, my focus and necessity eliminated any previous self-doubt I had about my work. I no longer wondered if my business idea was going to work. I simply knew that it *must* work. My family's survival depended on it. I was no longer a little girl playing pretend; I was a woman on a mission.

Every week, I would visit a holistic doctor who specialized in somatic healing. My intention with this work was to regain my power. To become strong again. Because when we're in codependent relationships, our belief is that our power is not enough, and therefore we must share it with another. Rather than realize that we each have a power source, we are under the impression that we are splitting one center of power between the two of us.

The patriarchal programming I grew up in taught me that in order to make a man (in this case Benny) feel more powerful, I would have to tone down my own power. As a result, I would limit my business success or my own spiritual awakening out of fear of making him feel insecure in my presence, outgrowing him, and ultimately losing him. Over the years, I had become a watered-down version of my true self. And in return, Benny had been handed too much power and responsibility that he was not truly prepared for or equipped to handle.

SPIRITUALLY OUTGROWING YOUR PARTNER AND OTHER RELATIONSHIPS

After years of working as a spiritual advisor, it is safe to say that what holds us back the most from living a truly soul-led life is the fear of outgrowing our loved ones. This is most evident in my students who are in romantic partnerships. Whether aware of it or not, they are afraid to spiritually outgrow their partners. The fear is that if they keep studying spiritual concepts, healing themselves, and stepping into their power, while their partners make no changes, they will soon be on completely different vibrations, causing a split in the relationship.

I feared this too. And after seven years of marriage, I met my greatest fear. We reached a point in our marriage where it was evident that it might break.

This is a very delicate dance. Not just for couples, but also for other relationships like friendships and parent-child relationships. Our fears of separation are not unfounded. I've seen many relationships become stronger when one person grows into their power, but I've also seen many relationships end. When we value a relationship so much, the thought of losing it is very scary.

PHASE ONE: BRING YOUR ATTENTION TO YOURSELF

If you find yourself in this situation, my first piece of guidance is to bring your attention to yourself. It is not time to make the decision to leave or stay. Forcing ourselves to make this decision prematurely can end a relationship that isn't necessarily over. For this reason, staying or leaving should not be the first point of action on the agenda. Regaining your power is the first step.

For me, regaining my power was achieved with my holistic doctor, week after week, for over a year, where I would revisit painful memories that made me believe that I was unworthy. It was also done through strengthening my pelvic floor and core in Pilates. And through investing in my business and myself.

During this first phase, it's important to note that by focusing on ourselves, we may accidentally neglect our partner. While it's not productive to pour into our partners at this time, if our resentment and disconnect is strong enough, we may give off the impression that we believe we are better than the other person. If we work on ourselves and simultaneously criticize our partners or friends for not doing the same, then we are still under the impression that we share a power source. We think we only get stronger as they get weaker.

What our actions convey is, "We're about to drown. And the only way for me to survive is for you to drown." We can only feel good and powerful about ourselves when we highlight the contrast between our successes and our partner's failures. This is why we gossip. Judging others gives us a false sense of power. But true power comes from realizing that there is enough for everyone. True power comes from being able to feel strong, even when the person next to us is just as strong — or stronger than us.

The balance we must attain during this phase is one where we are working on ourselves, while also holding a lot of love for the other person. Actions that can be helpful during this time are praying for the other person, speaking to the Divine and asking it to guide you and your partner to the highest outcome, and praying that your own inner healing may be a form of inspiration for the other person. Ask that your ego's instinct be completely removed.

Also, giving your partner permission to change can be miraculous. Remember, when we find ourselves in this codependent situation, we are perpetuating a pattern. When we act like this, they act like that. Change can only happen when someone penetrates the pattern.

Benny and I were in a pattern where he believed his worth was in providing. Subconsciously, he believed that I would love him only as long as he provided. I, too, was trying to prove my worth. I believed my worthiness lied in my ability to hold the family together, and that as long as I did that, he would not leave me. Underneath it all, this was our energetic agreement.

As I was working on my own power and recognizing Benny's decline, I looked at him one day and said, "Benny, I need you to know that I would love you in a cardboard box." I instructed him to look around at our beautiful house, at our children dressed in their private school uniforms, and told him, "You see all of this? None of this matters to me. This is just stuff. I would love you even if we were living inside a cardboard box on the streets."

I really meant that. We were nowhere near healing our relationship and foundation, but that day, I was able to give him permission to change. I was beginning to feel less afraid about losing all the material things, all the possessions that were keeping us trapped. I was willing to give it all up in exchange for healing.

That internal shift within me, where I no longer felt attached to the material life I had chased for so long, broke our pattern and created space for change. It was just a drop, but in that conversation, Benny started to feel some hope. *Maybe there's another way to live, other than the grind we've been living in?* He began to wonder.

When you are working on yourself — spiritually, emotionally, and physically — it can often seem like your partner is not. During these times, do your best to view your efforts as the best possible thing you can do for your partnership and your family. It may look like you're doing it alone, but when you understand that you're doing it for the greater good, you're less likely to create separation as a result of your guilt. When we grow, we feel guilty about leaving others behind. Eventually, that guilt causes isolation, which can unintentionally ruin the relationship.

By working on yourself and following your soul's callings, you're giving the relationship permission to change and evolve too. Throughout this process, it's important to vocalize how your behavior might have been upholding the dysfunction in the relationship. It took some time, but ultimately I was able to realize that I was enabling Benny's behavior, due to my own fear of survival and abandonment. He wasn't the bad guy. Neither was I. But I was just as responsible for the pattern we had created together. Communicating your aha moments to your partner will increase the chance of mending the union when the time is right.

Also, recognizing that they might be going about their healing in a different way can be very uplifting for your partner. My client Janie once asked me if I knew of a self-help book that had a cover that was interesting enough that her husband might pick it up. *If I could just trick him into reading a self-help book, he could change!* She thought.

While I loved her Nancy Drew plan, of strategically leaving a book on his nightstand as bait, I reminded her that our journeys all look very different. Reading books is not the only way. Sometimes our partners are learning to change by watching an obscure T.V. show, or by listening to their co-worker's stories about dating, or by working with their hands. Trust that your healing vibration is palpable, inspiring, and contagious. Truly walk your talk, and believe they can do the same.

PHASE TWO: IN OR OUT?

Two years after receiving the premonition that Benny was failing, I finally came to learn that he was suffering from an alcohol and drug addiction. Most Sundays, I would meet my best friend Caro for a soulful walk, these walks always seemed to solve life's biggest problems. During one of these epic walks, I vented to her about all the ways Benny was annoying me. She quietly listened for about 40 minutes, and when my rant felt complete, she looked at me and said, "You know, I think he's an addict."

An addict? I didn't even know what an addict was. In Miami, drugs and alcohol were about as common as a bowl of dip at any gathering. Sure, Benny drank, but overall he was a good husband, father, and provider. He never disrespected me. He loved his children. And he was a kind spirit. *Aren't addicts more destructive than this?* I thought.

While Caro was a close friend, she was also a new friend. We had met at a fundraiser for our kids' school. My oldest son and her youngest son were in class together, and we had become instant friends. Our bond was strong, but there was still so much we didn't know about each other's pasts, so it seemed every time we walked together, we learned something new.

Prior to that day, I had had no idea that her husband, a well-to-do attorney, had been an addict. She briefly shared her story, and the parallels to my current situation were undeniable. The similarities were almost eerie.

After our walk, she insisted that I come back to her house to talk to her husband (who had now been sober for years). He was so kind, and explained to me how addiction works and how it can manifest. Based on what I was hearing, Benny appeared to be a textbook case of a functioning addict. And without that fateful conversation with Caro and her husband, I might have never known the truth.

Looking back, the reality was that I was finally ready to see the truth. It had always been there, but my fear of losing him and my picture-perfect life had kept me in denial. After months of working on my inner power, I was ready, which ultimately brought me to that conversation with Caro and her husband.

I came home from that walk and went straight into our family RV camper, parked on the side of our home. Benny was constantly going in and out of the camper, but I was too busy with the kids and my life to notice, or care. After speaking with my friend's husband, I had a feeling that the evidence I had been looking for two years ago, proving my instincts around Benny's health, were probably hidden somewhere in this vehicle.

It wasn't hard to find. All I had to do was open a cabinet, and there were all the bottles. I had walked into that camper a dozen times. I had even traveled in it. But today, it was obvious that it was an addict's haven.

I felt so incredibly angry and betrayed by this. Without thought, I immediately grabbed a large black garbage bag, ran my arm across the camper's kitchen counters, and threw everything in the bag. The closets and cabinets were next. Within 20 minutes, the camper had been wiped clean by my rage.

I marched into our home with my black garbage bag filled with evidence ready to confront him. He was lying on the bed, probably nursing a secret hangover, when I showed him what I had discovered

His initial reaction was to diffuse my anger with laughter.

"I thought you were on a walk with a friend. What is all of this drama?" he said, downplaying the truth.

Although I had planned to fight with him, instead, something else took over. I dropped the bag on the floor, collapsed onto our bed, covered my face, and began to sob. "This is my fault," I admitted.

Despite spending the last few months retrieving my own

power, I still felt responsible for this dysfunction in my family and relationship. *My husband was sick, and I hadn't even noticed. I was a professional intuitive, for crying out loud! How had I missed this? What did that say about me?* My heart was broken, and Benny noticed.

"Your fault? Nikki, no, my drinking is not your fault. I have been stuck for a really long time," he explained, while comforting me with a one-armed hug.

I had every intention to lead with my anger, but somehow our hearts came online and we agreed to go through this very hard thing, together.

For the next two months, Benny tried to quit on his own, while I tried not to push or micromanage. I thought if he wanted to quit, he would just quit. But that was only because I didn't really understand addiction. Weeks had passed, and he just had not been able to do it. His addiction was becoming a threat to the safety of our family, and I knew I needed to take more drastic measures.

I called the only person I knew who could possibly get through to Benny: Maria. This was the friend who had introduced us at my best friend's engagement party. In a moment of panic, I called her and told her that she had gotten me into this mess and she needed to get me out of it.

By this time, Maria had gone through her own healing journey and had been sober for more than two years. She had grown up with Benny. They were as close as siblings. And quite frankly, she knew my husband better than I did.

She explained to me that in order to heal, he needed rehab. I knew he would refuse this, and I had no desire to force him.

What would be the most empowering thing I could do for myself,

I thought? What I knew about healing power issues was that I needed to remain in my own strength rather than try to manipulate the situation through force or by trespassing my boundaries.

By accessing my own power within myself, I grew the courage to ask Benny to leave. "I know you're trying, Benny. I see you trying each day to heal. But you can't do it here anymore. Not in front of our kids. You need to leave. And when you're sober, we can discuss the possibility of you coming back," I explained.

Within ten minutes, his bags were packed; he was out the door, and our family RV was hooked up to his truck. He had not expected this from me, and he was extremely upset. He did not know that I could be both compassionate and stern with him at the same time. This had not been a part of our previously established pattern. In our relationship, I was either extremely controlling or I would roll over. I had yet to master a balance between these two.

Benny leaving marked the end of our tug-of-war game over our joint power. I no longer cared who was wrong or right. But, most importantly, I was no longer afraid of being alone.

This energetic release was palpable, and Benny felt it. Within 24 hours, he was willing to check himself into a rehabilitation center. He was really ready, he knew he had too much to lose.

I am beyond grateful to report that Benny has been sober ever since, and his healing blessed our family beyond belief. I am also very aware that our story is not the norm. There were many factors that played into our success. For starters, Benny was ready and willing to heal. We had no control over his decision, and we are just thankful that he chose life.

Second, because I had spent many years walking my spiritual

talk, I knew how to support him, myself, and my family. It was as if I had been training all my life for that moment.

Lastly, our community of friends and family rallied behind us, sending us cooked meals, cleaning our home, and taking our children for play dates. The Divine used these relationships to embrace us during this time.

It really does take a village to heal. But this is not a story about addiction. This is a story about healing foundations. Benny's addiction was simply a symptom to the dysfunction of our family system. We had built the foundation wrong, and his addiction was the evidence that everything was about to crumble.

PHASE THREE: REBUILD

Benny and I had dreamt of a different life, beyond the endless rat race, for years. In fact, four years earlier, we had traveled to Asheville, NC in search of land. We were not yet ready to buy anything, but it didn't hurt to look.

Knowing now how land tends to call its stewards, I do believe that the weekend back in 2016 set into motion the following years of healing that our family experienced. Essentially, our dreams of a different life could not be sustained by the foundation we were standing on. As long as we kept dreaming that dream, our foundation was eventually going to have to change.

What I know now is that you can't build your dreams in a sustainable manner without standing on a solid foundation. This is why the more we reach for our dreams, the more our personal lives often feel like they are dysfunctional or falling apart.

Our life force, the energy within us, creates the life we experience. You want to imagine your life force as a tree. Your energy has roots, a trunk, and a crown just like a tree.

Funny enough, our life force can be divided into seven chakras that have names similar to those you would use to break down the parts of a tree. This system includes the root chakra found at the bottom of our spine, which also governs our legs (which happen to resemble the roots of a tree). And then we have our top chakra, found just above our head, also called the crown. In between the root and the crown are five other energy centers: the sacral, the solar plexus, the heart, the throat, and the third eye. These centers make up our "trunk."

I'm not going to go into detail about our energy because that's not the focus of this book, but I want you to understand how your root center will be challenged as you reach for the life of your dreams. This will explain why, when aspiring to live a soul-led life, life seems to get harder before it gets better. Without understanding this, you may tend to think that you're doing it all wrong.

Right above our root center is the sacral center. The sacral energy center is found hovering over our reproductive organs. This part of our body is what we use to create a literal life — a baby. Energetically, this center also represents birth, our ability to create joy, and live our passions. When we decide to live a soul-led life, we are trying to birth a new, joyful life into reality.

Our life force flows from the bottom of the root up to the crown. So if we're trying to get the juice of a well-balanced sacral center — the ability to create a joyful life — the center just below it (the root) needs to be solid. If the root is not built to hold our dream life, as you reach for that life, your foundation will begin to reveal its cracks. This is what happened to Benny and me.

Our foundation is made up of our family structure, how we

work, our home, and our personal passions. Rather than intentionally create our foundation based on what we feel is right for us, we tend to create our foundations based on the programming of our childhood. If we're not intentional, our foundation becomes a creation of our default path. Eventually, it creates friction against our dreams, and the cracks begin to show. For this reason, until these categories are a reflection of our truth, our lives will not reflect who we truly are. Let's observe each.

FAMILY STRUCTURE

Does yours work? Honestly, does your family structure work for *you?* You are the wheel that turns in order for your family structure to work. Based on how you work, everyone else settles into their role, which is how your family functions.

You now have the opportunity to change the structure, if you want to. The best part about that? You don't need to feel guilty because what is best for you is what builds a healthy foundation. And though family members may kick and scream along the way due to unwanted changes, ultimately everyone benefits from a healthy foundation.

For the first seven years of our marriage, I really tried to be a supportive wife and mother that put everyone else first. God, did I try. But it was killing me. I constantly felt like I had more to offer the world.

Benny, on the flipside, felt that playing the role of the male provider wasn't worth the hype. It was simply a show he didn't care to star in. Playing that role was, quite literally, killing him.

Being that we were the leaders of our family, if we were suffering, everyone else was, too. Even when it's not plainly obvious, other members of your family are not developing in the way their soul intended to, if we are not living authentically.

The good news is, this is your family. This is your life. Some days, it's hard to believe that someone left us in charge, but we are the adults! We make the rules.

Take a moment to close your eyes and imagine what your family and life would look like if the structure were really working for you. Try not to focus on others right now. If you were really listening to your needs and desires, how would you move within your family structure? What does it feel like to be you? Hold on to that feeling, and now open your eyes. Write down what you felt.

When I was restructuring my family and my role, I sought to feel truly empowered and worthy. I imagined myself moving within my family system unapologetically for my ambitions and my needs. Going forward, I made choices and changes based on a feeling of worthiness.

You may not know how to change your family structure. After all, what you are dreaming of has probably never been done before in your family lineage. I am the first woman in my family to work, manage a family, and creatively express myself. I've never seen it done before, which makes the vision hard to see most days.

You may feel blind as you walk this vision, which means you have to feel your way through. Allow that future feeling to guide you. Make small changes in your structure that bring you more of that feeling. After continuously putting that feeling first, you will wake up one day and realize that you — against all odds — made a beautiful family system that is authentic to who you are.

HOW WE WORK

Our middle child, Oliver, constantly tells me that school takes up way too many hours. He questions, with so much frustration, the reasoning behind a seven-hour school day. "Mom, all the important stuff happens in the first two hours of school."

I felt the same way after leaving my job as a magazine editor to work from home as a freelance writer. Somehow, what used to take me eight-plus hours at an office was taking me about three hours to complete from home. With the extra time, I took on more writing gigs and started to make more money! After this experience, I just knew that I could never go back to a full-time office job.

For some people, the eight-hour-plus-day works. But it seems like, the more we advance as a species, the less this old model seems to make sense. After all, the school system was created to train children to become factory workers (and also so their parents could work a full day). Technology has given us new ways to make money. As a result, the resistance to continue working this way is beginning to feel almost like our biology is evolving beyond the eight-hour workday.

If you are questioning the way you work, don't fight that feeling. Instead, get curious. If you could hold on to that feeling of discomfort in your body, what does it have to say? Close your eyes, feel it, and then write down what is coming through.

When Benny and I were restructuring, we were most bothered with the idea that everyone in the family had to leave the house at 6:30 a.m. only to return at 6 p.m. after school and work, only leaving time for dinner and baths. Benny started to wonder if owning a service-based business with a ton of employees was actually the right choice for him. Yes, his business was successful, but he was starting to believe that it just wasn't worth the stress. More importantly, he began to believe that there might be easier ways of making money than how he was currently doing it.

There has to be a better way, we thought. These curious thoughts are what led us to go all-in on my digital business. It gave us freedom of time and location, and the opportunity to earn money without a ceiling.

Reimagining how you work can take some time. Often, when we start this process, it can feel like a long frustrating road, especially if it points you in the direction of entrepreneurship or a new career path. It took us 10 years to get it right, but it has been worth it. What's 10 years if we can live in alignment for another 50?

We are constantly investing in our own self-development (like you are with this book) and our business skills. This combination, along with a teamwork mindset, is what has worked for us. We're in it together, and we're in it to win it.

If you're in the process of figuring out this puzzle, a great exercise is to make a list of all the people you know (or have seen on social media) whose work lives appeal to you. Maybe you even feel jealous of these people. That's perfect, because it's pointing you toward what you want. Write down the names of these people, and ask yourself why you feel attracted to the way they work.

Next, ask yourself, which work lifestyle you might be able to replicate. Once you pick a work lifestyle, I want you to imagine yourself living that lifestyle. See this version of yourself in your imagination. Once you see her in your imagination, ask her what you need to do now to create this reality. Write down any guidance you receive.

If you're in partnership, I recommend figuring out this puzzle with your partner if it feels safe to do so. I know as independent women, we want to figure everything out by ourselves. And honestly, sometimes, we're in a relationship with an unsupportive partner. I get it. But, if you can be vulnerable enough to let them in on the process of creating this vision, you will have double the manifesting power.

Instead of going out on date nights, Benny and I use our babysitting help for day dates. We start off the day with a visit to our favorite local coffee shop and we brainstorm, research and run ideas by each other. It's not always harmonious, often I'm annoyed at his input — like when he told me this book should have ended a few chapters ago. But when I'm brave enough to work together and receive feedback, I always make something better than I could have made on my own.

After coffee, we mayhead out to town to visit art shows, vintage shops, and thrift stores. We do this not because we're necessarily looking for something, but because there is no rhyme or reason to most of these stores. They're random and unexpected, which helps our minds get out of the same old thinking patterns. This is how we start to think creatively. This is how we start to think like trailblazers. And this is how we remain committed to designing our lives.

OUR HOME

Remember when you didn't care so much about where you lived? And then all of a sudden, 2020 hit and you started to realize that home is kind of a big deal? Well, that's because it is, and you deserve to have a home and space feel just right for you.

Home can feel wrong for two reasons. For one, you can be entirely in the wrong location, like we were when we lived in a busy metropolitan city. Secondly, the aesthetic, space, and feel can lack authentic expression of who you really are.

If you sense that you might be in the wrong location, focus on what is calling you rather than getting stuck on how much you hate your current circumstance. For years, Benny and I spent time complaining about where we lived, because we weren't courageous enough to admit where we were being called to go.

If you could live anywhere, where would it be? Even if this desire takes you to another country, let yourself feel it.

The good news about making the brave leap to live somewhere completely new is that it takes time. Meaning, you don't have to be afraid to hear the calling of your soul, because more often than not, you will have to make many adjustments to get to your dream destination. Which means that now is a perfect time to start envisioning yourself in a new land!

Make time to visit the places that resonate with you. Even see some properties while you're there! Start a savings account for this purchase or begin to organize your finances and documents. I find that taking these steps shows the Universe and the land that you are serious. Show your commitment. As a result, miracles begin to take form. When the time is right, you will feel it and take the leap, because you've been working on your bravery.

In the meantime, you can work on making sure your current home is an expression of who you are. For several years, I thought that interior design required a lot of money. Because I didn't have money, I just didn't do anything about my space and felt eternally frustrated.

Honestly, what I lacked more than money was vision and the courage to express myself. When thinking about feeling good about where we live, we need to ask ourselves what we need to thrive within our home. Maybe you need to feel happy, inspired, organized, or close to nature? What is it for you?

Sadly, in Miami, what I needed was to feel like I fit in, like I was worthy enough to belong. Therefore when decorating my home, my mind was focused on what people might like if they walked into my house. What would impress them?

Overwhelmed by this thought, I could barely furnish or decorate my house because I was afraid of making the wrong move. There was no possible way to make everyone happy with my design choices, so I just didn't make choices at all.

Our homes, inevitably, become a reflection of our insides. All of us love to walk into an artist's home because it is a reflection of their inner creativity. They are confident enough in who they are and their worthiness to express themselves, that they end up creating very unique spaces. We might not all agree with their design choices, but somehow we leave feeling inspired.

Funny enough, my favorite spaces in our Miami home were the kid's playroom and the outside playground. I designed the playroom to encourage play, imagination, and artistic expression. It was nothing special, but it was decorated with the kids' artwork, painting supplies, and toys. It was an expression of them.

The outside playground was an expression of Benny's inner child, which still makes me laugh. Because Benny owned a tree business, he was often involved in outdoor demolition projects, where clients would toss away old playgrounds, outdoor kitchens, and patio furniture. It's like the saying goes, "One man's junk is another man's treasure." Well, let's just say Benny was constantly bringing home what he considered to be treasure. To me, it seemed like the early stages of hoarding. Benny called it collecting.

He collected an old tree house and turned it into a play grocery store and later a bunny house. A rusted play airplane became a vibrant seesaw. Aly's old trampoline was restored and dug into the ground, making a safe jumping space for the kids that was inline with the ground. And he traded plants for artificial turf and mulch.

His greatest score was when he came across a local public school throwing away their giant playground set. One day, a massive truck arrived at my house to dump pieces of old colored metal, which Benny insisted were art. Guess what? He made a beautiful obstacle course for the kids from these found objects.

For a while, I was so embarrassed by our junk collection, but every time people would come over, they gravitated toward the playground. It was fun, interesting, and from the heart. It was a pure expression.

These days, I design my spaces based on how I want to feel rather than what I believe is expected of me. After all, if we create our homes based on what we think others will like, we're constantly going to feel less than worthy in our own space.

Pick one room or even just one wall in your home and express yourself. Try not to let money get in the way. Soul-led living is all about living outside the box, believing that there is a way to create your vision. Which means, even if we lack some resources, we always have the ability to create.

What can you do today to make your home feel more soul-led? And how can you work toward making your *future* home completely soul-led?

OUR PERSONAL PASSIONS

Once we start to intentionally explore our family structure, how we work, and our home, it's time to make some space for our personal passions. Why would personal passions matter in making a healthy foundation? Because the other three areas can quickly become too serious.

Our personal passions are the things we do without agenda. I grow flowers because I want to. Not because I'm going to sell them or make something out of them. I'm not even sure they make me happy, because they're a lot of work! I do it, because I feel drawn to them, and I don't worry about why my path is taking me here.

Our personal passions often give our minds the space to, without force, solve our foundation problems through creative solutions. Engaging in personal passions takes us out of ourselves for a while. When we leave our predictable selves, we gain the energy and clarity we need to continue along our unique soul-led path.

Maybe you already know what your personal passions are. Traveling, gardening, drinking wine. Amazing! Make time for them. Fit them into your rotation of family, work, and home. If your foundation was a pie sliced into four, your passions get a whole entire piece.

If you don't know your passions yet, ask yourself: what are you drawn to, but don't pursue because you don't see the point? Maybe you are being drawn to something but think you're supposed to do it for a living. All that pressure doesn't allow you to move forward.

Can you pursue something that pulls you even if it has no purpose? Can you give yourself permission to make a bracelet just because? Or learn a language just for fun?

Our personal passions lead us to remember parts of our souls. And for that reason alone, they are worthy of our time and attention.

CHAPTER ELEVEN

The Creation Process

As an imperfect person who has created so much in her life, I have come to clearly understand the stages of creating a dream life.

Stage One:

I want it.

I am longing for it.

I need it.

Stage Two:

I can almost see it.

I believe it.

Stage Three:

I know it's happening.

In stage one, we are frustrated, jealous, and contracted. In stage two, we allow ourselves to be foolish enough to try and set out on the hero's journey to accomplish it. And in stage three, we finally begin to believe that we deserve it. Our vibrational imprint becomes that of someone who has it, so shortly after, the dream comes our way.

When we know we're worthy — or are at least ready to reclaim that innate worth — the creation process is quite simple. What is often not simple at all for humans is understanding our intrinsic value.

In 2008, I received my first ever self-help book. "You Can Heal your Life," by Louise Hay was gifted to me by my co-worker. After I had inappropriately burst into tears at a casual work lunch over the mention of my ex-boyfriend, she wanted to share a book with me that had worked for her when she was going through a hard time.

A few chapters in, I remember thinking to myself *Wait a second, I can better myself to the point that I can have everything I want?!* As a girl who felt deeply unworthy after growing up in a patriarchal society, I was hooked. It became my mission to fix myself so that I could have it all — and maybe even, get my ex-boyfriend back.

As a newly single woman, I would spend my weekends on the floor of Barnes and Nobles jotting down notes from the best self-development books. Living off an assistant editor's salary meant I was too broke to buy the books, so I read and took notes instead.

Guess what? A year and half later, I met my future husband and began to land a few dream jobs. *Wow, this stuff actually works*, I thought to myself.

Life felt great until I became a wife, then a mother, and then a business owner, at which point life began to feel extremely hard. It felt worse than when my beloved ex-boyfriend had broken up with me years before. I reached for the personal development books again and consulted with the psychics. Hoping that I could once again earn my dreams, earn my happiness, and earn my worth.

It worked. Kind of. Temporarily. At times.

But I couldn't quite sustain it. Some days were great because the self-help practices I was learning seemed to be working. Other days were so painful, I would find myself dissociating from my body, desperately trying to seek relief from the inner pain I was experiencing. It was an uncontrollable stress I could not seem to manage.

The scariest part? My life was not awful. Hard, yes. But I had a beautiful family, a husband, a house, friends, health, work... all the things. Sure, they weren't perfect, but my dissatisfaction and overall stress about it often felt excessive and exhausting. Most days, I would shame myself for not being able to find gratitude for what I did have. But I just couldn't seem to find it.

I was stuck in a loop of shame. I would shame myself for wanting to fix something that wasn't awful. And then I would shame myself for not having what I wanted because I wasn't fixed within myself.

The self-help practices, messages, and books that had helped me so much just a few years before were no longer serving me. I was beginning to believe that I needed to earn my dreams by fixing myself in order to have them.

Sick, tired, and scared, I kneeled down next to my bed one night and prayed.

"God, please help me. I am lost," I pleaded.

I cried myself to sleep, and the next morning I woke up with phrases in my head. As a writer, I was used to this. Phrases going in and out of my mind, in no particular order, teasing me for a chance to become alive. I began to write.

You don't need to achieve more.
You are more.
You don't need to accomplish more.
You are accomplished.
You don't need to work smarter.
You are smart.
You don't need to prove or make yourself loveable.
You are loveable.
You don't have to work towards that future moment.
You are the moment.
You just are.

To really believe these words is to understand our intrinsic worth. When we envision our dream life, we think it's in the future, beyond us, and that we must earn it. Yet, when I asked the

Divine to help me, all that I received was the reminder that "I am."

You are. I am. We are.

To know that you are whole, you are enough, and you are your dream life is to stop chasing. That anxious feeling of needing to work, earn, climb, and accomplish can finally end — leaving you with the peace you deserve and seek. This truth is available to us right now.

Yes, I know that the embodiment of this truth does not give you the physical manifestation of your dream life. I know it doesn't give you the dream house, the successful business, or the loving partnership that is your soul's true path.

I just want you to know that it will not hurt you to believe that you're worthy of it, right now, as you are. Knowing that you are enough will not take away your competitive advantage or your ambitious nature. Feeling loved will not delay your dreams.

On the contrary, hating ourselves, wishing we were faster, better, stronger does cause a delay. Doing this is the equivalent of whipping ourselves, in order to move. But all we're doing by continuously hurting ourselves is perpetuating wounds that ultimately need care in order for us to move forward.

We are creators. At a soul level we understand this, which is why we are often unsatisfied with what we see. The most potent creation power in the Universe is made from the energy of feeling loved, worthy, and deserving. We don't need to overcomplicate it by thinking we're missing something and therefore don't have what we want.

Yes, even when we feel loved, worthy, and deserving, physical manifestations take time. I might feel this today, but not see that energy in my bank account until next year. But what you will instantly have is less anxiety, more presence, more joy, and more trust.

We fear that state, because we worry that once we're there, we won't want more. And then what? But I say, let's be brave and find out.

There is a journey to feeling good enough to experience our dreams — especially the bigger our dreams get. Therefore, we explore our past, looking for moments where we can take back our power and sense of self-worth so that we can create bigger dreams from a place of wholeness. This is why I wrote this book. So that you can reclaim your power, rather than feel like you need to earn it.

May you look back at your own stories and find the moments where you accidentally forgot who you truly are: a powerful soul made for really big things.

Acknowledgments

First and foremost, thank you to me. Thank you to all parts of me. The broken parts. The divine parts. All of it. Thank you for courageously walking through this. You are a bright star.

Thank you to my husband, life partner, and the father of my children, Benjamin Essig. Thank you for holding me when I couldn't hold myself, which was often throughout this process. You are the king to this queen. I will love you for many lifetimes.

My deepest gratitude to my team, my sisters, the midwives of this book: Danika Colucci and Kat Morzewska. Thank you for believing in me before I knew how to.

To my three children: Aly, Oliver, and Ethan. Thank you for lending your mom to the readers of this book. You allowed me a year to complete this work and never complained — even if it was only because of all the extra screen time you got in exchange. You supported me and cheered me on when I felt doubtful. At such a young age, you unselfishly gave up your time with your mom because you knew how important this was to me. Thank you for loving me unconditionally.

Thank you to my mother for always encouraging me to reach for the stars. Thank you to my father for instilling in me a love of books and words. And thank you to both for their deep love and for modeling the work ethic needed to reach for those stars (and write this book).

Thank you to my friends and family who had to endure the pain of listening to me speak about this book for a year. As you know, I need to process things out loud. I love you. Specifically thank you to Caro de Posada, Jordan Younger, Sisi Smit, Giselle Navarro, and my sister-in-law Rebecca Novo — all who patiently listened to me as I bounced ideas off of them.

Thank you to my very talented and patient therapist, Crystal Nero, who held space for me as I processed many of the thoughts and concepts in this book. She encouraged me, but also taught me how to encourage myself. For that, I am forever grateful.

Thank you to the team of wildly talented creatives who brought this book to life. Thank you to my editor Danielle Goodman, who encouraged me to even start this book.

Thank you to Kat Morzewska who curiously read every word I wrote, offering me the feedback to make this book what it is.

Thank you to my final editor, Marisa Leon, who made my writing so much better than I could have ever done. (You should probably edit this sentence.) She came in at the final inning and knocked it out of the park. Sharing a love of writing with my childhood friend has been one of the greatest joys of this process.

Thank you to Laura Wrubleski for another great book cover and design. I'm sorry (but not sorry) for tracking you down to work together again.

And thank you to the very talented Natalia Aristizabal for sharing your gifts with me and the soul-led community. Your design and book cover are a dream come true.

Last but not least, thank you to my community of clients and students. Not only do you inspire me, but you have held me through this process and throughout my career. I love you deeply. Thank you, truly.

Made in the USA
Columbia, SC
25 May 2024